THE CHINESE IN PAPUA NEW GUINEA

PAST, PRESENT AND FUTURE

THE CHINESE IN PAPUA NEW GUINEA

PAST, PRESENT AND FUTURE

**EDITED BY ANNA HAYES,
ROSITA HENRY
AND MICHAEL WOOD**

Australian
National
University

ANU PRESS

PACIFIC SERIES

Australian
National
University

ANU PRESS

Published by ANU Press
The Australian National University
Canberra ACT 2600, Australia
Email: anupress@anu.edu.au

Available to download for free at press.anu.edu.au

ISBN (print): 9781760466398
ISBN (online): 9781760466404

WorldCat (print): 1427411132
WorldCat (online): 1427411723

DOI: 10.22459/CPNG.2024

Cover design and layout by ANU Press.

Cover photograph: The Wong family in Papua New Guinea circa 15 Jan 1954. Image courtesy of Vyvyen Wong.

This book is published under the aegis of the Pacific editorial board of ANU Press.

Contents

List of illustrations

Maps

Tables

Figures

List of acronyms

ADB	Asian Development Bank
ADC	Assistant District Commissioner
APEC	Asia-Pacific Economic Cooperation
ATM/s	automatic teller machine/s
BPP	Borneo Pacific Pharmaceuticals
BRI	Belt and Road Initiative
CHEC	China Harbour Engineering Company
CITES	Convention on the Trade of Endangered Species
CMC/s	Chinese multinational corporation/s
DSTP	deep sea tailings placement
DA	defence attaché/s
DRC	Democratic Republic of Congo
GST	goods and services tax
HPAL	high-pressure acid leaching
JCU	James Cook University
KMT	Kuomintang (Nationalist Party)
LBC	Lae Biscuit Company
LMG	like-minded group
MCC	Metallurgical Corporation of China
MOU	memorandum of understanding
MP	member of Parliament
MRA	Mineral Resources Authority
NFA	National Fisheries Authority
NGO/s	non-governmental organisation/s

OECD	Organisation for Economic Co-operation and Development
PIC/s	Pacific Island Country/ies
PLA	People's Liberation Army
PNC	People's National Congress
PNG	Papua New Guinea/n
PNGBC	PNG-born Chinese
PNGDF	Papua New Guinea Defence Force
PRC	People's Republic of China
RH	Rimbunan Hijau
SOE/s	state-owned enterprise/s
TNC	The Nature Conservancy
UK	United Kingdom
US	United States
WWI	World War I
WWII	World War II

Contributors

Alexandra Y. Aikhenvald is Professor at the Jawun Research Centre of Central Queensland University (Cairns), and Australian Laureate Fellow. She is a major authority on languages of the Arawak family from northern Amazonia and has written grammars of Bare (1995) and Warekena (1998), plus *A Grammar of Tariana, from Northwest Amazonia* (CUP, 2003) and *The Manambu Language of East Sepik, Papua New Guinea* (OUP, 2008), all based on extensive immersion fieldwork, in addition to essays on various typological and areal topics. She has edited numerous books, among them *The Oxford Handbook of Evidentiality* (OUP, 2018) and, jointly with R. M. W. Dixon, *The Cambridge Handbook of Linguistic Typology* (CUP, 2017). Her other major publications include *Classifiers: A Typology of Noun Categorization Devices* (OUP, 2000), *Language Contact in Amazonia* (OUP, 2002), *Evidentiality* (OUP, 2004), *Imperatives and Commands* (OUP, 2010), *Languages of the Amazon* (OUP, 2012), *The Art of Grammar: A Practical Guide* (OUP, 2014), *How Gender Shapes the World* (OUP, 2016), *Serial Verbs* (OUP, 2018), *The Web of Knowledge: Evidentiality at the Crossroads* (Brill, 2021), and *A Guide to Gender and Classifiers* (OUP, forthcoming), in addition to a general interest book *I Saw the Dog: How Language Works* (London, Profile Books). Her current focus is on the integration of language and society and the ways of conceptualising disease and well-being in minority languages and cultures, and investigation of languages and cultures of Amazonia and New Guinea, including a comprehensive grammar of Yalaku, from East Sepik.

Vincent Backhaus is a Research Fellow based at The Cairns Institute where his current research explores the engagement of Reef Traditional Owners across the Great Barrier Reef and the ways Traditional Owner values inform, lead and govern crown of thorns research and management. Prior to this he taught across the suite of Indigenous studies subjects offered through the Indigenous Education and Research Centre at James Cook University and continues to supervise master's and doctoral candidates. He is also part of the development team for the JCU–CSIRO strategic partnership, which has a key focus on building Indigenous research capacity in the North. Vincent's specialities range across Indigenous education, anthropology and psychology as well as Indigenous studies and the politics of knowledge. He has an emerging research focus on environmental governance, sociality, Indigenous/ traditional ecological knowledges and education pathways across terrestrial and marine environments.

Laurie Bragge spent more than 45 years living and working in Papua New Guinea after taking a job with the Australian administration as a patrol officer (a.k.a. kiap) in 1961. During this time, he developed a deep appreciation and respect for Papua New Guinea and the peoples of the Sepik. He spent most of his time in the Sepik area but also in other parts of the country such as the Highlands, Milne Bay and the Gulf Province. In 2018 he generously donated what we now know as the Bragge Collection to James Cook University. The collection features two intimately connected components—more than 600 material culture artefacts collected by Laurie Bragge during the time he lived and worked in Papua New Guinea, and the extensive personal library he amassed containing various resources, which he used extensively when writing his multi-volume history of the Sepik.

James Chin is Professor of Asian Studies at the University of Tasmania. He was also the inaugural Director of the Asia Institute, University of Tasmania. In the late 1990s, he joined University of Papua New Guinea's Political Science Department where he served as Chair of the department in the early 2000s. Although he is widely regarded as a leading scholar in contemporary Malaysian politics, he has also maintained a close interest in the political landscape in Papua New Guinea and Fiji.

Simon Foale is an Associate Professor in the College of Arts, Society and Education at James Cook University where he teaches anthropology, political ecology and development studies. His primary research interests include coastal small-scale fishery management (including commodity fisheries), socially sustainable and culturally informed approaches to biodiversity conservation, sustainable livelihood development, and the role of local ecological knowledge in fishing and fishery management. He has also worked on the social and economic impact of mining. Simon has done most of his research in the Solomon Islands, Papua New Guinea and the Western Pacific.

Shaun Gessler is an anthropology PhD candidate from the Australian National University's Department of Pacific Affairs. His thesis investigates the relationship between the Chinese majority-run Ramu Nickel Cobalt Project in Papua New Guinea and the indigenous communities on whose land the mine is located. Shaun has professional experience in Papua New Guinea working and volunteering in international development, which underpins his research interests in the anthropology of development, the social impacts of resource extraction and China's rise in the Pacific.

Cathy Hair has broad experience in tropical aquaculture and fisheries. She has been involved with projects in the Pacific Islands region for more than two decades, working on aquaculture commodities for livelihoods and food security. In 2020 she completed her PhD, a multidisciplinary thesis on development of community-based sea cucumber mariculture in Papua New Guinea. Cathy is an Adjunct Fellow within the College of Arts, Society and Education at James Cook University and the School of Science, Technology and Engineering at the University of the Sunshine Coast.

Anna Hayes is a senior lecturer in International Relations in the College of Arts, Society and Education at James Cook University, Cairns. She is also an Honorary Research Fellow at the East Asia Security Centre. Anna specialises in non-traditional threats to security, with a particular focus on China. She has presented numerous papers in Beijing on topics ranging from the situation in Xinjiang to how the Belt and Road Initiative has been viewed outside of China, as well as the Quad and the Indo-Pacific from an Australian perspective. Anna has published numerous articles, book chapters and edited books on these topics. She is coeditor of *Cultures in Refuge: Seeking Sanctuary in Modern Australia* (Ashgate, 2012, with Robert Mason), *Migration and Insecurity: Citizenship and Social Inclusion in a Transnational Era* (Routledge, 2013, with Robert Mason) and *Inside Xinjiang: Space, Place and Power in China's Muslim Far Northwest* (Routledge, 2016, with Michael Clarke).

Rosita Henry is Professor of Anthropology at James Cook University. Her research concerns relationships between people and places in Australia and the Pacific as expressed through the politics of public performances, cultural festivals, museums and cultural heritage, and gender and development. Professor Henry is author of the book *Performing Place, Practicing Memory: Indigenous Australians, Hippies and the State* (Oxford and New York: Berghahn Books, 2012). She is coeditor of the book *The*

Challenge of Indigenous Peoples: Spectacle or Politics? (Oxford: Bardwell Press 2011) and coeditor of *Transactions and Transformations: Artefacts of the Wet Tropics, North Queensland* (Memoirs of the Queensland Museum [Culture], Volume 10, December 2016). More recently, she edited and contributed to an 'ethnographic autobiography' titled *A True Child of Papua New Guinea: Memoir of a Life in Two Worlds* (McFarland 2019), based on ethnographic field research in the Western Highlands of Papua New Guinea over a timespan of more than 20 years.

Kulasumb Kalinoe (Kula) is a PhD candidate in anthropology and law at James Cook University. Her research project is titled 'PNG Heritage in the Archives: A Legal Anthropology of Cultural Property'. This focuses on the cultural heritage issues concerning collections held in public institutions such as museums, galleries and libraries. There will be a particular emphasis on collections from Papua New Guinea with a focus on the Bragge Collection in the James Cook University Library. The Bragge Collection contains cultural artefacts and oral written histories from the Sepik region in Papua New Guinea. Currently there are no set guidelines in Papua New Guinea to protect traditional knowledge in public institutions, particularly when it could be secret/sacred knowledge. This project will analyse issues of access, ownership, gender and repatriation. Kula is also a Digital Editorial Fellow for *PoLAR: Political and Legal Anthropology Review*, where she is curating a feature *Cultural Rights are Human Rights: Decolonizing Museums through Repatriation & Source Community Partnerships*. Kula is a lawyer by profession and her broader research interests are human rights, social justice and Papua New Guinea.

Jeff Kinch is the Principal of the National Fisheries College in Papua New Guinea, supervising the Nago Island Mariculture and Research Facility, and is also an Adjunct Research Fellow in the Pacific Livelihoods Group at Curtin University in Western Australia. He has over 25 years' experience in project management in various donor-funded fisheries development management programmes and projects with the European Union, United Nations and the Asian Development Bank. Jeff has also worked for the Secretariat of the Pacific Regional Environment Program and the Pacific Community. On a practical level, he has experience in socioeconomic and environmental impact assessments, analysis of market chains, and issues surrounding climate change impacts on fisheries-focused livelihoods. He has also conducted several evaluations for government, NGOs and regional agencies in the Pacific Islands Region with a particular focus on Melanesia and Papua New Guinea. He has authored or coauthored peer-reviewed journal articles and many other technical reports, proposals, evaluations, reviews and education and awareness materials on a wide range of topics relating to fisheries and their management and development in the Pacific Islands Region.

I-Chang Kuo received his doctorate in December 2022 from The Australian National University's Crawford School of Public Policy. He is a postdoctoral researcher at Taiwan's National Science and Technology Council. His dissertation combines his expertise in anthropology and gender studies to examine employees' shifting power dynamics and personal identities in a Chinese nickel refinery in Madang Province, Papua New Guinea. The anthropology of mining, gender and masculinities studies, studies of the labour process, place and time, and global China studies are all his areas of interest.

Daniela Vávrová was born in Bratislava, in the former Czechoslovakia. Before completing her PhD in Australia, she studied social and cultural anthropology at the University of Vienna in Austria. She is currently Adjunct Research Fellow and a founder of The AV Lab Productions and ALTAR research group at The Cairns Institute and College of Arts, Society and Education, James Cook University. Along with her interest in different cultures, she explores the relationship between anthropology and visual communication, between written accounts, photography and ethnographic filmmaking. Since 2005 her field site has been situated in the East and West Sepik provinces of Papua New Guinea. Her PhD thesis and film, *'Skin Has Eyes and Ears': An Audio-Visual Ethnography in a Sepik Society* (2014), explores how people shape and are shaped by their social and cultural environment through their sensory experiences. www.danielavavrova.net.

Vyvyen Wong is the Research Communications Officer at The Cairns Institute at James Cook University. Prior to this role, she was the key Project Officer for the collaboration 'University of Papua New Guinea and James Cook University's Twinning Project/Partnership'. Vyvyen was born in Papua New Guinea and is of Melanesian-Chinese heritage. She grew up speaking English, Cantonese and Tok Pisin, and is in the process of learning more about her mother tongue Taishanese. Vyvyen holds a Bachelor of Business with a double major in Marketing and Tourism Management; however, she is contemplating further studies in the research area.

Michael Wood is an Adjunct Senior Lecturer at James Cook University in the College of Arts, Society and Education. He is currently interested in the new wave of carbon projects in Papua New Guinea, new forms of regional violence and the role of patrol officers in Papua New Guinea's transition to Independence. He is also interested in how all three may be related and how reading George Orwell might help him in making such connections.

1

The Chinese in Papua New Guinea's past, present and future

Michael Wood, Anna Hayes
and Rosita Henry

Collections of essays derived from a conference or workshop often reflect the disparate interests of the contributors and organisers while introductions to such collections typically provide a degree of coherence and justification by outlining an encompassing foundational origin story. This collection emerged from a workshop held at James Cook University (JCU) in Cairns in early November 2020 that was funded with the explicit aim of enhancing research capacities within the social sciences and humanities at JCU. This partially explains the number of JCU contributors to the collection.

The workshop had a rather ambitious title: Re-Visualising the Past, Imagining the Future: Race, Governance and Development in Papua New Guinea. Such ambition reflected the initial aim of the workshop, which was to consider the importance of a vast collection of documents, patrol reports, diaries and transcripts of interviews, and more than 600 material culture artefacts donated to JCU in 2018 by former officer of the Australian administration in Papua New Guinea (PNG), L. W. Bragge. This assemblage of archives and artefacts derived from Bragge's more than 45 years of living and working in PNG after he took up a job as a patrol officer in 1961. A further aim was to develop a research programme based on the Bragge Collection that would explore histories of Australian governance, race relations and development in PNG building on prior work on the colonial archives (McPherson, 2001). We thought a project on the role of patrol officers in the de-colonisation of PNG in the period between 1945 and 1975 might provide an interesting perspective into the archives of the period.

There was some debate about such a project. It was suggested that the emphasis on patrol officers' archives like the Bragge Collection could be seen as another example of colonial studies emphasising the European experience. One response was to move the emphasis of the proposed workshop beyond existing accounts of Australian colonial governance and race relations.[1] We argued that such works often deployed an approach that focused on the dualism of white Australian and black Papua New Guinean interactions and inter-cultural zones of exchange. Building on prior work (Bashkow, 2006; D'Arcy, Crowl & Matbob, 2014; Smith, 2012a, 2013b; Wood, 1995) we proposed that the workshop would move beyond such limited framing of colonialism and post-colonialism. It would do this by exploring how interactions, governance and development in PNG were also structured in response to the presence of the Chinese in PNG. Such a Chinese-centric re-imagining of PNG history would help destabilise understandings of PNG's colonial history as just a black and white experience. Further research on the Chinese presence in PNG's colonial histories would help develop new ways of reading both the Australian colonial archive and the personal archives of patrol officers like that created by Bragge. Such an emphasis promised to make the Chinese more central to any accounts of the colonial and post-colonial histories of PNG. The workshop emerged as a response to the broader absence of the Chinese in histories of PNG. There also seemed to be a lack of such material in accounts of Australian colonial and post-colonial relationships with PNG (a point developed below).

We thought the colonial records related to New Guinea might offer some promising leads on Chinese voices, perspectives and actions but there were some limits to such a project. In the colonial era, Asians and Chinese were not the dominant concern of patrol reports and other records and many of New Guinea's archival records were destroyed during World War II (WWII). Moreover, following German colonisation of New Guinea in 1884, it was

---

1   A related response was to develop a research project that would explore how the patrol officers' daily activities were linked to ongoing global and national political debates about the colonial and de-colonial implications of such activities. These debates often centred on what political institutions could best secure post-colonial independence and modern citizenship.

primarily New Guinea, and not Papua, which received Chinese and Asian immigrants. At the time of its Federation, the Australian Commonwealth Government passed the *Immigration Restriction Act 1901*, which sought to prevent and tightly control Asian immigration to Australia. This act was applied to Papua when it became a territory of Australia with the result that virtually no Asians were allowed into Papua until the mid-1950s. What this meant is that the Papuan colonial archive was defined by a complete absence of Chinese and Asians until the 1950s.

New Guinea's history in reference to Asians was different to Papua's. After World War I (WWI), in 1920, German New Guinea became a Mandated Territory of the League of Nations under Australian control, and the Australian Immigration Restriction Act was then used to profoundly restrict Chinese and Asian movement into New Guinea. The governance of New Guinea (and Papua) was a fundamentally racialised process (Wolfers, 1975) and the Chinese in New Guinea were incredibly significant subjects of such racial ordering. The process of regulating the Chinese generated a large body of archival material, especially concerning their movement between states and their living conditions in New Guinea.

Beyond the archive: Towards the politics and power shifting of the Chinese in PNG

As we moved towards finalising the workshop it became clear that our participants had effectively expanded the range of topics to be addressed well beyond the archival emphasis developed by the initial proponents of the workshop (Henry, Wood & Backhaus).[2] Most of the papers presented at the workshop provided accounts of contemporary Chinese in PNG and their experiences of politics, power, and difference. By detailing the agency of the Chinese, and those they engaged with, presenters foregrounded a distinctly interactive analysis of social relations, conflicts and politics, but did so without abandoning analysis of power differences and inequalities. Many of the papers provided detailed descriptions of the multiple, and different, scales of integration of the PNG Chinese into the wider world and highlighted the continually transforming, contextually specific nature of this integration over time. Another feature of the workshop (and this

---

2   Chris Ballard and Jude Phillip presented papers on patrol officers and colonial collectors, but their papers unfortunately did not become part of this collection.

collection) was that differences between domains such as local, national and global did not always function as central analytical concepts (Gulliame & Huysmans, 2019). Some participants avoided assuming they could present one political domain—such as a state or regional geo-politics—as usefully distinguishable from another realm of politics located in a 'local' everyday world of Chinese in PNG. They refused to place agency in powerful state or corporate elites 'outside' the past or current colonies and 'beyond' the reach of those living in the colonies.

Such arguments also emerged in workshop discussions of the colonial state and the idea of multiple or partial sovereignties. Rabaul, the capital of New Guinea, was an important site for Chinese engagement with, and the enactment of, forms of government, state power and sovereignty that were different to those deployed by the Australian colonial regime. Crucial here was the role of the Chinese state—represented by the Nationalist Government and later by the Communist government (see Liu, 2011; Liu & Van Dongen, 2016)—and the United Nations as the overseer of Australia's trusteeship. Post-WWII, New Guinea was never simply just an exclusively white Australian colonial government, but at times it was an interactive site for competing claims by states to influence policies relevant to the Chinese in New Guinea. The Australian colonial government's practices and policies in reference to New Guinea Chinese were partly formed in response to the perceptions of, and pressures created by, the UN and the Chinese state. Other states such as Indonesia, India and Russia were also at times influential (Inglis, 1972). To summarise, the Chinese in New Guinea were the subjects of multiple governments rather than just a monolithic Australian colonial government.

Given such arguments, analysis based on the centrality of national sovereignty or methodological nationalism seemed, at times, to limit insights into the history of the Chinese in PNG (Wimmer & Glick Schiller, 2002). Some participants were trying not to privilege the nation-state and its institutional order in their analysis. Instead, they wanted to explore the role of non-state forms of trans-local or diasporic power (Gilroy, 2000). They descriptively highlighted how states, such as New Guinea and Australia, were themselves shaped by global and trans-national forces that limited their ability to decide policy and control migration flows. Such contributions reiterated the point that the experiences of the Chinese in PNG have always been deeply influenced by trans-national connections and perspectives that are not just defined by nation-states (Smith, 2014).

While recognising the undoubted power and influence of often imperial-like configurations of states and corporations, some presenters took the view that the influence and power of these configurations was defined, debated and transformed in specific, always local, contexts of interaction. Power shifts have been less clearly observed or are less visible within strands of the PNG-specific literature (Pan et al., 2019; Pan, 2014; Connolly, 2020). Perhaps power shifts, like many other developments in PNG, cannot fit easily into a single clear narrative, but emerge as outcomes of political conflict and contradictory processes.

On the other hand, some participants were interested in developing arguments about a distinct shift in power to the state of China in PNG. In this collection, this view is reflected in Chin's argument that China is now a dominant influence on PNG politics and Hayes's concern that the Belt and Road Initiative (BRI) and the dream of Chinese global hegemony could intensify that dominance. Insofar as both are political scientists it is possible their response to the question of Chinese dominance in PNG reflects an international relations approach to explaining the Chinese in the Pacific as opposed to the more ethnographic approach adopted by other contributors to this volume.

Emphasis on the power shift to China tends to focus attention on the regional and geopolitical levels of analysis rather than on specific countries or accounts of specific interactions. Except for D'Arcy, Matbob and Crowl's (2014) recent collection, work on Asian and Chinese engagements and power shifts with the Pacific can make PNG seem a marginal figure in debates about Chinese expansion (Crocombe, 2007; Wesley-Smith & Porter, 2010; Smith & Wesley-Smith, 2021). Talk of the 'Pacific' or 'Asia-Pacific' or 'Indo-Pacific' highlight the vast scale of the strategic interests at stake in the power shift to China, whereas an emphasis on PNG material offers a narrower, less dramatic sense of geo-political relevance, crisis or conflict. This may be because the Pacific continues to be a site of unresolved conflict between China and Taiwan for recognition, whereas PNG recognised China in 1976. It may be that China's direct investment and expenditure via the BRI does not actually convert into the kind of influence expected in the power shift accounts. The fact that answers to such questions are often hard to find, or infrequently provided, implies there has been a kind of epistemological marginalisation of PNG in debates about power shifts between states in the Pacific, their projects of empire, their geopolitical strategies and their visions of a Chinese future. We think this should change.

Histories of the Chinese diaspora in PNG

In the workshop some participants argued that current debates about the shifting spaces and locations of power ('look North', 'take back PNG') could, and should, be re-thought by considering the histories of movement that crucially constituted the experience of all diasporic Chinese in PNG. Such histories multiplied the places of origin of the Chinese in PNG and diversified their social differences and ongoing connections with multiple nation-states, regional trade networks and claims to citizenship.

These movements in and out of what we now call PNG have a long history. Early Chinese visits to PNG date back to the Ming dynasty (1368–1644) (Waley-Cohen, 1999, p. 53). The Chinese who arrived in PNG were part of a long history concerning other overseas Chinese and their treatment by the Chinese state and recipient communities. Manchu rulers of the later Qing state (1644–1911) regarded overseas Chinese as being subjects of China and the localities in which they resided were seen as 'part of China's domain' (Gamer, 2012). Elements of this kind of thinking still have influence today in the Chinese state's attempts to incorporate the diaspora into itself and in this way 'terminate diaspora dispersal' (Gilroy, 2000, p. 124).

The history of Chinese movement in and out of PNG intensified with German colonisation of New Guinea in 1884. Chinese indentured labourers emigrated there to work in the emergent tobacco and copra industries. By 1895 many of those indentured labourers had died and most of those who survived returned home once their term of service had ended. The Chinese in New Guinea during this time mostly came from Sumatra (ruled by the Dutch), Singapore (ruled by the British), Hong Kong (ruled by the British), Malaysia and Australia (Biskup, 1970; Ichikawa, 2004, 2006; D'Arcy, 2014; Firth, 1976). Therefore, they were a mix of ethnic Chinese who were born into the overseas community in their adopted locale, perhaps from families who had lived there for generations, or they had left China for those adopted locales then re-migrated to New Guinea. In 1886, Chinese porters from Australia were recruited into a scientific expedition in New Guinea. This is believed to be the first example of trans-migration from Australia to New Guinea by the Chinese (Biskup, 1970). From 1898, Chinese migrants were beginning to settle in Rabaul, Kokopo, Kavieng, Lae and Madang. At this point, we also see the emergence of the first distinction between old Chinese and new Chinese (Biskup, 1970). This dualistic framing, which still exists into the present day, was originally intended to distinguish those Chinese who were from existing overseas Chinese communities (they were the old Chinese) from the newer arrivals from mainland China (Hokkian: *singkeh* or 'new chums'). As Ichikawa (2006) explains, multiple terms have been used to try to encapsulate some of the different peoples within this diverse group including *huaren* (ethnic Chinese), *huaqiao* (overseas Chinese) and *huayi* (Chinese descendants). Such terms reflect the significant diversity of the prior residential locations, and associated experiences, of the Chinese in New Guinea.

In 1920, German New Guinea became a Mandated Territory of the League of Nations, under Australian control as part of the Versailles Treaty following WWI. Under the Australian regime, Chinese residents who had migrated to New Guinea before 1922 were classified as 'alien residents', while those arriving after that date were only permitted limited stays in the territory (Wolfers, 1975). These policies made family reunification or chain migration from China exceedingly difficult. Many of the Chinese living in New Guinea at this time were single men, now unable to invite Chinese women to join them in New Guinea as their wives. Hence, some Chinese men married New Guinea women. Children born from these marriages were often educated and socialised as Chinese, within the Chinese community (Wu, 1982).

In the mid-1950s, changes to the Immigration Restriction Act in Australia meant that it was now possible for Chinese migrants to become Australian citizens. Many New Guinea Chinese took this option, regarding it to be a good opportunity given that their business and educational links were now more oriented towards Australia. In addition, some were concerned over what might happen to them when PNG inevitably gained its independence from Australia (Wu, 1982). Chinese communities in Indonesia, Burma and other newly independent Asian and African states were subject to violence (Mark, 2012, p. 65; Chang, 1980). Fears over PNG's post-independence stability, and possible ethnic violence, led some Chinese in PNG to migrate to other countries, most frequently, Australia. Others stayed but remained concerned about what may lie ahead (Wu, 1982; Ichikawa, 2006). In some cases, older Chinese in PNG who had sent their children to school and higher education in Australia found themselves alone in PNG when, rather than returning home, their children preferred to find work and settle in Australia. Therefore, the parents migrated to Australia to be reunited as a family unit. For others, Australia was the preferred location for living out their elder years especially as economic, social and political security within PNG became more fractious following Independence (Ichikawa, 2006). A slumping *kina* post-independence, and increasing crime rates, were also push factors driving out-migration from PNG (ibid.).

From the 1970s onwards, PNG also attracted a wave of 'new Chinese' migrants from Indonesia, Singapore, Malaysia, Taiwan, Hong Kong and mainland China (Chin, this volume, 2008; Smith, 2014). These new groups added to the diversity of the Chinese in PNG, based on their former site of residence as well as home provinces in mainland China, which now extended beyond Guangdong and Fujian to include cities like Shanghai and Beijing. The new Chinese appeared in provinces across PNG, including Western Province and Sanduan, rather than the urban centres (such as Port Moresby, Rabaul/ Kokopo and Lae) favoured by the old Chinese. The ability to become a PNG national, thereby being free to conduct business inside of PNG, was a major pull factor for migration (Ichikawa, 2006, pp. 123–7). The departure of Australia from PNG after Independence opened up 'economic niches' for overseas Chinese, other Asians and the more recent newcomers from the People's Republic of China (PRC) (Smith, 2012a, 2013b). PNG could also be used as a 'stepping-stone', allowing re-migration to Australia, New Zealand, Guam or further afield. Hence, PNG remains a destination for Chinese migration flows, both in and out, sojourner and settler.

The Chinese in PNG were never a single homogenous group, but a complex series of historically and culturally unique groups with different origins, languages and histories (Chin, this volume, 2008; Ichikawa, 2003, 2004; Inglis, 1997; Smith, 2014; Wu, 1982, 1994, 1998). Describing and analysing the histories of these Chinese and their interactions was the complex task we found ourselves immersed in during the workshop. We found ourselves re-thinking who the Chinese in PNG were and what types of geographies of power, politics and sociality were implicated in their movement in and out of colonial and post-colonial PNG. All the chapters in this collection show how Chinese lives in PNG have always involved complex conjunctions of local, state and trans-national interactions and relations.

Developing power, resources and the Chinese in PNG's future

In addition to issues of how to think about the past and its impact on Chinese identity, agency and history, the workshop also explored a variety of colonial and post-colonial projects that promised to develop a good future for an independent state of PNG and its citizens. We were interested in the Chinese engagement with development, broadly understood as a set of influential ideas, policies and projects concerning the relationships between elements of PNG's past, present and its imagined future.[3] While development is often understood to imply a linear sense of a purposeful and progressive unfolding of events over time, the projects we considered, especially those concerned with natural resource extraction, did not always develop in this manner.

In our discussions, colonial and post-colonial developmental logics and projects, along with their material outcomes, were often described as transformative and unstable sites of wealth creation, conflict, compromise, exploitation and resistance. We also questioned the assumption that the current PNG nation-state was the natural and necessary organisation for the creation of a modern society. Presenters highlighted how the colonial and post-colonial states of PNG did not always have the ability and resources to deliver the full promise of modernity. They also highlighted the multiple forms of capital and corporate organisation that the Chinese created in their various economic activities in PNG. Here participants refused to assume that there was one dominant form of capitalism or market organisation that would ensure development in PNG.

The accounts that emerged in our workshop outlined different histories concerning PNG's future to those found in still influential narratives of progress, modernisation and linear continuous development towards key goals. A number of the chapters outlined processes of development that involved generating new forms of domination and inequality. Another topic involved the post-colonial collapse of the PNG nation-state as a political institution that could effectively create equitable development. Our attention was often centred on popular criticisms linking the Chinese and the current corruption of the PNG state. For example, Malaysian Chinese influence

---

3   This interest in development is evident in the chapters in this volume by Gessler, Foale et al., Kuo and Hayes.

in PNG's forestry sector has forged an association between the Chinese, the corruption of the PNG government and the exploitation of PNG natural resources. Such associations echo earlier colonial representations of the Chinese as a racialised, fetishised body that is systematically linked to money (as in Gessler's chapter where some Chinese are defined as 'money face'), corrupt business deals and capital accumulation that is impossible to comprehend or fully explain. Other associations position the Chinese as possessing extra-ordinary powers and knowledge of business, political influence and money-making in ways that are opaque and hidden. These powers are often considered both unhealthy and dangerous—they have long been presented as a disease within the European white body politic (Anderson, 2002) and now the same imagery is applied to the PNG body politic. Earlier talk of 'tough and clever Chinese' who are 'culturally adapted to the requirements of business in cultural frontier situations' (Rowley, 1967, p. 13) has been recently supplemented by talk of a 'Chinese mafia' in PNG (Windybank, 2008, p. 36) and criminal gangs (Wani, 2018).

The November 2021 riots in the Solomon Islands were a reminder that Chinese people in PNG are also intermittently, but regularly, subject to incidents of violence that are partly linked to stereotyping of Chinese.[4] There are certain important, yet to be documented, vulnerabilities and emotional intensities involved in daily life under such conditions of permanent threat. Wu notes that when PNG was preparing for self-government in 1973 some Chinese believed 'that if they did not make plans well ahead they might be stranded in isolated towns (Rabaul was a major one) when a riot suddenly erupted' (1982, p. 147). There was a view that while the Australians would send troops to rescue expatriates some thought that given what happened to the Rabaul Chinese in WWII it would be 'Europeans first and Chinese second: by the time it was the turn of the Chinese they could already have been slaughtered' (Wu, 1982, p. 147). Jumping forward about 50 years to 2021, Matbob observed that over recent years 'there have been numerous attacks on and killing of the Chinese in PNG' (2021, p. 457). Such attacks generate extensive commentary in PNG's social media, but relatively little interest from scholars. In November 2019, when two Chinese storekeepers were murdered in a remote logging camp in the Western Province of PNG some comments by Papua New

4   See: Walden, Max, Seselja, Edwina, & Graue, Catherine. (2021, November 24). Protesters teargassed as they call for Solomon Islands Prime Minister to step down. *ABC News.* www.abc.net.au/news/2021-11-24/protesters-demand-solomon-islands-prime-minister-step-/100647536. For other accounts of earlier riots see: Allen, 2008; Smith, 2012b; and Chin, 2010.

Guineans implied that these murders were an appropriate response to the Chinese exploitation of the region's forests and landowners (Wood & Brooksbank, 2021). Such violence, and its justification, are some of the negative consequences of merging critical representations of the Chinese with their role in PNG's development.

Our participants negotiated these kinds of difficulties of adequately representing the Chinese in PNG by adopting a diverse range of approaches. Perhaps it is true those with the greatest knowledge of the state of China (Hayes) and the Chinese in PNG (Chin and Gessler) are more critical of the Chinese than other contributors. But this apparent outcome is also a function of the topics chosen by our authors—something we now address.

Chapters and perspectives

Our account of the Chinese in PNG begins with Section 1 of this volume: 'The Chinese in PNG: Their travels and multiple histories'. This examination is opened with a discussion by Rosita Henry, Daniela Vávrová and Laurie Bragge of what might be discoverable in the colonial archive about the Chinese in the Sepik region as represented in patrol reports and other material in the Bragge Collection. In their chapter, Henry, Vávrová and Bragge explore how writing histories from such sources requires developing a unified analysis of both archival records and artefacts (Henry, Otto & Wood, 2013). They argue that artefacts and archives are different aspects of the same entity or event and are to be treated symmetrically. Notwithstanding differences in their material forms, regulatory institutions and social relations, an archival record should be analysed as an artefact and an artefact can be understood as an archival record. Hence, the narratives of the Sepik elders recorded by Bragge have become 'archival artefacts' understood to be materialised images of events and their effects. These artefacts hold narratives about the Chinese, Europeans and people living in the Sepik region. Henry, Vávrová and Bragge make an original contribution to our understanding of the Chinese in PNG history by opening up the possibility of Sepik histories of the Chinese. They note that while rich ethnographic data on Sepik social life and culture can be found in the Bragge archive, based on personal accounts by Sepik elders, the lives of Chinese migrants to the region are relatively less well documented. Henry, Vávrová and Bragge provide us with one of the first accounts of how the Chinese appear in the archives of European patrol officers. In doing this, they lay the foundations for further research into the multiple histories of the Chinese in PNG.

In Chapter 3, Michael Wood and Vince Backhaus argue that Australian histories of the decline and end of the Immigration Restriction Act have tended to ignore perspectives and voices from the colonies such as New Guinea. More specifically these have ignored Chinese voices. The voices from the colony that Wood and Backhaus highlight rely on forms of liberal thinking circulating at that time. Wood and Backhaus argue relations of discrimination were transformed by liberal ideas and practices circulating within the PNG colony and beyond. This liberal thinking was mobilised to de-racialise policies regarding the New Guinea Chinese, but other aims linked to these debates involved the removal of the Chinese from PNG and its future. The chapter highlights the tension within liberalism; on the one hand, it is concerned both with creating equalities based on enhancing human capabilities by making access to such capabilities less dependent on race, gender and class, while on the other hand it promotes forms of equality based on a sameness that, in this case, reproduced substantive inequalities linked to the removal of the Chinese from PNG and their assimilation into Australian culture. The chapter shows how liberal ideas circulating in different media between Chinese and Europeans sometimes came into conjunction to effect change or at least put change on the agenda. In such an account, liberalism is treated as a bundle of highly responsive and changing ideas and linguistic conventions that define specific political technologies of social ordering (such as Hasluck's re-naming of minorities) and which, as they travel, transform some of the terms of debates and policies concerning the Chinese.

Wood and Backhaus also argue that both the history of the Chinese in PNG and the development of the colonial state are fundamentally about urban infrastructure. Current accounts of the role of the Chinese in Australian projects of state building are too confined to the policing of borders, regulated crossing and social categorisation. Wood and Backhaus suggest that a greater focus on state building and urban infrastructure may highlight additional important roles of the Chinese in PNG colonial history.

One of the most pleasing and significant outcomes of the workshop was that some participants with a variety of PNG affiliations became aware of their own historical connections to events that were outlined in various presentations. Participants such as Vyvyen Wong and Kulasumb Kalinoe are both examples of this happenstance and they have enriched the volume with reflective vignettes. Both have commented on their experience of such processes and these comments emerge as part of their own histories of their relationships with, and experiences of, PNG.

Such contributions reflect a move away from nation-state models of the agents, bearers and makers of history towards diasporic (Rienmenschnitter & Madsen, 2009) or sojourning (Ichikawa, 2006) histories. These histories, as reflected in Wong and Kalinoe's contributions, emphasise spatial and temporal distances, movement, dis-junctures and conjunctions, and, sometimes, forced movement and exile. Their stories are more personal than state centric in emphasis and reflect our contributors' complex movements and entanglements with multiple places of belonging and residence. Along with the chapter by James Chin, Kalinoe's and Wong's accounts provide bridges between the Chapter 2 by Henry, Vávrová and Bragge, and Chapter 3 by Wood and Backhaus, about pasts represented in archival records, and the rest of the chapters in this collection, which are concerned with developments that have occurred between 2000–2020 and are less constrained by reliance on archival sources.

Kulasumb Kalinoe is a lawyer and anthropology PhD student at JCU working on intellectual property issues concerning material collected by Bragge from her home communities in the Sepik region. She has developed a PhD project that would engage appropriate parts of the Bragge archive with the current descendants of those whose histories he recorded during his work as a patrol officer in the Sepik. The project could involve these communities' developing protocols for regulating public access to this material. Kalinoe will explore and perhaps actively instigate ways Sepik memory owners might engage with the Bragge Collection to create their own histories of colonialism and their past. She will explore how new colonial and post-colonial histories and memories might be re-imagined by custodians and owners of the archives by developing 'archival affordances that depart from those associated with imperial rule' (Basu & De Jong, 2016, p. 5). In her reflective vignette, Kalinoe reflects on the nature and value of the archived interviews with Sepik elders that Bragge collected, one of which Henry, Vávrová and Bragge refer to in their chapter.

Kalinoe argues that the Chinese who came to New Guinea a long time ago are now recognised as belonging to specific provinces and hence are part of the PNG nation-state. Such recognition by other Papua New Guineans is only one component of what is a far more complex and contradictory set of understandings. Nonetheless, Kalinoe stresses the existence of a widely recognised sense of a rightful, possibly de-racialised, place-based Chinese belonging in PNG (Ang, 2022). Kalinoe is effectively inviting us to rethink our understanding of Chinese in PNG by taking seriously the PNG dimensions of this Chineseness.[5] She argues that such understandings of the 'PNG Chinese' or 'Sepik Chinese' are already well developed within Sepik affiliated communities. What also needs to be further explored is how these Sepik Chinese self-define, or otherwise make, themselves Papua New Guineans in their own right, just as they simultaneously make themselves 'Chinese' and 'Australian'. In raising such issues Kalinoe's reflections, and other contributions in this volume, highlight the need to move away from dualistic to multiple understandings of Chineseness in PNG.

Vyvyen Wong, was born in Rabaul in East New Britain Province, the last of nine children born to James and Winnifred Wong. James's father, who was from Fujian Province in China, originally came to New Guinea on his own, but later sent for his Chinese wife, who gave birth to James and his siblings in Rabaul. Winnifred's father also left a Chinese wife behind to travel to New Guinea for work, but she did not end up joining him in New Guinea. Thus, Winnifred is mixed Chinese and Melanesian. In her reflective vignette, Wong discusses her childhood growing up as part of the Chinese community in Rabaul, her understandings of race relations among the Chinese and the impact of Australian administrative policies and processes on the lives of her family members. Her discussion of her father's application for Australian citizenship provides an example of the practical application of such policies and debates regarding PNG Chinese that are raised by Wood and Backhaus in their chapter. Wong's text highlights the relative absence of detailed ethnography of Chineseness in contemporary PNG that provide new insights into race as involving mechanisms of privilege and power. Wong's account of her family is an argument for types of racial analysis that pays attention to those of mixed Chinese and Papua New Guinean heritage (Fozdar & McGavin, 2017; Goddard, 2017). Her family has long grappled with the legacies of the power and privilege of more racially 'pure' Chinese, Papua New Guineans and white Europeans. Wong's account points to how these legacies continue to matter (and not matter) in contemporary times.

---

5   Some phrasing in the section derives from Hendriks (2017).

James Chin's chapter in this collection further develops his interest in the Chinese living in PNG. He updates his now classic 2008 article on the Chinese in Port Moresby. Both works are full of lively anecdotes delivered in an engaging style. Chin's work is part of a broader body of research on Chinese living in urban PNG. Much of the first wave of this research began in 1970s and focused primarily on Rabaul (Wu, 1982; Cahill, 2012). The second wave has focused more on Chinese life in Port Moresby and the emergence of the most recent 'new Chinese' in PNG generally (Chin, 2008; Ichikawa, 2006; Smith, 2014).

In his chapter, Chin argues that the mainland Chinese have now become a dominant economic and political force in PNG. They dominate the local Chinese community and rival Australia for influence in national politics. He also makes suggestions about what might happen in the future. He thinks the PNG elite will play Australia and China against each other and that China is seen is as 'more flexible' and less concerned with issues of corruption than Australia. Chin argues that China will replace Australia as the most influential external actor in PNG politics. While PNG will move closer to China on political issues, it will remain more aligned with Australia culturally. He argues that these power shifts within PNG reflect the rise of China on the global stage (Chin, 2021). Chin's chapter concludes Section 1 of the volume.

Chapter 5 by Simon Foale, Cathy Hair and Jeff Kinch opens section two of the book, which examines 'The Chinese as transformers of PNG and its political economy'. Their chapter outlines the role of Chinese traders in the fisheries sector via a case study of the market for sea cucumber. Their chapter demonstrates how the trade is structured by differences in the value Chinese buyers and PNG producers attribute to sea cucumbers. The Chinese regard sea cucumbers as a type of high value food that imparts vitality to consumers. In contrast, producers do not typically consume their product and regard it as without value. The market is also crucially defined by the fact that Chinese control all elements of the supply chain from the buyer to the Chinese consumer and that this market chain is profoundly opaque to non-Chinese. The chapter by Foale, Hair and Kinch emphasises a persisting, perhaps intensifying, sinification of all relevant aspects of the supply chain, paying particular attention to transactions at the point of sale. At the same time, it is difficult to assess the effectiveness of regulations on this trade by the PNG National Fisheries Authority. This is compounded by the lack of interest in the sea cucumber market by environmental non-governmental organisations, meaning the impact of this trade on sea cucumbers is unclear.

Foale, Hair and Kinch's chapter transitions the book into discussions of current Chinese investment in natural resource extraction in PNG. Their chapter is followed by chapters from I-Chang Kuo and Shaun Gessler, who provide accounts of social relations in the Basamuk nickel processing factory that is part of the Ramu Nickel mine. The conjunction of these three chapters points to the possibilities of a comparative analysis of Chinese capital in PNG. If Foale, Hair and Kinch highlight the dominance of the Chinese throughout the supply chain, Kuo's chapter points to the different ways Chinese practices of industrial relations in PNG, and hence the price of labour, have been effectively trans-nationalised. Furthermore, Foale, Hair and Kinch's account of sea cucumber markets provides a contrast to Gessler's account of the Chinese–PNG interactions in food markets. In Foale, Hair and Kinch's account, both buyers and sellers of sea cucumber appear relatively happy with their trade partly because sellers can realise high financial returns from the sale of sea cucumber which, to them, is a low value product. In contrast, PNG sellers in the Basamuk food market are not able to establish a fair price for what they think is the true value of their product. All three chapters provide interesting insights into the development of markets influenced by the Chinese in PNG.

In his chapter, Kuo uses a labour process compromise theory to examine how industrial relations are influenced by Australian-imported standards and indigenous cultural values. The mine is run by a Chinese state-owned enterprise and was, until recently, the largest investment by China in any project in the Pacific region. The chapters by both Kuo and Gessler build upon a considerable body of prior research on the mine (Imbun, 2017; Leach, 2011; Smith, 2013a, 2013b; Zimmer-Tamakoshi, 2014). Kuo develops an account of Chinese–PNG work relations as they emerge within the company's industrial relations practices concerning promotion, training, health and safety. Utilising neo-Marxist theoretical perspectives developed in work relations studies and comparative material derived from China and Africa, Kuo provides one of the first accounts of industrial relations in a Chinese factory in PNG. He outlines how compromises between Chinese management and PNG staff were generated in contexts where power was sometimes complexly dispersed rather than tightly structured and where protocols and expectations could be restructured. In developing his discussion, he highlights how officials from the PNG state were at times influential and at other times absent and also highlights how representatives from the Chinese government played little direct role in the company's resolution of industrial disputes or disputes with landowners. Kuo offers a subtle account of dispute resolution that highlights some of the limits of the Chinese ability to dominate or exploit PNG workers.

Gessler's chapter provides the first detailed account of Chinese engagement with a market in PNG, the Marmar marketplace outside of the Basamuk nickel refinery. He examines how different understandings of market practices inform the way Chinese male buyers and PNG female sellers interact in the marketplace and how their interactions reproduce forms of sociality that are gendered, often antagonistic and at times racialised. For Gessler, the Chinese buyers come to the market with a price-centred understanding of market transaction as involving a commodity where it is appropriate to haggle and barter. The female sellers do not accept these practices and seek to define a social relationship where the price is accepted without further negotiation. As a result of these differences, market transactions fail to create a shared moral economy that can work across inter-cultural differences and inequalities. Rather, they become sites for the generation of conflicting values, stereotyping and forms of denigration and resistance.

Kuo and Gessler both make a significant contribution to understanding how the Chinese communicate with speakers of other languages. Kuo shows how the Basamuk nickel refinery is the origin place of a new male-only workplace pidgin in PNG. Through their focus on communication and what Gessler calls 'foreigner talk', both make an important contribution to our understanding of the production of cultural imaginaries at the level of interaction and linguistic practices that scaffold understandings of, and by, Chinese. In this, they build on and significantly develop the insight that Graeme Smith brought to his earlier analysis of the Chinese in PNG, which was significantly based on his own command of the Chinese language. The importance of these new forms of linguistic interaction highlighted by Gessler and Kuo is further developed in a commentary provided by Alexandra Aikhenvald.

Aikhenvald provides us with the first overview of the linguistic practices that emerge from attempts by Chinese and PNG speakers of other languages to communicate with each other. Relying on the preliminary data found in Gessler's and Kuo's chapters, she also contextualises her analysis of developments in PNG within the wider global literature on the Chinese engagement with pidgins, Creoles and foreigner talk. Having provided us with the necessary conceptual and comparative background, she makes explicit the significance of the workplace pidgin at the Basamuk nickel refinery outlined in Kuo's chapter. She does this by arguing it is unique in that no other Chinese-based pidgins have been documented in PNG. She further highlights this uniqueness by reviewing the relatively small number of accounts of Chinese workplace pidgins that have developed in other parts of the world. She wonders why we have no record of other Chinese pidgins in PNG and suggests that the emergence of Tok Pisin may have made a Chinese-based pidgin redundant. It is also possible that other Chinese pidgins in PNG may have been ignored and never recorded. She argues that up until the 1980s, Papua New Guineans may have perceived the Chinese as less relevant to their social and political relationships than the Europeans. Hence, there was little need to develop other forms of communication with Chinese beyond Tok Pisin.

Aikhenvald also considers Gessler's account of gendered foreigner talk in the Marmar market, which is adjacent to the Basamuk nickel refinery. This foreigner talk occurs only between Chinese men who buy food and PNG women who sell food to the men every morning when their shift ends. Aikhenvald highlights the use of mock Chinese by the women. She argues that while foreigner talk involves a specific form of convergent accommodation between two parties, mock Chinese involves the opposite by attributing a negative value to a mocked target. In drawing out such implications of Gessler's and Kuo's work, Aikhenvald outlines how there needs to be further research on the often racialised understanding of the Chinese as linguistically and socially inferior. As she notes, more research is needed to fully document these different types of meanings currently linked to the Chinese living in PNG. Such meanings help constitute the politics of difference in PNG today.

Anna Hayes's chapter outlines the increasing influence of China in the region but does so through the lens of the BRI and the intensifying geopolitical competition between the United States (US) and China, noting the implications of both for PNG's politics. Hayes argues the BRI, as part of Beijing's 'China Dream' grand strategy, seeks to transform the international system into a Sino-led international order, thereby replacing the US as the world's leading power. In addition, given the Pacific region is viewed as the southern extension of China's desired Maritime Silk Road, and its geostrategic location within Island Chain theory, the region is increasingly being drawn into this contest, alongside Australia. Hayes follows Hillman

(2020) in thinking the BRI constitutes Chinese imperialism that seeks to defy international rules and norms and concurs with Schuman (2020) that the BRI is the reestablishment of the tribute system via a China-centric trading system.

Following O'Dowd (2021, p. 415) Hayes also argues BRI investments may further exacerbate PNG's challenges with corruption, public sector management and poor governance, as well as questionable development projects and a lack of transparency and accountability over both loans and projects. Hayes outlines how high interventionist development models applied within China have resulted in cronyism, land grabs, local disempowerment and poor environmental outcomes, noting similar models may be applied in PNG. She highlights how PNG's landowners have already been identified as a 'problem' for Chinese investment in PNG because they truly do have rights over their land, unlike in the PRC. By exploring such possibilities, Hayes provides an astute and thought-provoking account of the negative effects of the BRI and the Chinese state's increasing influence on PNG's governance. Certainly, she and Chin both highlight how the PNG government's engagement with the BRI is occurring in the context of rapidly intensifying geopolitical competition in the Indo-Pacific region between the US and China, with Australia drawn into the contest. This is generating considerable political, economic, strategic and, increasingly, academic interest. Hayes usefully concludes our collection because her chapter asks: what is the future of China in PNG?

Concluding thoughts

In putting this volume together, our key concern has been to encourage focused research on histories of different Chinese peoples in PNG. We have challenged the treatment of the Chinese as a single homogenous group and have sought to foster recognition that there is great historical, political and cultural diversity among the people in PNG who have been 'orientalised' under the single category of Chinese.

We hope that the collection of chapters we have curated here will serve as a reminder of the importance of the Chinese in PNG's history and future. We also hope that the collection will be seen as invitation for others to create their own unique, 'irreducible' (Fanon, 1967) histories of their time with, or as, Chinese in PNG. This may not fully explain, nor fully predict, the yet to come world of the Chinese in PNG, but more stories of the past and present Chinese presence in PNG will certainly help us to better understand PNG's future as it emerges.

Acknowledgements

We thank the Cairns Institute in collaboration with the College of Arts, Society and Education, JCU, for funding and hosting the Humanities, Arts and Social Science Research Focus workshop on November 4–6, 2020, that seeded this volume. Vyvyan Wong and Helen Clarkson wonderfully organised the publicity, logistics and food for our workshop under the difficult and challenging constraints of COVID-19. We thank JCU Library staff for facilitating access to the Bragge collection, other scholars who participated in the workshop, including Chris Ballard, Colin Filer, Jennifer Gabriel, Stewart Lockie, Jude Philp, Kearrin Sims, Borut Telban and Maria Wronska-Friend, and community participants who enlivened the workshop discussion, especially Patricia Kassman, Mai Bragge, John and Christine Wong and Richard Cheong. Thanks also go to our student participants from the JCU PNG Student Association. Wood and Henry acknowledge the support of the Australian Research Council DP140100178 towards the research concerning PNG citizenship that informed issues relevant to this volume.

References

Allen, M. (2008). Politics of Disorder: The Social Unrest in Honiara. In S. Dinnen & S. Firth (Eds.), *Politics and State Building in Solomon Islands* (pp. 39–63). ANU Press. doi.org/10.22459/psbs.05.2008.02

Anderson, W. (2002). *The Cultivation of Whiteness: Science, Health and Racial Destiny in Australia*. Melbourne University Press.

Ang, I. (2022). On the perils of racialized Chineseness: race, nation and entangled racisms in China and Southeast Asia. *Ethnic and Racial Studies, 45*(4), pp. 757–77. doi.org/10.1080/01419870.2021.1990979

Bashkow, I. (2006). *The Meaning of the Whiteman: Race and Modernity in the Orokaiva Cultural World*. University of Chicago Press. doi.org/10.7208/chicago/9780226530062.001.0001

Basu, P., & De Jong, F. (2016). Utopian archives, decolonial affordances. Introduction to Special Issue. *Social Anthropology, 24*, pp. 5–19. doi.org/10.1111/1469-8676.12281

Biskup, P. (1970). Foreign Coloured Labour in German New Guinea: A Study in Economic Development. *The Journal of Pacific History, 5*, pp. 85–107. doi.org/10.1080/00223347008572166

Cahill, P. (2012). *Needed—but not wanted. Chinese in Rabaul. 1884–1960.* CopyRight Publishing.

Chang, C. Y. (1980). Overseas Chinese in China's Policy. *The China Quarterly, 2,* pp. 281–303.

Chin, J. (2008). Contemporary Chinese Community in Papua New Guinea: Old Money versus New Migrants. *Chinese Southern Diaspora Studies, 2*, pp. 117–26.

Chin, J. (2010). Papua New Guinea in 2009: anti-Chinese rioting and the liquefied natural gas deal. *Asian Survey, 50*(1), pp. 247–52. doi.org/10.1525/as.2010.50.1.247

Chin, J. (2021). Papua New Guinea in 2020: China rising and Bougainville independence. *Asian Survey, 61*(1), pp. 160–65.

Connolly, P. (2020). The Belt and Road comes to Papua New Guinea. *Security Challenges, 16*(4), pp. 41–64.

Crocombe, R. (2007). *Asia in the Pacific Islands: Replacing the West.* University of South Publications.

D'Arcy, P. (2014). The Chinese Pacifics: A Brief Historical Review. *The Journal of Pacific History, 49*(4), pp. 396–420. doi.org/10.1080/00223344.2014.986078

D'Arcy, P., Crowl, L., & Matbob, P. (Eds.). (2014). *Pacific-Asia Partnerships in Resource Development.* Divine Word University Press.

Fanon, F. 1967. *Black Skin White Masks.* Pluto Press.

Firth, S. (1976). The Transformation of the Labour Trade in German New Guinea, 1899–1914. *The Journal of Pacific History, 11*(2), pp. 51–65. doi.org/10.1080/00223347608572290

Fozdar, F., & McGavin, K. (2017). Introduction: 'Mixed race' in the Australo-Pacific region. In K. McGavin, & F. Fozdar (Eds.), *Mixed Race Identities in Australia, New Zealand and the Pacific Islands* (pp. 1–15). Routledge. doi.org/10.4324/9781315559391

Gamer, R. (2012). China Beyond the Heartland. In R. Gamer (Ed.), *Understanding Contemporary China* (pp. 171–215). Lynne Reinner Publishers.

Gilroy, P. (2000). *Against Race: Imagining Political Culture beyond the Colour Line.* The Belknap Press of Harvard University Press.

Goddard, M. (2017). A categorical failure: 'mixed-race' in colonial Papua New Guinea. In K. McGavin, & F. Fozdar (Eds.), *Mixed race identities in Australia, New Zealand and the Pacific Islands* (pp. 133–146). Routledge. doi.org/10.4324/9781315559391

Guillaume, X., & Huysmans, J. (2019). The concept of 'the everyday': Ephemeral politics and the abundance of life. *Cooperation and Conflict, 54*(2), pp. 278–96. doi.org/10.1177/0010836718815520

Hendriks, T. (2017). A darker shade of white: Expat self-making in a Congolese rainforest enclave. *Africa, 87*(4), pp. 683–701. doi.org/10.1017/s0001972017000316

Henry, R., Otto, T., & Wood, M. (2013). Ethnographic Artifacts and Value transformations. *HAU Journal of Ethnographic Theory, 3*(2), pp. 33–51. doi.org/10.14318/hau3.2.004

Hillman, J. (2020). *The Emperor's New Road: China and the Project of the Century.* Yale University Press.

Ichikawa, T. (2003). Transformation of Chinese Migration Patterns and Their Community in Papua New Guinea. *Journal of Asian and African Studies, 65*, pp. 181–206.

Ichikawa, T. (2004). Malaysian Chinese Migration to Papua New Guinea and Transnational Network. *The Journal of Malaysian Chinese Studies, 7*, pp. 99–113.

Ichikawa, T. (2006). Chinese in Papua New Guinea: Strategic Practices in Sojourning. *Journal of Chinese Overseas, 2*(1), pp. 111–32. doi.org/10.1353/jco.2006.0005

Imbun, B. Y. (2017). The Chinese, Political CSR, and a Nickel Mine in Papua New Guinea. In A. Verbos, H. Ella, & A. Perdro (Eds.), *Indigenous Aspirations and Rights: The Case for Responsible Business and Management* (pp. 47–59). Routledge.

Inglis, C. (1972). Chinese. In P. Ryan (Ed.), *Encyclopaedia of Papua and New Guinea* (pp. 170–74). Melbourne University Press.

Inglis, C. (1997). The Chinese of Papua New Guinea: From Settlers to Sojourners. *Asian and Pacific Migration Journal, 6*(3–4), pp. 317–41. doi.org/10.1177/011719689700600304

Leach, J. (2011). Twenty Toea has no power now. Property, Customary Tenure and Pressure on Land near the Ramu Nickel Project Area, Madang, PNG. *Pacific Studies, 34*(2/3), pp. 295–322.

Liu, H. (2011). An Emerging China and Diasporic Chinese: historicity, state, and international relations. *Journal of Contemporary China, 20*(72), pp. 813–32. doi.org/10.1080/10670564.2011.604502

Liu, H., & Van Dongen, E. (2016). China's Diaspora Policies as a New Mode of Transnational Governance. *Journal of Contemporary China, 25*(102), pp. 805–21. doi.org/10.1080/10670564.2016.1184894

Mark, C.K. (2012). *China and the World Since 1945: An International History.* Routledge.

Matbob, P. (2021). On-the-Ground Tensions with Chinese Traders in Papua New Guinea. In C. Smith & T. Wesley-Smith (Eds.), *The China Alternative? Changing Geopolitics in the Pacific* (pp. 451–72). ANU Press. doi.org/10.22459/ca.2021.15

McPherson, N. (2001). *In Colonial New Guinea. Anthropological Perspectives.* University of Pittsburgh Press.

O'Dowd, S. (2021). Bridging the Belt and Road Initiative in Papua New Guinea. In G. Smith & T. Wesley-Smith (Eds.), *The China Alternative? Changing Geopolitics in the Pacific* (pp. 397–425). ANU Press. doi.org/10.22459/ca.2021.13

Pan, C. (2014). Rethinking Chinese power: a conceptual corrective to the 'power shift' narrative. *Asian Perspective, 38*(3), pp. 387–410. doi.org/10.1353/apr. 2014.0016

Pan, C., Clarke, M., & Loy-Wilson, S. (2019). Local Agency and Complex Power Shifts in the Era of Belt and Road: Perceptions of Chinese Aid in the South Pacific. *Journal of Contemporary China, 28*(117), pp. 385–99. doi.org/10.1080/ 10670564.2018.1542220

Riemenschnitter, A., & Madsen, D. (Eds.). (2009). *Diasporic Histories: Cultural Archives of Chinese Transnationalism.* Hong Kong University Press.

Rowley, C. D. (1967). *The New Guinea Villager: The Impact of Colonial Rule on Primitive Society and Economy.* Praeger.

Schuman, M. (2020). *Superpower Interrupted: The Chinese History of the World.* Public Affairs.

Smith, G. (2012a). Beyond the Reach of the Whip: Chinese Investors in Papua New Guinea. *African East-Asian Affairs, 73*, pp. 4–10. doi.org/10.7552/73-0-69

Smith, G. (2012b). Chinese Reactions to Anti-Asian Riots in the Pacific. *The Journal of Pacific History*, *47*(1), pp. 93–109. doi.org/10.1080/00223344.2011.653482

Smith, G. (2013a). Nupela Masta? Local and Expatriate Labour in a Chinese-Run Nickel Mine in Papua New Guinea. *Asian Studies Review*, *37*(2), pp. 178–95. doi.org/10.1080/10357823.2013.768598

Smith, G. (2013b). Beijing's Orphans? New Chinese Investors in Papua New Guinea. *Pacific Affairs, 86*(2), pp. 327–49. doi.org/10.5509/2013862327

Smith, G. (2014). Fuqing Dreaming: 'New' Chinese Communities in Papua New Guinea. In L. D'Arcy, L. Crowl, & P. Matbob (Eds.), *Pacific-Asia Partnerships in Resource Development* (pp. 131–37). DWU Press.

Smith, G., & Wesley-Smith, T. (Eds). (2021). *The China Alternative? Changing Geopolitics in the Pacific*. ANU Press.

Waley-Cohen, J. (1999). *The Sextants of Beijing: Global Currents in Chinese History*. W. W. Norton & Company.

Wani, D. (2018, February 12). Illegal group exists. *The National.* www.thenational. com.pg/illegal-group-exists/

Wesley-Smith, T., & Porter, E. (2010). *China in Oceania: Reshaping the Pacific*. Berghahn Books.

Wimmer, A., & Glick Schiller, N. (2002). Methodological Nationalism and beyond: Nation-State Building, Migration and the Social Sciences. *Global Networks*, *2*(4), pp. 301–34. doi.org/10.1111/1471-0374.00043

Windybank, S. (2008). The Illegal Pacific, Part 1: Organised Crime. *Policy, 24*(1), pp. 32–8. www.cis.org.au/wp-content/uploads/2015/04/images/stories/policy-magazine/2008-winter/24-2-2008-sue-windybank.pdf

Wolfers, E. P. (1975). *Race Relations and Colonial Rule in Papua New Guinea*. Australia and New Zealand Book Company.

Wood, M., & Brooksbank, V. (2021, October 14). Draft Notes on kidnapping in the rainforests of PNG [Paper presentation]. Anthropology Research Seminar, Cairns, James Cook University.

Wood, M. (1995). 'White Skins', 'Real People' and 'Chinese' in some Spatial Transformations of the Western Province, PNG. *Oceania, 66*(1), pp. 23–50. doi.org/10.1002/j.1834-4461.1995.tb02529.x

Wu, David Y. H. (1982). *The Chinese in Papua New Guinea: 1880–1980*. Hong Kong University Press.

Wu, David Y. H. (1994). The Construction of Chinese and Non-Chinese Identities. In W.M. Tu (Ed.), *The Living Tree: The Changing Meaning of Being Chinese Today* (pp. 148–66). Stanford University Press.

Wu, David Y. H. (1998). The Chinese in Papua New Guinea: Diaspora Culture of the Late 20th Century. In L.-C. Wang & G.-W. Wang (Eds.), *The Chinese Diaspora: Selected Essays* (Vol 2, pp. 206–16). Times Academic Press.

Zimmer-Tamakoshi, L. (2014). Natural or unnatural partners? Inequality and the Gende's relations with mining companies. In P. D'Arcy, P. Matbob & L. Crowl (Eds.), *Pacific-Asia partnerships in resource development* (pp. 88–103). Divine Word University Press.

Section 1:
The Chinese in PNG:
Their travels and
multiple histories

2

Archives as artefacts of knowledge: A Sepik philosopher and a Chinese trader in Papua New Guinea

Rosita Henry, Daniela Vávrová
and Laurie Bragge

Introduction

The archive produced by officers of the Australian Administration in Papua New Guinea (including not only patrol reports, field diaries and other written records, but also photographs, and material culture collections) has much to contribute to our understanding of the colonial state and its legacy in Papua New Guinea (PNG). In this chapter, we approach this archive as an artefact of knowledge, focusing on the collection made by former government officer Laurie Bragge.

Laurie Bragge was sent to the Sepik area of PNG as a patrol officer in 1964. After he served at various patrol posts in the area, the Australian colonial administration appointed him Assistant District Commissioner of the Ambunti district, East Sepik Province in 1970.[1] The appointment included responsibility for maintaining peace, order and good governance among

---

1   In the Sepik area, Bragge was first put in charge of the Green River Patrol Post, then the Imonda Patrol Post before a stint in the Amanab subdistrict followed by a posting to Telefomin.

tens of thousands of speakers of over 50 indigenous languages, spread over thousands of square miles of the middle and upper reaches of the Sepik River, as well as any expatriates living in the area—including Chinese. At that time, Sepik people referred to government officers like Bragge as *kiaps*, or sometimes just as *gavman*—the government, in Tok Pisin. The Chinese were termed *kongkong*, while Europeans were referred to as *waitskin* (Mihalic, 1989 [1971]).

We consider the question of race relations during the colonial era by focusing on two characters who feature in the Bragge archive, especially his five-volume manuscript on the history of the Sepik region—a Chinese trader named Chu Leong and a Sepik man named Kolion, a widely respected Sawos elder from Nogosop Village in the East Sepik. Chu Leong and Kolion would have crossed paths during their lifetimes, as Chu Leong traded for sago with Sawos people (Bragge, personal communication, April 14, 2021). Certainly, Kolion would have known Chu Leong, by reputation at least.

Bragge's papers include an account of his meeting with Kolion, a description and photograph of the man and a transcript of an interview that he did with him in 1973. However, references by Bragge to Chu Leong's life and activities in the Sepik are based entirely on secondary sources. According to Bragge, he was on patrol in the Sawos area of the Sepik when he heard of Chu Leong's death in December 1966 (Bragge, personal communication, April 14, 2021). Bragge never met Chu Leong himself and, even if he had, he is unlikely to have interviewed him, as he did Kolion. Australian government officers were instructed to conduct patrols and area studies specifically focusing on the indigenous people, including their social and cultural practices, economic and political activities, land tenure and migration histories as well as demography. They were also instructed to report on the 'business activities' of non-indigenous people in these areas (Australia. Territory of Papua New Guinea. Department of Native Affairs, 1966).[2] As Bragge notes,

---

2   The Departmental Standing Instructions (Australia. Territory of Papua New Guinea. Department of Native Affairs, 1966, Volume 1, p. 162) includes under the heading 'Non-Indigenes' instructions to 'List all plantations, factories and commercial establishments owned and operated by non-indigenous persons in the area being surveyed'. We assume that the category 'non-indigenes' included Chinese, but they were not singled out as a racial category. Perhaps this reflects the liberal agenda of the Australian Minister of Territories (1951–1963), Paul Hasluck, and others as discussed by Wood and Backhaus (in Chapter 3 of this volume), which was to reduce the population of PNG to two categories, by giving the Chinese in PNG 'full Australian citizenship, with the right of permanent residence in Australia and to give every possible encouragement to all of them to identify themselves with Australians as part of a single immigrant community' in PNG (Hasluck, 1976, p. 31).

The Chinese were a fact of life but were ignored basically … On our patrols, each census division occasionally required an area study and the Standing Instruction book has got the headings laid out … I have no memory of any requirement to write about the Chinese … We were supposed to find out everything possible about the indigenous population of that census division … There definitely was a heading for Europeans. There was not a heading for Chinese; definitely not from my memory … There is a whole chapter on area studies, telling us what headings we needed to write under. I'm sure there was nothing about Chinese. (personal communication, April 14, 2021)

Thus, while the Sepik elder Kolion has a voice that is discoverable in the archive, albeit only via a transcript of an interview that Bragge did with him, Chu Leong is unfortunately knowable to us only through the little that Bragge was subsequently able to glean from other sources about him while doing post-retirement research for his manuscript entitled *History of the Sepik Region, PNG* (Bragge, 2018 a–e; hereafter referred to as Bragg's Sepik history). The Chinese were largely rendered invisible in the reports of Australian government officers, patrol officers or *kiaps* by colonial administrative reporting requirements (see also Wood & Backhaus, this volume).

Bragge's observations of Chu Leong and Kolion in his Sepik history (Bragge, 2018 a–e), highlight how different kinds of histories were constructed around the figure of the Chinese migrant and the Sepik elder in the reports of colonial agents. These differences continue to define forms of inclusion and exclusion that influence how 'we'—Australian academics, Papua New Guineans, those of Sepik heritage and Chinese—now write or otherwise record histories of PNG. What is discoverable in archives inevitably frames how histories of origin, migration, race and governance are represented, understood, forgotten and remembered today.

Archives as artefacts of knowledge

Stimulated by Riles's (2006) approach in her edited volume *Documents: Artifacts of Modern Knowledge* and Strathern's (1990) extension of the concept of artefact to performance and to event, we argue that treating archival collections as artefacts draws attention to the material conditions of the creation of these collections in the on-the-ground, embodied encounters between colonial state agents and the subjects of colonial governance.

For example, in the encounter between Bragge and Kolion, the exchange was initiated by Kolion, who specifically came to see the government officer to offer his testimony. By recording and transcribing Kolion's oral narrative, Bragge inevitably became an agent in transporting it beyond the bounds of the Sepik community (see Johnson, 2008, p. 110).

We see the colonial documents—texts, photographs, audio-visual recordings and so on, not just as technocratic artefacts of colonial bureaucratic state practice, but also as co-created products of performative encounters between government officials and the people they were sent to govern. They are materialised enactments of 'the tensions and discontinuities of empire' (Edmonds, 2006, p. 84).

Yet, if Bragge's archive is an artefact of knowledge, then we must also consider the limitations of that knowledge. In other words, what might be missing from the archive? What performances and events are not materialised in the archive? What does this absence tell us about race and governance in the colonial period? While Bragge included an account of the Chinese in his Sepik history and referred to their activities and to colonial government policies and practices regarding them (see especially Bragge, 2018b, Ch 9 'The arrival of the Chinese and introducing Chu Leong' and Bragge, 2018e), his material is much richer in detail about Sepik people. The colonial era archives produced by government officers, as artefacts of racialised governance, have long framed understandings of PNG history and culture, which are dominated by stories about Papua New Guineans in reference to Europeans, leaving little or no space for Chinese stories. Interestingly, what is discoverable about the Chinese presence in PNG is by virtue of the fact of their very absence in the archive.

Kolion's story: Origins, migration and the circulation of wealth

Bragge interviewed Kolion, a Sawos elder of the Niaui moiety, on February 21, 1973, in the rest house where he was staying during his two-day patrol visit to Nogosop Village, which, according to Bragge (2018d, p. 730), is regarded by Iatmul and Sawos people to be very near to their legendary place of creation. Although Bragge recorded Kolion's story as part of his duties as a patrol officer, it is not just another one of the many 'artefacts of bureaucratic labor duly performed, artifices of a colonial state declared to be in efficient operation', as Stoler (2009, p. 2) puts it. Kolion's story is much more than this. Kolion sought Bragge out himself. He came to the rest house in the evening specifically to offer his testimony and Bragge recorded it beyond the call of his duties, driven by a deep scholarly interest in the history and culture of the people among whom he had been placed to work.

Bragge later transcribed Kolion's testimony, subsequently including the whole transcript in his official patrol report (Bragge, 1972–73; in Appendix A 'Anthropological Notes') and again, over 40 years later, in his Sepik history (Bragge, 2018a). As Bragge notes, Kolion's 'statement is a fascinating blend of traditional religious belief as influenced by the impact of Christian teachings, including the adaptation of Jesus and the Sawos cult hero Mai'imp ...' (2018a, p. 730). At the same time, Kolion's story encourages reflection on the different historicities and values that might be discoverable in the archive, including Sepik understandings about the origins and nature of Europeans and Chinese and their activities in PNG.

In the following extract from Bragge's transcript of his interview with Kolion (who is referred to by Bragge as 'a Sepik philosopher'), Kolion expresses a particular understanding of 'sameness' and 'otherness' (identity and difference).

> Now what about this ground? You are a white-man and I am a black-man. Now what about this ground? It is the same (as us). There is white ground and there is black ground ...

> I am black and you are white. When I was born and I lay on my mother's lap, I was the same as you. I stood on this (black) ground and I became a black-man. It works the same with white ground, or red ground or yellow ground. Who changed it? Are you the big brother and I am the small brother? Our skin colour follows the colour of the earth we break. (Kolion in Bragge, 2018d, pp. 731–32)

Here Kolion is at pains to claim identity with Bragge ('I was the same as you'). This is an example of a well-recorded tendency in PNG to treat 'white people' as 'lost kin' (Burridge, 1969; Connolly & Anderson, 1987; Bell, 2016; Bashkow, 2006; Lattas, 2010). Bell (2016), for example, discusses such a claim by an elder named Ivia, in Baimuru (Gulf Province) in 2001. As Bell (2016, p. 28) writes:

> Through this shared cosmological beginning, Ivia sought to establish a moral relationship with me, as a representative white person. Ivia's story is of a genre, called 'cargo talk'. Possessing affinities to the Tok Pisin formulations of *kago* in terms of its metaphoric and relational aspects, cargo talk is a mode of critique (Robbins, 2004)

and a means by which to express hope (Crapanzano, 2004). It is a means by which speakers seek to elicit and reconfigure relations to transform their social, political and economic realities … As a performance of history, cargo talk helps enact the realities it purports to see by revealing the hidden potentialities in its subjects.

Yet, Kolion was not just conveying his ontological identity with Bragge that night in the guest house. He was also conveying his difference from Bragge, that is, not only the fact of their sameness but also the origin of their otherness, but not in the western sense of racial otherness where skin colour is a criterion in a quasi-scientific system of social classification based on human biology. While Kolion distinguishes between 'black-man' and 'white-man', these terms do not carry the same racialist meaning that they have in the West. Rather, skin colour, according to Kolion, is a product of the ground (land/earth). 'Was your ancestor a white woman and mine a black woman? No! It was the white ground and black ground' (Kolion in Bragge, 2018d, pp. 730–736). By extension, while he does not specifically mention Chinese, he notes that red ground gives rise to red-skinned people and yellow ground to yellow-skinned people. Skin colour is a loaded visual signifier of something Sepik people value above all else—place (*ples* in Tok Pisin)—that is, clan-based ground or land. In turn, *ples*—the ground itself —is imbued with something else that is highly valued—knowledge:

> The sago grows on this ground. The mother of the ground will not go far away; she stays at the base of the sago. We men are different, we get up and walk around, but she stays. You [white-men] went away and now you have come back. I stayed here and now you have come to see me and to teach me. You have books to hold your knowledge. We keep it in here [stomach indicated—popularly believed to be the mind; the repository of knowledge]. I cannot write like you can and I cannot read. I remember it all and I store it in here. My book is filled [again stomach indicated].

> Mai'imp [ancestral being] died and through his death knowledge was hidden from us black people … The knowledge is hidden and we do not know it … Our mother's vagina was closed against us and we obtained no further knowledge from her …

> We had no way to get knowledge, and then you white-men came back and you had books with knowledge and you gave more knowledge to us … You teach us but you do not give us all the secrets … Look at yourself and look at us. We are the same. Five fingers … Our difference is in our knowledge. Some knowledge is hidden from us. (Kolion in Bragge, 2018d, pp. 730–36)

Knowledge is seen as something that confers power and that can be taken away (or stolen), hidden and kept secret. In Kolion's worldview, differences between peoples of the Sepik and the various outsiders that entered their world—Germans, British, Australians and Chinese, Japanese and others— like gender differences, were founded on the assertion and enactment of the ownership of knowledge (or the material representations thereof; that is, the valuables or 'cargo' that these outsiders had brought with them). The nature of the relationship between the 'white-man' and the 'black-man' is like that of the relationship between Sepik men and women. In the cosmogonic past, as Kolion related, men appropriated from women the sacred images (objects) of knowledge that conferred to women their power and dominance. He referred to women as having been the 'big brother' (that is, as being dominant) while men were the 'small brother' until their roles were reversed. After the men took the sacred objects from the women, they hid them from the women. They kept the knowledge secret from women, thus securing the dominance of men over women. Similarly, according to this cosmology, when the white ground split away from the black ground, the 'white-man' took knowledge away and now keeps this knowledge hidden from the 'black-man', perhaps generating a masculinity crisis for Sepik men. 'Are you the big brother and I am the small brother?' Kolion rhetorically asks of Bragge (Kolion in Bragge, 2018d, pp. 730–36).

In his discussion with Bragge, Kolion used the Tok Pisin term *save*, referring to knowledge, understanding and wisdom (Mihalic, 1989 [1971]). Interconnecting with the views of the authors, Kolion sees different skins— that is, different peoples—as producing knowledge according to their own historicities, or 'modes of temporal being and awareness' (Ballard, 2014, p. 103). Bragge's patrol reports and his Sepik history reveal differences between the historicities of Sepik peoples and the agents of the colonial state, according to their different cosmological and ontological frames of reference, but reveal little about the historicity of Chinese in the Sepik.

In his Sepik history, Bragge draws heavily on Sepik people's stories, in which the ground/land/earth itself is thought of as knowledge, heritage and skin/ body. The concept of the transformation of the ancestral body is seen in the story of Mai'imp, as told to Bragge by Kolion that evening in Nogosop Village. Mai'imp was a powerful being who would provide an abundance of fish to women in exchange for intercourse with them at his market. When their husbands discovered this, they devised a plan to kill Mai'imp. They decided to carve two wooden images and bury them in the earth, the source of ancestral power. Kolion continues,

> Mai'imp came up to the market and stepped over the two buried images. The images got up and fought him and Mai'imp fell down … dead … The Mai'imp's bung [market] was an Old Testament law and the sago bung is of the New Testament. Now we are people of the New Testament. The people of the Old Testament are once again in the ground … This is the New Testament as we do it now. Before there were no enemies, no death, no poison and no sorcery, but now in the New Testament we have all these things and we follow all these fashions [ways]. Do you understand what I am saying? Now it is his [Mai'imp's] body we eat. It is like this 'now you eat my body' and his blood became the fish and all the things edible in the water … Are you still with me? Now we eat sago and we eat fish. We call his blood in our language 'Kami' and his body we call 'Nau'. Nau is the word for the sago which we eat. (Kolion in Bragge, 2018d, pp. 730–36)

'The Christians nearly got it right', says Kolion after telling the story of Mai'imp, clearly associating him with Jesus Christ and the Catholic ritual transformation and consumption of Christ's body and blood. The knowledge that each party, the 'white-man' and the 'black-man', has is only partial, according to Kolion. For each to be complete in their knowledge, exchanges between the two brothers are required. At the time, Bragge understood Kolion's words as 'cargo cult talk' (personal communication, April 14, 2021). Bragge took Kolion to mean that Bragge, like other Europeans, knew the secret of how to get the material goods they had brought with them but had a vested interest in not sharing that secret and, therefore, was hiding access to it from his 'small brother'.

One of Bragge's tasks during the 1972 patrol when he stayed overnight in Kolion's village was to inform and educate Sepik people about the coming of PNG Independence. In his report following this patrol, Bragge writes that one of the main fears among Sepik people was that the Australians would leave without first sharing the knowledge they had been keeping from them (Bragge, 1972–1973). Regarding Sepik views on the Chinese, Bragge reminisces (personal communication, April 14, 2021):

> The only thing contentious … which I didn't follow up … was that in cargo cult terms they said that the cargo would be in the Chinese stores at Independence … It was just something I heard before Independence … picked up from a patrol somewhere. I think the common theme from cargo cult belief is that the ancestors made this cargo for you and that it has been sidetracked from you by the Europeans and that it was held in the Chinese stores …

Chinese in the Sepik: The story of Chu Leong

Apart from noting that, like 'white people', there were also 'red' and 'yellow' people, based on the colour of the 'ground' from which they hailed, Kolion did not specifically focus on the Chinese in his account to Bragge, who he classed as a 'white-man'. Would Kolion have asked the same question of the Chinese trader Chu Leong as he asked of Bragge? 'Are you the big brother and I the small brother?' Would he have included the Chinese traders or Japanese soldiers, who were in the Sepik during World War II, in the category of 'big brothers' who had appropriated knowledge in the cosmogonic past and kept it secret from the 'black' man? Kolion certainly had encountered at least one Chinese trader who was active in the Sepik area—Chu Leong—but did not mention him in his interview with Bragge. Some Australian government officers in PNG, however, thought that Papua New Guineans did not distinguish Chinese from the 'white-man'. Bragge (2018d, p. 8) quotes Robert Melrose, an Australian government officer working in New Guinea between 1921 and 1949, as writing that 'Wild natives are incapable of distinguishing between Europeans and Asiatics for they group them all as Whiteman.'

So, what is discoverable in the archive about Chu Leong and other Chinese in the Sepik? The following account has been gleaned from Bragge's account in his Sepik history, which is based on secondary sources, and on written and oral history accounts by Chu Leong's daughter, Anna Chu, as well as research conducted and shared with her by Dr. Adam Lui, compiled while researching his own family history in the Sepik.

Born in 1888, Chu Sai Leong originally came from Canton (Pak Kong Village, Hoi Peng County, Kwang Tung Province) to New Guinea in 1913 under the German administration. He was already a married man with a son, but his wife and child remained behind in China. In 1930, Chu Leong moved to Marienberg, a Catholic Mission settlement and patrol post on the Sepik River. It was here that J. K. McCarthy (1905–1976), then a patrol officer for the Australian administration posted to the Sepik, met him in 1930 (Chu, 2008). McCarthy remembered that 'The establishment of Chu Leong's store on the Sepik was welcomed by the small community [of Australian government officers, European missionaries and entrepreneurs] on the river' (McCarthy, 1972, p. 26). McCarthy also noted that Chu Leong was 'one of the first of my many Chinese friends'

(1972, p. 26). The key point that McCarthy made in his article eulogising Chu Leong was that the Chinese had, in general, been overlooked in PNG history. Reflecting on the increasing number of books written about PNG, McCarthy (1972, p. 26) wrote:

> The indigenous people and the Europeans play a great part in these books, but one race is seldom mentioned. I refer to the Chinese who are—and have been for the past 80 years—part of New Guinea's expatriate population. With the courage and diligence of their race, these folk from Canton are among the pioneers of the Territory, and they should be given the recognition they deserve.

After arriving in Marienberg, Chu Sai Leong married a Sepik woman— Elekama of Kiwim village in the Banaro area on the Keram River, a tributary of the Sepik (Chu, 2008). His first child to Elekama was born in 1936, followed by seven more children (Chu, 2008). When the Australian administration moved its post at Marienberg up the Sepik River to Angoram in 1933, Chu Leong relocated his trade store and settled there. Establishing his store at Angoram was not only a good business venture for him, but also felicitously contributed to the growth of the new government station. Whether other Chinese traders were foundational in the early establishment of townships across New Guinea warrants further research (see also Wood & Backhaus, this volume). Certainly, Australian government officers all over the Territory relied on the Chinese storekeepers for provisions. Bragge notes that he had accounts at such stores, and that Chu Leong was the sole Chinese person living in Angoram and plying his trade along the river; most Chinese appear to have preferred to set up businesses in already established urban areas. Other Chinese who ventured into the Sepik area settled in the coastal town of Wewak. Bragge mentions a few Chinese families who had settled in Wewak before World War II. These included the Chow family, the Ning Hee family, the Seeto Nam family and the Tang Mow family (Bragge, 2018c, Ch. 23, p. 80, notes of Adam Liu).

According to Cahill (2012, p. 211), the Australian administration denied an application by a Chinese storekeeper in Wewak to bring Chinese shop assistants from China in 1948. The storekeeper was told he should employ assistants from within the existing PNG Chinese community but was unable to do so as most were resident in Rabaul and unwilling to settle in areas where there were fewer 'social amenities', especially so soon after World War II.

Australian policies regarding Chinese were inconsistently applied on the ground in PNG during the war. For example, Bragge (2018c, Ch. 23) provides a detailed account of the fate of the Sepik Chinese during World War II. While Chinese in Rabaul were never evacuated and ended up at the mercy of the Japanese military, most of those in the Sepik were flown to Australia in 1943. Unfortunately, three Chinese families missed joining the evacuation from the Sepik. According to Adam Lui (cited in Bragge, 2018c, p. 80) the three families from Wewak were the Ning Hee family, the Seeto Nam family and the Tang Mow family. Of these, only the Tang Mow family remained in PNG for the duration of the war. The other two families eventually made it to Australia. According to Bragge (personal communication, April 14, 2021):

> In 1942, the European women and children were evacuated. The Chinese then came and said, "What about us?" And there was no instruction for them … The administration didn't want them or need them. They were something the Australian government had inherited without the wish to do so from the German New Guinea period … The Chinese were originally all left behind. Then as the Japanese started to approach the Sepik the administration officers who were there, Bates in particular, rounded up the Chinese and walked them out through the Ramu into the highlands to Bena Bena and at Bena Bena they were loaded on to planes and taken to Australia.

The Australian officers who led the evacuation of the Chinese in December 1942 were Captain C. D. Bates, former District Officer at Maprik, Captain T. G. Aitchison, former Assistant District Officer at Wewak, Captain J. S. Milligan, former patrol officer at Aitape, and Wireless Operator Kevin Minogue. However, the arduous journey would not have been possible without the assistance of hundreds of Sepik carriers and other Papua New Guineans along the way. Bragge's archive includes an interview he did with a Sepik man, Nonguru Kemerabi of Japandai, who provides details of what he and others did to assist in the evacuation:

> … we doubled big canoes and evacuated all the Chinese from Wewak. We took them down river as far as Kambaramba where we left the double canoes. We took single canoes then to move the Chinese through the Grass country and into the Ramu River system … (Bragge, 2018c, p. 77)

The journey took six weeks. Among the group evacuated was Chu Leong, although he did not join the group until later. From Bena Bena, he and the other Chinese were flown to Port Moresby and then to Australia.[3]

> He wasn't in Wewak when they rounded the rest up. They found him along the way ... One story I got about him in that regard was that one of the Chinese women was very pregnant, so walking to Bena Bena was not a very nice option for her. So Chu Leong got her and took her to his village in the Keram River area and stayed with her until the baby was born; and the baby was left with the women in that village and then he walked with her to follow up the patrol to Bena Bena; and, after the war the child was collected by the Chinese. That's the story I got. I can't remember where I got it from, but [caring for the pregnant woman] is typical [of the man] that Chu Leong was. (Bragge, personal communication, April 14, 2021)

Whatever the truth of this story, before he joined the Chinese being evacuated, Chu Leong took his Sepik wife and children to live with her family in Kiwim village, instructing them to paint the children with black ash and to shave their heads so the Japanese would not know they were 'mixed race Chinese' (Chu, 2008, p. 13). Chu Leong was in his sixties. He spent the rest of his war years in Australia as a refugee (McCarthy, 1972, p. 26). McCarthy recalls Chu Leong telling him stories about how hard he worked in Australia. Eventually, he 'was considered unsuitable for war work and was out of a job' (McCarthy, 1972, p. 26). Chu Leong said, 'I was all right ... The pay was high and I had saved my money, for I lived cheaply. I had met some Chinese in Australia, but I had to work ... I cooked Chinese food and there were thousands of American soldiers and sailors with plenty of money to pay for it. I could work as hard as I liked and there was no bloody foreman [referring to Australian war factories management] to stop me' (McCarthy, 1972, p. 26).

After the war, while many PNG Chinese sought to become Australian citizens and remain in Australia, Chu Leong returned to his family in the Sepik. Chu Leong first re-established his trade store in Angoram and then sent a policeman to bring his wife and children back to him from her village.

---

3   According to the Commonwealth of Australia Form of Application for Registration (For Aliens Entering Australia in Overseas Vessel on or Aircraft), Chu Leong (spelled Chew Leong on the form), born on 21 August 1889, arrived in Australia by army plane from New Guinea and landed at Brisbane on 11 November 1943. He first lived in Brisbane and later moved to Sydney.

He repaired his boat, the *Winon*, and continued with his trading, including suppling the trade stores along the Sepik River that he had encouraged Sepik people to set up.

Along the Sepik, Chu Sai Leong carried sago, artefacts and crocodile skins for other expatriate traders. His daughter, Anna Chu, recollects that 'he also traded for snake and crocodile gall and smoked cassowary feet which were sent off to his son from his first wife in Hong Kong' (Chu, 2008, p. 17). He travelled to Hong Kong in 1960 and again in 1962 to visit his son from his first wife and make business connections. While Chu Leong appeared to operate as a lone wolf along the Sepik River, he was clearly linked into a wider Chinese community both in PNG and overseas. He was a registered member of the Chinese Nationalist Party, the Kuomintang (KMT) in PNG and had business arrangements with other Chinese in the Sepik. Anna Chu (2008, p. 43) writes that within a week of his burial at Angoram, 'a Chinese representative from Madang arrived in a chartered aircraft to take away whatever money we had in the shop'. Chu Leong's wife and children were told to sell whatever goods were left in the shop and then close it. They eventually received a 'small portion' of his estate, but not until 1984. 'I think most of his estate went to his son from his first wife in Hong Kong who had moved there from Canton' (Chu, 2008, p. 43).

While Chu Leong's was the sole Chinese store in Angoram, other Chinese were active along the Aitape/Sepik coast and inland areas during and after German times, 'recruiting labour and hunting birds of paradise' (Bragge, 2018b, p. 333), but little is known of them. Their voices remain silent in the colonial archive 'as they tended to leave, neither reports on what they did, nor maps where they did it' (Bragge, 2018b, p. 333).

Kiaps such as Bragge were instructed by the Australian administration to write detailed 'area reports' based on their patrols. These were focused almost entirely on the indigenous population. A brief section in reports was devoted to non-indigenous people active in the area patrolled, but this was generally interpreted as meaning 'Europeans'. In Papua there simply were very few Asians and Chinese to be reported on because they were not allowed to live in that Australian territory. When Chinese activity in an area is noted, little was recorded about their lives, politics and worldviews. The relative absence of Chinese voices in patrol reports reflects the dualistic racialised political order of the colonial regime of the time (Wolfers, 1975). Yet, as we have shown in this paper, by reading them ethnographically 'along the archival grain' (Stoler, 2009), much can be gleaned from patrol reports that will assist us to understand how Chinese relations with the colonial state were expressed. Further research will enable us to explore how such colonial legacies continue to impact on Chinese relations with the post-independent nation-state of PNG, as described in several other chapters in this volume.

Discussion and conclusion: Knowledge, memory and history as image

We have focused in this chapter on the lives of two individuals who feature in an archive produced by a particular government officer, L. W. Bragge, serving the Australian colonial administration in PNG during the 1960s and early 1970s, just before Independence. There is a stark contrast between what is discoverable about Sepik and Chinese in the Bragge archive and in the five-volume history of the Sepik region that he produced from this archive—*History of the Sepik Region, PNG*. While Bragge made a great effort to include an account of the Chinese in his manuscript, there is little about their lives in the colonial archive that he was able to draw on, in comparison to the richness of material he had himself collected on Sepik people.

We have highlighted narratives created and directly shared by Kolion and other Sepik elders with Bragge that reveal Sepik understandings of origins, migrations and their relations with various colonial agents—Germans, Japanese, Australians. We have also focused on the comparatively little that Bragge was able to recount about the Chinese in the Sepik, particularly Chu Sai Leong. Kolion and Chu Leong's lives intersected in the Sepik. A unifying theme in their stories is one of migration; in Kolion's case, an original migration that separated the 'white-man' from the 'black-man', the big brother from the small brother, and in Chu Leong's case, an individual lifetime from Canton to PNG, to Australia and back, and continuous movement along the Sepik River where he made his home. What Kolion and Chu Leong may have thought of one another is not on record. In Bragge's view, Chu Leong was not classed by Sepik people as a 'white-man':

> I think he was just regarded as a one off. He certainly would not have been seen as European; and Europeans had some good reputations and some bad reputations, especially in the labour trade. He definitely would have been regarded as better than the *bad* Europeans. (Bragge, personal communication, April 14, 2021)

Encounters with strangers are understood as *effects* in the Melanesian context, according to Strathern (2013, p. 170). People construct images not only about the past but also about the present and future effects of encounters they have experienced, and these images are told in the form of what Foucault (1977) has termed 'effective histories'. Bell (2016) argues that the strategic telling of such 'effective histories' is intended to materialise 'utopian desires', which we argue is likely the case for any history, whether Melanesian or otherwise. As Bell (2016) puts it, in relation to the PNG context, such narratives:

> ... shed light on people's creative capacities when faced by the extreme pressures ... [of] uneven development ... Those who seek to enact effective histories ... tell narratives that claim intimate connections with the outside world (i.e., white foreigners are kin), and which confound distinctions imposed on them by outsiders. Doing so, they work to create space for other narratives to emerge, narratives that they hope can be used to readdress the current state of their own disenfranchisement. The acknowledgement of these intersections are one way individuals seek to create the grounds for the recognition of their moral equivalence.

Kolion's account as told to Bragge is an artefact that itself contains artefacts—images of past, present and future. His effective history provides evidence for Strathern's (2013, p. 169) point that such 'images are reflected self-knowledge' in that they are a means for people 'to construct knowledge about themselves and their relations with others'.

The narratives of the Sepik elders recorded by Bragge have become archival artefacts—materialised images of events and their effects. As such, they are potential agents for new aspirations and actions yet to come. The archive invites engagement with Sepik historicities and alternative accounts of colonial state governance, race, gender and development. As artefacts, the transcribed narratives of the Sepik elders not only hold histories but also carry memories, and if memory is 'the womb of history' (as Ricoeur, 2004, pp. 95–6 writes), then it carries not only the past, but also the present, and the future.

In contrast, the voices of Chinese migrants to PNG are relatively absent in the archive. They are knowable only through the accounts of others. For all we know, like Kolion, Chu Leong may also have been a philosopher of a kind, but what he may have thought or understood, his reflections on the origins of the world he found himself in, or his own migration experiences and journey through life is not readily discoverable, at least not directly.

Nevertheless, we argue that there is value in reading 'along the archival grain' for representations of the Chinese, as even the relative paucity of accounts in these 'artefacts of colonial knowledge' can be revealing. Adding Chinese stories is vital for the creation of 'effective histories' of PNG.

References

Australia. Territory of Papua New Guinea. Department of Native Affairs. (1966). *Departmental Standing Instructions: General Field Administration*. Port Moresby.

Ballard, C. (2014). Oceanic Historicities. *The Contemporary Pacific, 26*(1), pp. 96–124. doi.org/10.1353/cp.2014.0009

Bashkow, I. (2006). *The Meaning of Whitemen: Race and Modernity in the Orokaiva Cultural World*. The University of Chicago Press. doi.org/10.7208/chicago/9780226530062.001.0001

Bell, J. (2016). Dystopian realities and archival dreams in the Purari Delta of Papua New Guinea. *Social Anthropology/Anthropologie Sociale, 24*(1), pp. 20–35. doi.org/10.1111/1469-8676.12285

Bragge, L. W. (2018a). *History of the Sepik Region, PNG*. [Unpublished manuscript; Five Volumes]. Special Collections, James Cook University.

Bragge, L. W. (2018b). *Sepik II: The Winds of Change 1885–1941* [Unpublished manuscript]. Special Collections, James Cook University.

Bragge, L. W. (2018c). *Sepik III: The Sepik at War 1942–1945* [Unpublished manuscript]. Special Collections, James Cook University.

Bragge, L. W. (2018d). *Sepik IV: Coming to Grips with the Future—1946 to 1975 and Beyond* [Unpublished manuscript]. Special Collections, James Cook University.

Bragge, L. W. (2018e). *Sepik V: Department of District Services & Native Affairs Policies, Guiding Principles and Support Documents* [Unpublished manuscript]. Special Collections, James Cook University.

Bragge, L. W. (1972–1973). *Situation Report No 4: Ambunti Patrol No. 13/1972–73* [Unpublished report]. Special Collections, James Cook University.

Burridge, K. (1969). *New Heaven, New Earth: A Study of Millenarian Activities*. Schocken Books.

Cahill, P. (2012). *Needed—But Not Wanted: Chinese in Rabaul 1884–1960*. CopyRight Publishing Company.

Chu, A. (2008). *Kapiak Tree: Memories of Papua New Guinea*. MaskiMedia.

Connolly, B., & Anderson, R. (1987). *First Contact*. Viking.

Edmonds, P. (2006). Imperial Objects, Truth and Fictions: Reading 19th Century Australian Colonial Objects as Historical Sources. In P. Edmonds & S. Furphy (Eds.), *Rethinking Colonial Histories: New and Alternative Approaches* (pp. 73–87). RMIT Publishing.

Foucault, M. (1977). Nietzsche, Genealogy, History. Foucault Reader. In D. F. Bouchard (Ed.), *Language, Counter-Memory, Practice: Selected Essays and Interviews* (pp. 139–64). Cornell University Press. doi.org/10.1515/9781501741913-008

Hasluck, P. (1976). *A Time for Building: Australian Administration in Papua and New Guinea, 1951–1963*. Melbourne University Press.

Johnson, M. (2008). Making history public: Indigenous claims to settler states. *Public Culture, 20*(1), pp. 97–117. doi.org/10.1215/08992363-2007-018

Lattas, A. (2010). *Dreams, Madness, and Fairy Tales in New Britain*. Carolina Academic Press.

McCarthy, J. K. (1972, January 28). Chu was a pioneer of the Sepik. *Papua New Guinea Post-Courier*, p. 26.

Mihalic, F. (1989 [1971]). *The Jacaranda Dictionary and Grammar of Melanesian Pidgin. PNG*. The Jacaranda Press.

Ricoeur, P. (2004). *Memory, History, Forgetting*. University of Chicago Press.

Riles, A. (2006). *Documents: Artifacts of Modern Knowledge*. University of Michigan Press.

Stoler, A. L. (2009). *Along the Archival Grain: Epistemic Anxieties and Colonial Common Sense*. Princeton University Press.

Strathern, M. (1990). Artifacts of history: Events and the interpretation of images. In J. Siikala (Ed.), *Culture and History in the Pacific* (pp. 25–44). Finnish Anthropological Society.

Strathern, M. (2013). *Learning to see in Melanesia*. Masterclass Series 2. HAU Society for Ethnographic Theory.

Wolfers, E. P. (1975). *Race Relations and Colonial Rule in Papua New Guinea*. Australia and New Zealand Book Company.

Vignette—Reflection: Research with the Bragge Collection and Reflections on Sepik Chinese

Kulasumb Kalinoe

I first discovered the existence of the Bragge Collection in 2018. There was a seminar at James Cook University (JCU) run by the JCU Papua New Guinea (PNG) Wantribe Student Association and they brought in some scholars and other Papua New Guineans to speak. Laurie Bragge was one of the speakers. He was speaking of his time in Ambunti in the middle Sepik River area and he gave out handouts from his presentation. My dear friend Lisa Kune from Ialibu took one of the handouts. I was not able to attend at that time, but Lisa told me about it and said, 'Oh you should have come, because there was a *kiap* there and he was in Ambunti and apparently he spoke to all these elders there and did interviews with them'. She then passed on to me one of the handouts that Laurie had given out.

A couple of days later I looked at the handout and saw that some of the interviews Bragge had done were with men from my father's village. The handout was an index page to the interviews that Bragge had done. I thought, 'Oh this is amazing', because our village is just so remote, so for him to have done those interviews was astonishing to me. At the time, I thought I should try to get in touch with Laurie because he had these interviews, but it took me a year and a bit to find him.

Fast forward to 2019. I went to the JCU Library, and they had brochures in the foyer announcing that the Bragge Collection was now at JCU and if you were interested to contact the Library. So, I spoke to the Library Manager,

Kate Wanchap, and she was thrilled and said I had to contact Professor Rosita Henry. When I met Rosita, that just changed everything. One day Rosita invited me into the storeroom to look at the artefacts in the Bragge Collection and then she turned around and suggested that this would make a great PhD project for me. My first reaction was disbelief, as I didn't think that I was cut out for it and at the time a PhD was not on my bucket list; but then one thing led to another and here I am well into the second year of my PhD. This decision didn't come lightly but after a year of weighing up my options and with Rosita's faith in me to pursue legal anthropology I decided that it was fate.

I thought 'what are the odds', like in Cairns, in Smithfield, just down the road from where I lived were these interviews! It was about three months after my dad's sudden death. During that time there was a lot of sadness with trying to navigate through life without him so finding the Bragge Collection had a special significance for me. My late father was a patriotic Papua New Guinean and a proud Sepik River man. He was deeply connected with his kin in the village and the community, and he was accustomed to performing his customary obligations—*man blo wokim kastom wok*. He tried to instill these cultural values into my siblings and me. He told us many stories of his carefree childhood as a village boy coming from very humble beginnings. I believe his childhood shaped him into the person that he was—humble, thoughtful, resourceful and, of course, a hard worker.

In one of our last conversations my dad had advised me that pursuing research would be best for my career and that it would take me places just like it had done for him. It was only after he had passed away, and I had realised how easily this research project came to me, that I remembered his words. In a way it does feel that he had a hand in bringing this opportunity to me. This is an area that he was interested in both professionally and personally. I do feel very honoured, but also obligated, to complete it to honour my father's memory and the stories of his forefathers.

My PhD research is basically on the cultural heritage issues around PNG collections, whether held in museums, galleries, archives or public institutions, using the Bragge Collection as a case study. I am looking at issues around access, ownership, repatriation and gender. I will be examining the current state of our cultural heritage legal framework to see how it can be improved to protect not just our cultural objects but also the knowledge that is attached to the objects and the knowledge from archives, records and documents. There will be a focus on our current legal options such as customary law to examine how it can provide protection. PNG is an oral tradition society and with traditional knowledge being passed down without written records and documentation, that knowledge is becoming endangered and at risk of exploitation. To determine ownership rights and access rights over customary land and natural resources, courts consider traditional knowledge that includes migration stories, oral histories, creation stories, myths and legends. For example, *Re Hides Gas Project* [1993] PNG LR 309 involved a dispute between two different tribes who claimed ownership over the Hides Project site in the Southern Highlands Province. This case saw both tribes give evidence that included detailed genealogies from several generations back to their first ancestors who arrived on the land. With land being an invaluable resource to Papua New Guineans, it is important that such knowledge is protected.

I have not read all the interviews that Laurie Bragge did with the Sepik elders; because of my background, culturally I am aware that this type of knowledge and these stories that the elders told Laurie could be secret/sacred. I feel that I may not have the right to read all of them or even any of them. The one interview that I did read was very superficial. It did not go into depth with land, names and myths. I know that type of information is secret and only meant for certain men.

Bragge's comprehensive index of the interviews he conducted has given me a lot of comfort and context as well. It allows me to know what material might be contained in each interview. The index is detailed enough, in that it lists which interviews have myths and legends and names in them, for me to know that I don't need to read all the interviews' transcripts—in fact that I should not read them—to do this research project. I feel comfortable just working with the index.

My plan is to eventually go to the Sepik for field work. I hope to take copies of the index pages there to gauge from discussions with people there—men and women—their thoughts on the type of information and knowledge contained in the interviews. What do they think? Is there likely to be knowledge in the interviews that should be kept secret? Should the interview transcripts be restricted or is it appropriate for them to be publicly accessible to anyone? What might they want done with the transcripts? What protocols should there be regarding access and use by researchers and members of the public? Although I felt that the transcript of the interview that I did read did not have any secret/sacred knowledge in it, I am uncertain about the other interviews. Only someone with the cultural standing to read them could tell for sure.

Regarding the Chinese in PNG, these views are my own and I only speak for myself from my personal lived experiences. Ambunti and our villages of Avatip and Yaumbak are isolated, and from my own understanding people had fewer interactions with the Chinese compared to people living in places like Wewak. Sepik people living in the town would have had more interactions with the Chinese.

Sepik people distinguished white Australians and *ol Kong Kong*, Asians. They weren't just all lumped under one umbrella as foreigners. In Wewak, there are big Chinese shops such as Tang Maw and Garamut Enterprises. People in the Sepik know that they are owned and run by the Chinese, *ol Kong Kong* or *Sinaman*. Even with Garamut Enterprises moving to Port Moresby and creating Boroko Foodworld and Waterfront, big supermarkets in Port Moresby, Sepik people in Port Moresby refer to them as *ol Kong Kong blo Sepik*. Sepiks recognise them as starting from Wewak, so we are supportive and proud of them. That's from what I can remember growing up.

Kong Kong blo Sepik (Sepik Chinese) are distinguished from *Kong Kong blo Rabaul* (Rabaul Chinese) or *Kong Kong blo Kavieng* (Kavieng Chinese). When Sir Michael Somare passed away, Garamut Enterprises, *Kong Kong blo Sepik,* closed their shops in Port Moresby, joining the other business houses in Wewak out of respect ('Waterfront closed for business in Port Moresby', 2021). There is respect and recognition, *luk save*, between the Sepik people and *Kong Kong blo Sepik*. I don't know firsthand but what I do understand is that the respect has to do with these Chinese having been in Wewak for so long, even before Independence. I think we respect that. *Yupla kam na yupla stap*. You came and are still here being a part of this community.

My best friend Bernadine Rabia, who is Tolai, told me that once when she was flying to Port Moresby she was sitting near an elderly Chinese couple. She overheard them speaking the Tolai language (Kuanua) to each other. She was surprised that these Chinese were fluent in Kuanua. The Chinese who settled in PNG during the colonial era have become so much part of PNG that some speak *the tok ples* (the vernacular) of the places where they settled.

I can't remember there being tensions with the old Chinese in Wewak. Papua New Guineans differentiate between the old Chinese and the new Chinese who come to do business. Regarding the Chinese government recently coming to PNG and having a presence with their services and the roads that have been built throughout Port Moresby, I was told when I returned to PNG, 'This is the work of the Chinaman' ('Chinese president opens new six-lane road in PNG capital', 2018). There was appreciation among people I talked to. I think that PNG is becoming friendly with China these days out of appreciation for the help we are being given (Latimer, 2018; Whiting, 2019).

However, there has been anti-Chinese sentiment and violence, particularly in 2009. This was due to Papua New Guineans resenting the flood of new Asians, particularly the Chinese, into PNG; they saw them as engaging in unfair business practices, illegal activities, corruption and organised crime in PNG. Chinese-owned shops in Madang, Kainantu, Goroka and Port Moresby were looted ('Asians attacked as PNG violence flares', 2010; 'PNG police protect Chinese shops from looters', 2009).

Recently there has also been tension among local designers and the Chinese who allegedly have been copying and making prints on fabric for sale (Kari, 2021; Sete, 2019; Zoriry, 2021). The appropriation of PNG images, patterns and designs has angered PNG designers. Annette Sete, a prominent designer, has stated: 'Chinese imitations of local designs and fake or counterfeit products will continue to flood our markets. This past week my total of Chinese copies reached eight. Six of those we attempted to fight against, but high legal costs meant we can't afford to do it all' (Sete, 2019). In one of the first copyright infringement cases, Annette Sete filed a lawsuit in 2020 against Kenny PNG Ltd and Tropicana Ltd alleging the copying of her tabu fabric designs.

People distinguish between old and new Chinese. While there are some tensions about the new Chinese businesses, I think there is no resentment against the Chinese that have been in PNG for generations and have made PNG their home. Some of them have become naturalised PNG citizens themselves. We see them as part of us. We respect the old Chinese who have made it in PNG, just like we respect other Papua New Guineans who have built successful businesses.

I grew up in Port Moresby and I didn't have Chinese friends, nor have I been to any Chinese clubs. There was definitely a distinction between us and them, like they were Chinese or half-Chinese, and they had their own clubs, communities and groups. There was respect, but also separation. We referred to the Chinese as *Kong Kong man* and *Kong Kong meri* or *Sinaman* and *Sinameri*.

References

Asians attacked as PNG violence flares. (2010, September 13). SBS News. www.sbs.com.au/news/article/asians-attacked-as-png-violence-flares/8z7l66wjn

Chinese president opens new six-lane road in PNG capital. (2018, November 17). Radio NZ. www.rnz.co.nz/international/pacific-news/376109/chinese-president-opens-new-six-lane-road-in-png-capital

Kari, J. (2021, September 17). Comp Stiff for Women in Fabrics Business: Sete. Post Courier. postcourier.com.pg/comp-stiff-for-women-in-fabrics-business-sete/

Latimer, C. (2018, September 24). From bus stops to bridges Chinese influence in PNG a 'wake up' call. The Sydney Morning Herald. www.smh.com.au/world/oceania/from-bus-stops-to-bridges-chinese-influence-in-png-a-wake-up-call-20180914-p503ro.html

PNG police protect Chinese shops from looters. (2009, May 18). ABC News. www.abc.net.au/news/2009-05-18/png-police-protect-chinese-shops-from-looters/1686852

Sete, A. (2019, August 18). Chinese counterfeits are killing PNG's embryonic fashion industry. My Land, My Country. PNG Attitude. www.pngattitude.com/2019/08/chinese-counterfeits-are-killing-pngs-embryonic-fashion-industry.html

Whiting, N. (2019, April 16). Syndicate spending $414m on Chinatown in Port Moresby as battle for PNG influence escalates. ABC News. www.abc.net.au/news/2019-04-16/chinatown-for-port-moresby-as-beijing-influence-grows-in-png/11004362

Waterfront closed for business in Port Moresby. (2021, February 26). Post Courier. postcourier.com.pg/waterfront-closed-for-business-in-port-moresby/

Zoriry, J. (2021, March 2). Designer Annette Sete calls for others to join fight. EMTV News. emtv.com.pg/designer-annette-sete-calls-for-others-to-join-fight/

3

What was colonial in extending Australian citizenship to New Guinea Chinese?

Michael Wood and Vincent Backhaus

Standard histories of the dismantling of White Australia policies can imply New Guinea Chinese had, at best, a minor role in such processes. While this may be true, these histories tend to assume that policies flow from the centre to the colony and that nothing much came from the periphery with the result that what gets written is largely Eurocentric (Thomas, 1994, p. 106; Anderson, 1998). Such histories are sometimes confined to, and conflated with, the values of a single nation-state, as when Tavan noted, perhaps somewhat over-enthusiastically, that the dismantling of the White Australia policies was 'largely a pragmatic response by political leaders to the changing circumstances in which Australia found itself and to the *changing values of Australian society*' (2005, p. 238, italics in original).[1]

Responding to this kind of methodological nationalism (Wimmer & Glick Schiller, 2002), we argue New Guinea Chinese should be made more central to the history of the White Australia policy. We do so by examining the granting, in 1957, of conditional Australian citizenship to Chinese residents in both Australia and New Guinea. In this chapter we merely point toward

---

1   Along with Tavan's work there is a vast range of scholarship on the history of the White Australia policy (Jones, 2005; Jordan, 2006, 2018; Mann, 2012; Meaney, 1995).

something less Eurocentric than 'Australian values' as the central analytic. While we do not adopt a Chinese or Asian approach to policy history, we build on earlier attempts to rethink the history of Australian immigration from a trans-national perspective, from outside Australia (Lake & Reynolds, 2008; Lake, 2010) and, in this case, include perspectives of Chinese and other actors who lived in New Guinea. Policy reform of Asian immigration was more than something internal to the Australian government and its colonial rule. At times it involved different, perhaps barely recorded, perspectives to those promoted by the Australian government, its archives and some Australian histories of the White Australia policy.

One response is to highlight the agency of New Guinea and other Chinese in overturning Australian policies. King (2002, 2005) made a useful start to such a project by considering how some 330 New Guinea Chinese war refugees in Australia were, in the early 1950s, granted permanent residency in Australia. King presents these refugees as productive actors in the creation of a significant breach in the White Australia policy. This shift occurred in the face of the Australian government campaign to forcibly repatriate the New Guinea Chinese and other non-European refugees, which culminated in the passing of the *War-time Refugee Removals Act 1949*. However, High Court cases, wide public support and a change of government prevented the Removals Act from being implemented (Neumann, 2006; Brawley, 2014). King's account of the New Guinea Chinese refugees' agency shows how it was enabled by complex networks of actors, institutions and social relations. What is also clear from his account is that openings into a distinctly New Guinea Chinese perspective on reforms of Australian immigration policy are limited and constrained by the available archival data.

Rather than just promote Chinese agency (and constraining structures) as the key analytic of our narrative, this chapter positions arguments about Chinese citizenship in the tensions, overlaps and contradictions between the racialised ordering of New Guinea Chinese (and other Asians) and certain strands of post-World War II (WWII) liberal anti-racism. Such tensions helped generate policy reforms concerning Chinese citizenship in both New Guinea and Australia. These reforms developed from within emerging configurations of global mid-twentieth century liberalism that were arguably 'more equitable than any version of liberalism that came before or after it' (Stewart, 2020, n.p.). This liberal order provided a language and global structures, such as the UN, for imagining and creating citizens who were not restrictively defined by racial difference, biology or culture. Versions of this new political subject were found throughout the British Empire—

such discourses circulated throughout the colonies, from 'legislative council chambers and Colonial Office memoranda to youth clubs and debating societies'—including New Guinea (Kumarasingham, 2018, p. 815).

While such global flows of various liberal ideas and practices were important in constituting possibilities of reform, it was Paul Hasluck, the Minister of Territories from 1951 to 1963, who initiated a unique set of policies in regard to the Chinese in Papua and New Guinea. In this chapter, we aim to extend MacWilliam's (2019) and Wright's (2002) analysis of Hasluck's liberalism in reference to land issues in Papua New Guinea (PNG) to his reforms of New Guinea Chinese citizenship and immigration. Hasluck's policies rested on two underlying assumptions: first, the New Guinea Chinese, like the Chinese in the Australian settler state, were disposable (De Genova & Roy, 2020) and should be removed from New Guinea so that Papua New Guinean interests could be protected. The aim was to de-racialise the colony by removing the Chinese from New Guinea to Australia. The second assumption involved the post-WWII attempts to shift the economy of Papua and New Guinea from one centred on the white plantation (Lewis, 1996) towards an economy centred on an indigenous land-owning farmer who engaged in cash crop production (MacWilliam, 2019). The colonial government sought to protect its native subjects from the consequences of the Chinese presence in New Guinea and justified such protectionism by deploying liberal arguments for Chinese access to Australian citizenship and permanent residence in Australia. The Chinese, long portrayed as destabilising internal others, were redefined as suitable subjects for removal from pre- and post-Independence PNG. We highlight how the transformations of Chinese into Australian citizens involved reproducing certain racial and cultural distinctions and exclusions and highlighted the fundamental 'disposability' (De Genova & Roy, 2020) of the Chinese in liberal policy of the time. However, the policy of granting rights to citizenship and permanent residence in Australia failed to clear PNG of all the New Guinea Chinese, many of whom relocated to and colonised Port Moresby and other urban centres in PNG.

We develop these points by first outlining aspects of the racial ordering of Chinese in New Guinea and Papua and then present Paul Hasluck's ideas concerning PNG development, race and the New Guinea Chinese as potential citizens of Australia. We then consider a report (Thomson, 1952), commissioned by Hasluck, on the social conditions of people of 'mixed blood' in Papua and New Guinea as a case study on how Australian citizenship was conditional on the capacity of potential citizens to 'assimilate' to European society. We highlight how liberal reforms of social categories and naming practices attempted to eliminate the use of ethno-racial terms in a manner that paralleled the development of social policies promoting the removal of all 'Chinese' and 'Asians' from pre-Independent PNG via offers of Australian citizenship.[2] The semantic simplification of social categories used in PNG was an attempted epistemic equivalent to removing the Chinese and Asians from PNG.

Another element in our account of similar liberal policy interventions concerns a New Guinea Chinese high school student, Brian Cheung, who wrote to Hasluck to argue for the abolition of Rabaul's Chinatown and its replacement with a new de-racialised urban settlement and greater citizenship rights for the Chinese residents. The student's arguments relied on the work of Simon (Simon & Hubback, 1935; Ku, 2018; Olechnowicz, 2000) an influential British liberal educationalist and practitioner of new forms of urban planning for the improvement of the working class. We argue this urban emphasis of Cheung prefigured how some New Guinea Chinese effectively reworked the government's intentions concerning Australian citizenship by largely settling in urban centres in both Australia and PNG. This material suggests what is needed is a revaluation of the role of the Chinese in urban processes of colonial and post-colonial state formation.

Racial regulation of New Guinea Chinese

The White Australia policy as it applied to Chinese in Papua and New Guinea was more emphatically enacted in Papua than in New Guinea. Papua was, since 1906, a possession of Australia and the indigenous population were considered British subjects. As Papua was part of Australia, Australian laws and ordinances such as the *Immigration Restriction Regulations Ordinance* of 1907 were used to prevent any Chinese and other Asians from residing in Papua. By 1955, there were apparently only four Chinese in all of Papua (Cahill, 2012, p. 268).

---

2   For an outline of Australian debates, especially between Elkin and Hasluck, concerning the biological, cultural and social relations of assimilation see Moran (2005).

In contrast, New Guinea was not part of Australia and the indigenous population were not British subjects, nor after 1948 understood to be Australian citizens. New Guinea was, after World War I (WWI), a Trust Territory mandated by the League of Nations and then, after WWII, by the United Nations.

In the period of German rule of New Guinea many Chinese and other Asians were classified as 'non-indigenous natives', but in 1922 the Australian administration, in accordance with assumptions about Asians operating in Australia's immigration policies, redefined them in more exclusionary terms as 'permanent alien residents'. In the inter-war years the fundamental aim of the Australian colonial administration in reference to the Chinese was to suppress any expansion of the Chinese economy and population in New Guinea. Taking Rabaul town as the site where colonial government power and infrastructure were most fully implemented, Chinese life in New Guinea was defined primarily as within an urban enclave linked to systematic exclusions from an economy and social order largely defined by white plantations and a governing bureaucracy (Wu, 1982; Cahill, 2012; Wolfers, 1975).

Chinese seeking entry to New Guinea, like those seeking entry to Australia, were obliged to carry an alien registration card; to undertake a dictation test or secure a renewable certificate exempting the bearer from the dictation test; and to secure temporary entry permits (Jones, 2005, pp. 39–47). Permits were also required for any New Guinea Chinese resident in New Guinea who wished to visit their homeland. Entry of family members and spouses to New Guinea was strongly regulated with many applications for kin and wives to enter PNG being rejected or excessively delayed (Wu, 1982, p. 164). As one member of New Guinea's Legislative Council noted, the Australian administration's attempts to apply the White Australia policy in New Guinea had the effect that by the 1930s, the Asian community appeared to have been 'legislated almost out of existence' (Wolfers, 1975, p. 102).

However, many New Guinea Chinese were citizens of China and actively engaged with the New Guinea Kuomintang after it was founded in 1924. After 1945 the Rabaul community regularly sent delegates to Taiwan to attend National government meetings. Wu reports that when he arrived in Rabaul in 1971 *ching-fu* 'our government' was often used to mean the Nationalist Government in Taiwan rather than the Australian administration (Wu, 1982, p. 107). The New Guinea Chinese status as Chinese nationals ensured that political relations mediated through the Chinese Nationalist government were important in generating some reforms to the colonial administration's anti-Asian immigration policies.[3] In 1931, the Chinese Consul General, then located in Sydney, wrote to the Prime Minister's Department noting that certain types of Chinese were exempt from being fingerprinted when they arrived in Australia. He asked that the same exemptions be applied to Chinese entering New Guinea. In response, the Prime Minister's secretary indicated that certain kinds of Chinese entering New Guinea would be exempt from fingerprinting; this included those 'Chinese of superior standing who were known to the Customs authorities', 'Chinese visitors to New Guinea of superior standing', or those who could furnish two photographs 'in lieu of fingerprints' (The Secretary, Prime Minister's Department Letter to Acting Consul General China 18/12/31 NAA: A981, NEW G 46:4). Such material suggests that the Chinese community in New Guinea was not simply subject to the sovereign power of the Australian state but was, at times, able to effectively position itself within the albeit limited power and overlapping sovereignty of the Chinese state. A more complete history of Chinese in New Guinea would take greater account of Chinese sovereignty over its citizens. Here we merely point to the entanglement of Chinese, Australian and the United Nations claims to sovereignty in New Guinea. New Guinea and, perhaps especially, Rabaul, were sites where multiple, if unequal, sovereignties were enacted.

In WWII, Australian policies regarding Chinese in New Guinea coalesced into a statement of colonial neglect, structural marginality and exclusion when the Australian administration failed to organise an evacuation of Chinese residents in Rabaul. Those left in Rabaul were placed in camps by the Japanese and subject to harsh and often violent treatment (Nelson, 2010, 2008). Moreover, Wu noted that, in the decade after WWII, the Chinese in New Guinea received no better treatment than before the war: 'racial segregation was pronounced and the Chinese were still disliked by Europeans' and all Chinese visitors to New Guinea were treated as 'potential' illegal immigrants (Wu, 1982, p. 43, 46).

---

3   In this paper all references to the Chinese government are to the Nationalist government, located in Taiwan, that was recognised by Australia up until 1972.

Questions of citizenship and Hasluck's liberalism

By the late 1940s, racial discrimination in Australia's immigration policies and in the UN Trust Territory of New Guinea had become a 'sensitive issue' for the Australian government. After the war, New Guinea Chinese could leverage the UN's influence to make demands for reform of racial discrimination and for Australia citizenship. Concerns about racial discrimination against Chinese in New Guinea were raised by the Nationalist Government delegate on the Trusteeship Council at the UN meetings in November and December 1946. The New Guinea Chinese Union started to directly petition the UN Trusteeship Council, requesting, among other things, Australian citizenship, permanent residence in New Guinea, and access to land. The petitioners also argued they should have the same rights to permanent residence as enjoyed by Chinese in other countries such as New Zealand and Canada (NAA: A452, 1956/993 PART 1:81).

The Australian government responded to such demands in 1951 by making all persons born in New Guinea, who were not British subjects, Australian Protected Persons.[4] Such persons were entitled to vote and stand for election in the Legislative Council in PNG, to travel on an Australian passport and to receive 'all the protection and assistance normally given to Australians while travelling' (Cahill, 2012, p. 246). However, in practice, they were prohibited from entering Papua and were highly restricted in travelling to Australia. In addition, as Rowley noted, an 'Asian Australian Protected Person' had limited opportunities to acquire freehold property or leases over property (1956, p. 7). The administrative practices that resulted in such discrimination were usually justified, first by the Germans and then by the Australians, on the grounds that Asians were not permanent residents of New Guinea (Rowley, 1956, p. 7).[5]

It was in this context that Paul Hasluck became the Minister for Territories. MacWilliam (2019, p. 84) argues Hasluck's policies in PNG often involved a liberal developmentalism that was anti-conservative, paternalistic and

---

4   Taylor and Boyd (2022) provide a detailed analysis of the concept of 'protected person' as it applied to people from PNG.
5   A *Pacific Island Monthly* (PIM) (July 1, 1957, p. 22, 28) reporter noted how the offer of citizenship to New Guinea Chinese meant that they would be eligible to enter both Australia and the Australian Territory of Papua as permanent residents. PIM noted a concern among people that the movement of Chinese into Papua might mean 'saying goodbye' to European businesses in that part of Australia.

actively protectionist. Hasluck stressed colonial rule in Papua and New Guinea was justified because the underlying paternalism, 'in its true nature', was good. It was necessary for the colonial government to exercise guardianship over people threatened with disruption to their existing modes of living by an otherwise exploitative mode of development (McWilliam, 2019, p. 86).[6] Hasluck argued:

> We have to contemplate in the long term the problems that may be set up by the early creation of a landless, urban proletariat … We have to be careful that they do not lose their social anchorage in the village before we can be sure that they find an equally safe social anchorage … as wage-earners in the town. (Cited in Wright, 2002, p. 62)

Hasluck's use of state power to direct development to avoid creating such a future came under attack from sections of the PNG expatriate community. The *Pacific Islands Monthly* observed that the Minister 'may be nominally a Tory; but his record up to date … suggests that he is mostly a Socialist planner' (Wright, 2002, p. 62).[7] Hasluck's use of class analysis may have given some support to this polemic.

For Hasluck, the aim of development in PNG was the creation of a 'community' of small property owners, or 'capitalism without a proletariat' (Wright, 2002, p. 65). Hasluck's defence of small property ownership reflected an agrarian bias combined with liberalism's defence of private property. He was open to a limited commodification of land, but in a form that sought to prevent indigenous landlessness. His defence of local interests in land was often explicitly liberal and exclusionary of any Chinese or Asian interests:

> (T)he liberal respect of property […] is a respect for small property no less than a respect for a large property and […] I assert that the private enterprise of every native villager is just as sacred to liberalism as is the private enterprise of any European. (Hasluck cited in McWilliam, 2019, p. 95)

---

6   Such arguments about future disruption were often deployed as a justification of colonial government in New Guinea (Commonwealth of Australia, 1920) and date back to Mill's argument that British colonialism involved a trustee relationship (Bell, 2010).

7   This kind of claim was echoed in Hayek's accusation that J. S. Mill's arguments for colonial trusteeship exercised through state power helped develop socialism (MacWilliam, 2019, pp. 86–7).

Sociological liberalism via Thomson and C. D. Rowley

In 1951, Hasluck established an inquiry that focused on the position of what were termed 'half-caste' residents in Papua and New Guinea. The Senior Social Welfare Officer of the PNG Education Department, Thomson was asked to undertake a survey and report his finding to the Executive Council of PNG. Thomson recommended that people of what he termed 'mixed blood' 'become increasingly assimilated and given Australian citizenship'. He recommended that the granting of citizenship to mixed bloods be conditional—it was to 'be a reward for effort and that such citizenship be granted on social status and not racial origins' (1951–52, p. 80).

This finding echoed Hasluck's wish 'to reduce the non-indigenous population to one immigrant group. This meant that the mixed-race people should be given the chance to identify themselves either with the Europeans or with the indigenes and to be received into which ever group they chose' (1976, p. 31). According to Hasluck, Papuan New Guineans' rejection of 'mixed race' persons meant that such persons 'would have to be accorded the same position in law and in social relationships as the Europeans' (Hasluck, 1976, p. 31).

As for the Chinese, he 'saw at once that the only way open was to give them full Australian citizenship, with the right of permanent residence in Australia and to give every possible encouragement to all of them to identify themselves with Australians as part of a single immigrant community' (Hasluck, 1976, p. 31). Citing the examples of racial issues in Fiji and East Africa, Hasluck was cautious about introducing further Asian labour into Papua and New Guinea:

> … my uppermost concern was to keep the population as uncomplicated as possible against the day when the indigenous people would make their own decisions on the composition of their county's population. This seemed to be as necessary as the parallel policy of checking the alienation of land from indigenous possession and occupation. (Hasluck, 1976, p. 31)

For Hasluck, control of the racial composition of PNG's population and ownership of the land was equivalent to control of the processes of development and class formation.

In developing his analysis, Thomson deployed a somewhat different mode analysis to that of Hasluck. Thomson relied more explicitly on anthropologists operating in the emerging field of race relations such as Felix Keesing (Paisley, 2015) and Sydney Collins (1951, 1952; Clapson, 2006, p. 259; Mills, 2008, pp. 129–147; Banton, 1973). Rather than focus on biological theories of race, Thomson argued race was a social process and it was therefore more important to end European discrimination against 'mixed bloods' and overcome 'the belief in the superiority of the people who dominate those of mixed blood' (Thomson, 1952, p. 11). For Thomson, mixed bloods were potential Australian citizens who could be brought 'into a more favourable position in society' (Thomson, 1952, p. 7) when discrimination by Europeans ended.

Like Hasluck (1988), Thomson thought speeding up the assimilation of mixed bloods into the European population should involve simplifying and eventually abandoning racial categories. Here the central assumption was that getting rid of both the categories and socialities of racially and culturally hybrid groups, along with those of the Chinese and Asians, was consistent with promoting the long-term welfare of PNG nationals (Van Krieken, 2004, p. 142). According to Hasluck, in PNG (and in Australia) there should be just 'one immigrant group alongside one indigenous group' (Hasluck, cited in Goddard, 2017, p. 139). Perhaps in response to such an argument, Thomson replaced the term 'half-caste' with 'mixed blood' because, in his view, the latter term avoided the possibility of 'considering the group as a homogenous entity' (Thomson, 1952, p. 4).[8] He argued racial discrimination would be reduced by de-emphasising the use of particular group names because such naming practices tended 'to set groups apart' (ibid.).[9] All social groups needed to be treated 'as a number of individuals rather than as a group with common origins, common standards of living and an entitlement to a common name. They have their own names as individuals which should serve all purposes apart from the occasional need for giving group references' (Thomson, 1952, p. 4). Given Thomson's liberal emphasis on the individual, there was no need for group

---

8   Current interest in critiquing the unqualified deployment of the term 'Chinese' as promoting racialised and essentialising understandings of the distinction between Chinese and non-Chinese (Ang, 2014) replicates some of these liberal concerns with the power of racial and ethnic categories (see also Gilroy, 2001).

9   Developing such ideas in 1953, Hasluck drafted an ordinance declaring all Northern Territory Aborigines as 'wards'. Identity group names such as 'Aborigine' had no role in their transition toward citizenship in a civilised state (McGregor, 1999, p. 244).

names—as potential Australians, they were to be detached from communal ties and be reconstructed as universal and interchangeable citizen isolates (Rowse, cited in Van Krieken, 2004, p. 145).

Reflecting these ideas, Thomson also recommended that 'individual applications for Australian citizenship be encouraged' from those with mixed blood, but not on a group basis:

> There can be no thought of giving Australian citizenship to the mixed-blood because he is of two or more racial origins. Because the group as a whole are subject to undue social stresses is reason enough for careful consideration of their claims. This does not call for a sentimental approach ... (Thomson, 1952, p. 26)

Thomson was rather quick to emphasise that the mixed blood communities themselves did not think Australian citizenship should automatically be extended to all 'mixed blood' in Papua and New Guinea. He explained:

> At a meeting of the Rabaul group, I was surprised to find that there was a quick appreciation of the necessity for citizenship to be earned. The fact that birth in Australia confers citizenship without the necessity for moral and social qualifications is accepted as the good fortune of Australians. (Thomson, 1952, p. 25)

Thomson also noted a number of the submissions he received argued citizenship should be only granted to those mixed bloods who had attained 'the living standard of the average white man by energetic work, good behaviour, cleanliness in housing and clothing' (1952, p. 23).

Thomson recommended applicants for naturalisation should provide sufficient evidence of 'moral worth' to a naturalisation board that could be set up to evaluate applications and the recommendations of the District Commissioner and others (1952, p. 27).[10] Thomson, in contrast to this

---

10 Thomson noted that two cases 'at present being considered will indicate the probability of success' (Thomson, 1952, p. 27). Both applicants were plantation owners from the Kokopo 'mixed blood group' and were 'to all intents and purposes treated as Europeans' (Thomson, 1952, pp. 23–4) such as being accepted as members of the European-dominated Kokopo club. There is perhaps another history of citizenship yet to be fully described. Such a history might require a more detailed look at Rowley's argument that 'the Commonwealth Nationality and Citizenship Act, Section 15 specifically recognises residence in New Guinea ... as qualifying a Protected Person to have his application for British Subject and Australian Citizen status considered (Rowley, 1956, p. 8). Rowley suggested 'there are obvious advantages to be gained from making available to Protected Persons on application the status which all persons born in Papua are automatically accorded' (Rowley, 1956, p. 8).

conditional extension of citizenship to mixed-blood people, did recommend an automatic extension of Australian citizenship to all Eurasians in Papua and New Guinea.

By way of contrast the Chinese, while not part of Thomson's terms of reference, emerged in one point in his report something like a threat to the white European colonial order. Such Chinese were said to be competing with Europeans for the loyalty of the Chinese 'mixed blood' group:

> In New Ireland it is reported that the Chinese are making overtures to the mixed blood group. It is not unreasonable to expect that, unless the mixed blood group find certain of their needs met by the European society, they will think more favourably of the Chinese community. We must consider this situation a direct challenge and … realise the advantages accruing from the mixed-blood group's desire to be as Europeans. We have, in fact, an incentive which needs only evidence of sincerity on our part to bring the mixed-blood group into a more favourable position in society. (Thomson, 1952, p. 7)

However, it was not until 1962, while Hasluck was still the Minister of Territories, that the 'mixed-blood' group became formally entitled to apply for Australian citizenship.

Such a move found further justification in Rowley's (1956) advice to Hasluck and the administration of Papua and New Guinea on how to de-racialise policy concerning the status of Alien Asians. Rowley thought that rights to movement and property needed to be based on legal and not racial categories. Indeed, he wanted to revise all legislation by deleting racial categories and replacing them with non-racial categories so that there could be no racial discrimination 'in administrative practice, or in the law, between the rights of Australian Protected Persons and British Subjects and Australian Citizens' (Rowley, 1956, p. 12). This recommendation, if implemented, would have gone a long way towards realising Hasluck's dream of there being only two types of person in PNG that Rowley, in his report, called 'villagers' and 'Australian citizens'.

Manchester liberalism and Chinese citizenship

Rowley's plans for complete de-racialisation of laws regarding Asians in New Guinea had been preceded by limited reforms in reference to the education of their children. During the 1930s, some Chinese children were sent to Australia for their education.[11] The Methodist Church in Rabaul played a role in organising some of these trips. In 1947, the Australian government resumed this pre-war practice of allowing Chinese students from New Guinea to enter Australia for educational purpose (NAA Series A518 BG /182/1).[12] In 1946, officials recommended several Chinese students from New Guinea be permitted to enter Australia with a two-year exemption under the Immigration Act providing they had secured guarantees about their maintenance.

Officials in Canberra and in New Guinea provided a number of other reasons for supporting Chinese students from New Guinea. They argued if the 'children of Asiatic residents of the Territory' were not permitted to come to Australia for educational purposes, then such a policy would provide 'a basis of criticism from Asiatic countries, in UNO [Organisation of the United Nations] and on the Trusteeship Council, on the grounds of racial discrimination' (NAA Series A518 BG 182/1:17). Suggestive of such pressures, a bureaucrat noted in 1947 that the Chinese Vice Consul in Sydney, Mr. Lui, in a visit to Rabaul, made representations to the Australian New Guinea Administrative Unit on behalf of New Guinea Chinese who sought permission either for themselves or members of their families to enter Australia.

One effect of this policy was that some Chinese students who came to Australia made further demands on the Australian government. Brian Cheung wrote to Hasluck in October 1953 on Barker College letterhead suggesting a degree of support from the college itself. Cheung argued the main problem in the Territory:

---

11   Servants, mainly from Papua and New Guinea, were also important early destabilisers of the White Australia policy (Davies, 2019).

12   Kuo and Fitzgerald (2016) outline how 400 students from China were granted visas to enter Australia between 1920 and 1925 through a significant Chinese government representative.

> ... is the strong existence of the 'Racial Barrier'. I feel that the New Guinea Government as well as every citizen should do something about this matter. The fundamental quality a citizen of democracy must have is a deep concern for the good life of his fellow man. He must have a sense of social responsibility and the general interests of his people in the common good: to do his full share in the working for the community. (NAA: M332, 51:3)

Cheung argued that Rabaul township was racially structured and that the Chinese and Malay residential areas were 'in ... revolting conditions compared with the European residential area'.[13] In 1955, the Rabaul Chinese quarter was described by the *Pacific Island Monthly* as a 'derelict shantytown' (Wu, 1982, p. 43).

Cheung was also referencing a longer history of racial segregation in Rabaul that was evident in the work of the Department of Public Health's Director, Dr. Cilento. In 1925, Cilento indicated that in Rabaul the 'demands of hygiene, racial inclination, and variations in the standards of living, all emphasise the desirability of ... subdivision, and the Department of Public Health has endeavoured to continue and develop this policy of racial segregation' (New Guinea Annual Report, 1925/1926, p. 73). Dr. Cilento authorised the removal of nine temporary Chinese residences from the general town area as they 'represented a continual menace to ... the neighbouring European buildings ... [because] several cases of bacillary dysentery had been definitely traced to them' (New Guinea Annual Report, 1925/1926, p. 73). The resulting evictions and demolitions emphasised the vulnerability of the Chinese to the colonial state's power to create racialised urban landscapes and ghettos.

Cheung's discussion of the conditions in Rabaul's Chinatown highlighted how this urban carceral ordering, rather than the plantation, was a crucial feature of Chinese life in colonial New Guinea (Wu, 1982, pp. 42–3). Cheung's emphasis on the living conditions in Chinatown suggests the salience in histories of New Guinea concerning the patrol, the plantation

---

13   Similar descriptions are provided in a 1953 survey of some 237 Chinese and Asiatic houses at Matupit Farm at Rabaul on land to be acquired by the government. The surveyor noted that most of the buildings 'can only be classed as hovels—their usual design being second-hand galvanised iron crudely fastened to bush timber frames. The flooring material is invariably earth; this being covered with seromat strips in the more elaborate establishments. There are over 1000 Asiatics living in the area—an area which might be able to house one third this number ... If we now prevent the higher class Chinese living in the European residential areas, we must further aggravate this position' (R. G. Matheson. Staff Surveyor Matupit Farm, typescript report, 6 August 1953. Fryer Library UQFL 387 Papua New Guinea Association of Australia Box 40 Folder 14).

and associated forms of controlled labour needs to be supplemented by accounts of the urban settlement and infrastructure of the colonial state and forms of racialised power developed in towns like Rabaul, Kavieng, Madang and Lae.

Cheung called for the removal of the Chinese enclave in Rabaul.[14] He argued there was a strong feeling of racial discrimination among the Chinese living in Rabaul that created a sense of 'hatred', which could only be destroyed when the government built a residential area where 'all people could live together closely'. In developing his arguments, Cheung cited Sir Earnest Simon's *Education for Citizenship in Secondary Schools* where Simon argued that it was public opinion that had forced all recent democratic governments to intervene and improve the standard of housing found in slums. Cheung stated that while he wished to make 'no comment' on whether such an argument applied to New Guinea conditions:

> I am very sure that the Government could improve the residential areas of these people had the Government thought of doing so. It is better still to set aside one central residential area which the Government had suggested three or four years ago, but nothing had been done. (NAA: M332, 51:4)

Simon was a former member of the British Liberal Party and, in the 1920s, he played a crucial role in creating the Wythenshaw estate, near Manchester, as a model town full of democratic citizens. Simon hoped to reform British class inequalities by designing a new town that would facilitate the poor's self-improvement. By the late 1930s, Simon regarded this reform as a failure partly because most of the residents were working class and as such were not really suitable as leaders of a model democratic community (Olechnowicz, 2000).

Simon also established an Association for Education in Citizenship in 1934. The object of the Association was to advance 'training in the moral qualities necessary for the freedom, tolerance, truth, justice, kindliness, public service, the co-operative habit and equality' (Simon, cited in Olechnowicz, 2000, p. 19). The training was aimed at encouraging 'clear and logical thinking', especially among secondary school pupils. Rational and moral perfectibility could be induced through education. His more political aim was to use schools as a means of strengthening liberal democracy in the

---

14   See K. Anderson (2018) for a more recent attempt to deconstruct the 'enclave framing' of Chinatowns. Cheung's intervention is a robustly practical and abolitionist approach to the same problem.

face of communist and fascist totalitarianism. For Simon, democracy was fundamentally about the freedom of the individual democratic citizen (Ku, 2018, p. 501). For such citizens of democracy to emerge it was essential that 'every child should be given a fair chance of growing up sound in mind and body, and making the best of its natural faculties' (Simon & Hubback, 1935, p. 15).

In his letter, Cheung approvingly echoed the elements of character that Simon thought were essential to any democratic citizen. Cheung repeated a key liberal idea that all people, given the right social conditions, were perfectible. Cheung thought the currently racially subordinated Chinese in New Guinea could, if given a 'fair chance', become model democratic citizens:

> The fundamental quality a citizen of democracy must have is a deep concern for the good life of his fellow man. He must have a sense of social responsibility and the general interests of his people in the common good: to do his full share in the working for the community … (NAA: M332, 51:3–4)

As Cheung suggests, the possibility of such a liberal democratic active citizenship existing for Chinese in New Guinea was severely limited by the persistence of racial barriers. Hasluck replied to Cheung's demands with a polite, if opaque, reference to current policy:

> In order that you may be more fully informed of the policy of the Government towards the Chinese residents of the Territory of Papua and New Guinea I am enclosing herewith a copy of a press statement which I recently made on the subject. (NAA: M332, 51:1 of 4)

Conditional citizenship achieved

Despite this response from Hasluck, similar appeals for Chinese citizenship gained support from a wide range of often surprising sources. In 1954, Arthur Calwell visited Rabaul and argued all New Guinea Chinese should be granted entry to Australia and that they should be naturalised. He said he regarded them as Australian citizens and pressured the Menzies government for naturalisation. He also impressed the Chinese community by speaking to them in Mandarin, even though his speech had to be translated into Cantonese (Cahill 2012, p. 252). In March 1954, *The South Pacific Post* wrote an editorial suggesting the government's next move 'toward progress and enlightenment must assuredly be the granting of full citizenship rights to the Territory Chinese' (cited in Cahill, 2012, p. 252). The possibility of Chinese becoming Australian citizens was raised in PNG's Legislative Council in 1955 and attempts were made to establish a select committee to investigate, recommending to the Australian government 'that Asian and mixed race of the Territory be granted Australian citizenship' (Cahill, 2012, p. 252). The motion was defeated largely because it might embarrass the Australian government and 'create a precedent' (Cahill, 2012, pp. 252–3).

Support for extending citizenship to the Chinese in PNG continued to grow within government circles. The Australian Security Intelligence Organisation strongly supported the policy shift, arguing that since only a small number of Chinese were involved, they would be 'absorbed' in the larger Australian population without undue difficulty. If they were left with their current status then there was some risk that they might eventually become easy prey for the advances of Communist China (NAA: A452, 1956/993 PART 1).

In September 1956, Hasluck decided that the Chinese in New Guinea should be granted citizenship and asked that a cabinet submission outlining such a recommendation be drafted in his name and that of Harold Holt, then Immigration Minister (NAA: A452, 1956/993 PART 1:132). In June 1957, cabinet made a decision to offer 'Asian residents' of PNG the chance to become naturalised Australian citizens. In August 1957, the Australian dictation test was abolished and Asians, and other non-Europeans in Australia, who had 'taken part in normal Australian life' could apply for naturalisation after fifteen years of living in Australia (Jordan, 2006, p. 236). Over the next eight years, several thousand Asians living in Australia did become citizens (Jordan, 2006, p. 237).

The New Guinea policies regarding naturalisation defined suitable applicants as 'Asians' a term which included persons of mixed European and Asian descent (Administrator Territory of Papua and New Guinea 9 September 1957, NAA: A452, 1956/993 PART 1:12), but not persons of mixed indigenous and Asian descent. Once naturalised such Asians could go to Australia under the same conditions as other Australians and stay there without restrictions on their movement or length of stay (Cahill, 2012, p. 255).

In an attempt to dampen opposition in Australia to the offer of citizenship to New Guinea Chinese, Hasluck stressed that only a particular kind of Asian would be eligible. They would in effect be European Asians:

> Those who will be affected by the decision are people living wholly in the European manner alongside, or integrated with the European community. They have no home except the Territory, and in all the implications of the term they can be regarded as good citizens. They have English education, are of Christian religion, and in every way are fitted by cultural and general social background to live on equal terms with other Australian citizens. (Hansard, 1957)[15]

On another occasion, Hasluck stressed 'that the established policy regarding the entry into the Territory of persons of non-European race has not been relaxed in any way' (Hasluck to Australian Natives Association 25/7/57, NAA: A452, 1956/993 PART 1:22). None of the reforms reduced the Commonwealth's power to exclude non-Europeans from Australia or New Guinea.

By 1958, sixty-four 'Asians' had participated in a naturalisation ceremony in the Rabaul District Court and the following year, 313 naturalisation certificates were issued (Cahill, 2012, p. 256). By 1963 of the 1,300 New Guinea Chinese who had applied, around 1,100 were naturalised (Wu, 1982, pp. 48–9). Those rejected were mainly older people who could not speak English. By 1966, there were only 282 Chinese in New Guinea who had Chinese nationality.

At the start of 1957 there were 2,448 Chinese in New Guinea (Wu, 1982, pp. 8–9). However, a 1966 census indicated there were roughly the same number—2,455—in the whole of PNG (Wu, 1982, Appendix 1). Wu argues the granting of Australia citizenship allowed the Chinese residential access to Papua with many New Guinea Chinese moving into Port Moresby while others moved to Australia. This movement into Papua co-occurred with the 'large scale migration' of the 1950s by the Rabaul Chinese into other towns in New Guinea such as Lae, Madang and Wewak (Wu, 1982, p. 42). Most of these movements involved establishing retail and wholesale business (Wu, 1982, p. 88; Ichikawa, 2006). Some Chinese who had initially moved to Australia started to routinely move between Australia and PNG. These various movements sedimented the Chinese position in PNG's emerging retail sector in a way that Hasluck hoped

---

15   See: historichansard.net/hofreps/1957/19570918_reps_22_hor16/#subdebate-20-0-s0.

would not occur. Rather than resulting in the removal and assimilation of the New Guinea Chinese into Australia, what emerged from Australian citizenship was a persisting Chinese emplacement in a complex set of racial, ethno-national and class distinctions in PNG that often involved blurring and differentiation of distinctions between migrant and citizen and between home, place of origin, place of return and place of citizenship.

Such possibilities influenced Brian Cheung's life. After graduating from Barker College in 1954, he returned to Rabaul and in 1961 became a director of Kwong Chong Bros Pty Ltd. He successfully expanded the business in Rabaul and after opening an outlet in Port Moresby he moved there in 1972, where he remained until his retirement in 1983 (*The Barker,* 2019, p. 67), when he moved to Australia. Brian's sons, one nephew and two granddaughters have gone on to attend Barker College (ibid.).

Concluding thoughts

The chapter is partly a response to the idea that changes to Australia immigration policies, and policies concerning New Guinea Chinese, could only reflect then hegemonic Australian values. We called for greater attention to New Guinea Chinese voices and examples of political activism and we located some of the possibilities for such a voice within then influential strands of liberalism that were global rather than just Australian.

It is arguable this could simply shift the emphasis from one form of the colonial power to another, involving a hegemonic white liberal post-war settlement and Hasluckian assimilationism understood as a project of decolonisation involving the racial and ethnic cleansing of PNG. Such an argument tends to ignore the context specific complexities and contradictions of what various strands of liberalism have facilitated, or denied, to New Guinea Chinese. Moreover, the focus of this paper on trans-national flows of liberal ideas tends to undercut any easy writing of histories just from the position of a single nation (Tavan's Australia) or from a single colonial enclave (Cheung's Chinatown in Rabaul).

We have pointed to some possibilities of rewriting PNG policy history from more of a New Guinea Chinese perspective. Cheung's letter outlined several liberal arguments for a de-racialised urban polity and opened up a model of development in PNG that was different to Hasluck's promotion of a future defined by an indigenous group of land-owning farmers and some helpful Europeans. Urbanisation has been given a relatively minor role in PNG histories and this has tended to amplify the absence of Chinese from PNG's history. Cheung's arguments, and his own life, invite us to rethink the role of urban Chinese in the development of PNG generally.

Finally, reading colonial policy 'against the grain', as did Brian Cheung and his father, we argued the post-citizenship movement of the Chinese out of Rabaul into both urban PNG and Australia was a practical political response to policies that promoted their removal from PNG. This response, which has yet to be fully documented, effectively transformed government policies into practices that ensured the Chinese created a better life more on their own terms than was previously thought possible by the colonial state.

Acknowledgements

Thanks are due to Marion and Peter Cahill, Michael Goddard, Margaret Jolly, Bruce Kapferer, Stuart Kirsch and Karen Sykes for their assistance with earlier versions of this paper. Chris Ballard, and especially Mark Dawson, generously enabled our access to King's 2002 honours thesis. Kelsey Halbert provided us with material by, and about, Sir Earnest Simon. Rachel Byrne, the archivist at Barker College in Sydney, and Stuart Braga helped in tracing Brian Cheung's engagement with the college. Research for this paper was funded by a grant provided to Wood by Nola Alloway and stimulated by work on an ARC-funded project (DP140100178).

References

Anderson, K. (2018). Chinatown dis-oriented: shifting standpoints in the age of China. *Australian Geographer, 49*(1), pp. 133–48. doi.org/10.1080/00049182. 2017.1327791

Anderson, W. (1998). Where is the Post-Colonial History of Medicine?. *Bulletin of History of Medicine, 72*, pp. 522–30. doi.org/10.1353/bhm.1998.0158

Ang, I. (2014). Beyond Chinese groupism: Chinese Australians between assimilation, multiculturalism and diaspora. *Ethnic and Racial Studies, 37*(7), pp. 1184–96. doi.org/10.1080/01419870.2014.859287

Banton, M. (1973). The Future of Race Relations in Britain. The Establishment of a Multi-Disciplinary Research Unit. *Race, 15*(2), pp. 223–39. doi.org/10.1177/ 030639687301500206

Bell, D. (2010). John Stuart Mill on Colonies. *Political Theory, 38*(1), 34–64. doi.org/10.1177/0090591709348186

Brawley, S. (2014). Finding Home in White Australia: The O'Keefe Deportation Case of 1949. *History Australia,11*(1), pp. 128–48. doi.org/10.1080/14490854.2014.11668503

Cahill, P. (2012). *Needed-but not wanted. Chinese in Rabaul.1884–1960.* CopyRight Publishing.

Clapson, M. (2006). The American Contribution to the Urban Sociology of Race Relations in Britain from the 1940s to the early 1970s. *Urban History, 33*(2), pp. 253–73. doi.org/10.1017/S0963926806003804

Collins, S. (1951). The Social Position of White and "Half-Caste" Women in Colored Groupings in Britain. *American Sociological Review, 16*(6), pp. 796–802. doi.org/10.2307/2087506

Collins, S. (1952). Social Processes integrating Coloured People into British Society. *British Journal of Sociology, 8*(1), pp. 20–9. doi.org/10.2307/587524

Commonwealth of Australia. (1920). *Royal Commission on Late German New Guinea.* Government Printer for State of Victoria.

Davies, L. (2019). A Regulated Labour Trade across the Torres Strait: Papuan and New Guinean Domestic Workers in Australia, 1901–50. In Victoria Stead and Jon Altman (Eds), *Labour Lines and Colonial Power: Indigenous and Pacific Islander Labour Mobility in Australia* (pp. 75–101). ANU Press and Aboriginal History Inc. doi.org/10.22459/llcp.2019.04

De Genova, N. & Roy, A. (2020). Practice of Illegalisation, *Antipode, 52*(2), pp. 352–64. doi.org/10.1111/anti.12602

Gilroy, P. (2001). *Against Race: Imagining Political Culture beyond the Color Line.* Cambridge, MA: Harvard University Press.

Goddard, M. (2017). A categorical failure: 'mixed-race' in colonial Papua New Guinea. In K. McGavin, & F. Fozdar (Eds.), *Mixed race identities in Australia, New Zealand and the Pacific Islands* (pp.133–46). Routledge. doi.org/10.4324/9781315559391

Hasluck, P. (1976). *A Time for Building.* Melbourne University Press.

Hasluck, P. (1988). *Shades of Darkness: Aboriginal Affairs, 1925–1965.* Melbourne University Press.

Ichikawa, T. (2006). Chinese in Papua New Guinea: Strategic Practices in Sojourning, *Journal of Chinese Overseas, 2*(1), pp. 111–32.

Jones, P. (2005). Chinese in Papua New Guinea and Pacific Island Territories. *Chinese–Australian Journeys: Records on travel, migration and settlement, 1860–1975, Research Guides* (pp. 233–49). National Australian Archives.

Jordan M. (2006). The Reappraisal of the White Australia Policy against the Background of a Changing Asia, 1945–67. *Australian Journal of Politics & History, 52*(2), pp. 224–43. doi.org/10.1111/j.1467-8497.2005.00416.x

Jordan, M. (2018). 'Not on Your Life': Cabinet and Liberalisation of the White Australia Policy, 1964–67. *The Journal of Imperial and Commonwealth History, 46*(1), pp. 169–201. doi.org/10.1080/03086534.2017.1391485

King, J. (2005). The creation of a 'recalcitrant minority': a case study of the Chinese New Guinea wartime refugees. *Journal of the Royal Australian Historical Society, 91*(1), pp. 48–57.

King, J. (2002). The wartime refugees and the consequences of humanitarianism: Australia's restrictive immigration policy. 1942–1955. Honours Thesis. Department of History. Australian National University.

Ku, H.-Y. (2018). Education for Democratic Citizenship: Earnest Simon's Ideals of Liberal Democracy and Citizenship Education in England, 1934–1944. *Historia y Memoria de la Education, 7*, pp. 499–532. doi.org/10.5944/hme.7.2018.19403

Kumarasingham, H. (2018). Liberal Ideals and the Politics of Decolonisation. *The Journal of Imperial and Commonwealth History, 46*(5), pp. 815–20. doi.org/10.1080/03086534.2018.1519250

Kuo, M. & Fitzgerald, J. (2016). Chinese Students in White Australia: State, Community, and Individual Responses to the Student Visa Program, 1920–25. *Australian Historical Studies, 47*(2), pp. 259–77. doi.org/10.1080/1031461x.2016.1156136

Lake, M. (2010). Chinese Colonists Assert Their "Common Human Rights": Cosmopolitanism as Subject and Method of History. *Journal of World History, 21*(3), pp. 375–92. doi.org/10.1353/jwh.2010.0011

Lake, M. & Reynolds, H. (2008). *Drawing the Global Colour Line: White Men's Countries and the Question of Racial Equality.* Melbourne University Press.

Lewis, David Charles. (c.1996). The plantation dream: developing British New Guinea and Papua, 1884–1942. *Journal of Pacific History.* openresearch-repository.anu.edu.au/bitstream/1885/132636/1/JPH_Plantation_Dream.pdf

MacWilliam, S. (2019). Anti-Conservatism: Paul Hasluck and Liberal Development in Papua New Guinea. *Australian Journal of Politics and History, 65*(1), pp. 83–99. doi.org/10.1111/ajph.12535

Mann, J. (2012). The evolution of Commonwealth citizenship, 1945–1948 in Canada, Britain and Australia. *Commonwealth & Comparative Politics, 50*(3), pp. 293–313. doi.org/10.1080/14662043.2012.692923

McGregor, R. (1999). Wards, Words and Citizens: A. P. Elkin and Paul Hasluck on Assimilation. *Oceania, 69*(4), pp. 243–59. doi.org/10.1002/j.1834-4461.1999.tb00372.x

Meaney, N. (1995). The End of 'White Australia' and Australia's Changing Perceptions of Asia, 1945–1990. *Australian Journal of International Affairs, 49*(2), pp. 171–89. doi.org/10.1080/10357719508445155

Mills, D. (2008). *Difficult Folk: A Political History of Social Anthropology*. Berghahn Books.

Moran A. (2005). White Australia, Settler Nationalism and Aboriginal Assimilation Australian. *Journal of Politics and History, 51*(2), pp. 168–93. doi.org/10.1111/j.1467-8497.2005.00369.x

Nelson, H. (2010). Chinese in Papua New Guinea. In T. Wesley-Smith and E. Porter (Eds.), *China in Oceania: Reshaping the Pacific?* (pp. 104–117). Berghahn Books.

Nelson, H. (2008). The Consolation Unit: Comfort Women At Rabaul. *The Journal of Pacific History, 43*, pp. 1–22. doi.org/10.1080/00223340802054578

Neumann, K. (2006). Guarding the flood gates: the removal of non-Europeans, 1945–1949. In M. Crotty and D. Roberts (Eds.), *The Great Mistakes of Australian History* (pp. 186–202). Sydney.

Olechnowicz, A. (2000). Civic leadership and education for democracy: The Simons and the Wythenshawe estate. *Contemporary British History, 14*(1), pp. 3–26. doi.org/10.1080/13619460008581569

Paisley, F. (2015). Applied Anthropology and Interwar Internationalism: Felix and Marie Keesing and the (White) Future of the 'Native' Pan-Pacific. *The Journal of Pacific History, 50*(3), pp. 304–21. doi.org/10.1080/00223344.2015.1078544

Rowley, C. D. (1956). Questions of Status, Movements etc. Involved in Territory of Papua and New Guinea Legislation. Typescript Report. AIATSIS Library MS 3774.4.1.

Simon, E. & Hubback, E. (Eds.). (1935). *Education for Citizenship in Secondary Schools*. Oxford University Press.

Stewart, I. (2020). On recent developments in the New Historiography of (Neo) Liberalism. *Contemporary European History, 29*(1), pp. 116–24. doi.org/10.1017/s0960777319000158

Tavan, G. (2005). *The Long, Slow Death of White Australia*. Scribe.

Taylor, S. & Boyd, J. (2022). Protecting Australian Protected Persons: Statelessness and Papua New Guinea's Independence. *Statelessness and Citizenship Review, 4*(2), pp. 213–36.

Thomas, N. (1994). *Colonialism's Culture: Anthropology, Travel and Government.* Princeton University Press.

The Barker. (2019). Obituaries: Brian Cheung. *The Old Barkers.* Issue 237, p. 67.

Thomson, R. (1952). *An Enquiry into the Social Conditions of the Mixed-Blood Population of Papua and New Guinea, July 1951–July 1952.* Canberra. Department of Territories. Typescript report. Mitchell Library.

Van Krieken, R. 2004. Rethinking Cultural Genocide: Aboriginal Child Removal and Settler-Colonial State Formation. *Oceania, 75,* pp. 125–51. doi.org/10.1002/j.1834-4461.2004.tb02873.x

Wimmer, A., & N. Glick Schiller. (2002). Methodological Nationalism and Beyond: Nation-state Building, Migration and the Social Sciences. *Global Networks, 2*(4), pp. 301–34. doi.org/10.1111/1471-0374.00043

Wolfers, E. P. (1975). *Race Relations and Colonial Rule in Papua New Guinea.* Australia and New Zealand Book Company.

Wright, H. (2002). A Liberal 'Respect for Small Property': Paul Hasluck and the 'Landless Proletariat' in the Territory of Papua and New Guinea, 1951–63. *Australian Historical Studies, 33*(119), pp. 55–72. doi.org/10.1080/10314610208596201

Wu, D. 1982. *The Chinese in Papua New Guinea, 1890–1980.* Chinese University Press.

Vignette—Reflection: History of a Chinese family in PNG

Vyvyen Wong

I was born in Rabaul in East New Britain Province. I was the last of nine children, five boys and four girls, born to James Yuen Yow Wong, but everyone knew him as Jimmy, and Winifred Loi Hay Wong, but everyone knew her as Winnie. We were not a wealthy family, but we had the richness of family. Mum and Dad worked very hard. We lived in Rabaul in the border area between Chinatown and Malaytown. The Chinese were only allowed to buy in certain places, so that's why Dad bought land there. His brothers lived nearby, so we grew up with all our cousins next door, and only a few doors down.

My father was a self-taught mechanic and worked with his brother until he branched out with his own workshop. It eventually became a reasonably successful workshop, which funded the purchase of their own house and some land in Australia. The main business that Dad had was the mechanic workshop, fixing cars and trucks, but he also did other things such as plumbing and oxywelding. We had water trucks to deliver water to households and a cargo truck, not a massive cargo truck, just several tons, which they drove to the wharf to pick up goods and deliver them wherever.

My mother used to run what we call a *haus kai kai*, which is equivalent to a diner. It was primarily aimed at the indigenous people, but anyone could go and eat there. Quite often as a child I would just rock up and say, 'Feed me.' There was a lamb curry, which was delicious, a fish curry and vegetables. The main staple was rice, of course, and they served tea or coffee. In the morning, they sold 'flour balls'; deep-fried delicious yellow-coloured balls of carbohydrate. They used to go down as a treat. A lot of our own workers and other indigenous workers from around the area used to have breakfast there. They used to do what we call *dinau*, that is they could run up a tab and then it would get docked from their wages.

Historically, there were two main waves of Chinese that came to PNG. I have been told that my paternal grandfather and maternal grandfather were among the second wave of Chinese that arrived. The first lot came as indentured labourers, but the second lot were free labourers, just people looking for work.

My earliest memory of our first generation of Chinese in PNG is of my paternal grandmother. Unfortunately, my grandparents on my mother's side passed away before I was born so I did not get to know them. All I know are the stories told to me. We estimate that it was sometime between 1909 and 1919 that both my paternal and maternal grandfathers came to the New Guinea Islands from China in search for a better life, like most immigrants. They came from different provinces, which I am still trying to research. I've worked out that my paternal grandfather is from Guangdong Province. He had a wife in China. He came out first, found work and then sent for his wife, my grandmother. She still wore the traditional Chinese mandarin-collar type clothing. She was probably very endearing, but I was always a little bit scared of her. She gave birth to five boys, including my dad, and three daughters, so she had eight children in total. Two of my father's sisters died early, but all his brothers survived.

I remember my grandmother would stay in turn at each one of her sons' houses and she had a stint at our place. She used to live in what we called 'the back room'. When she went to live with my Uncle Martin, my mother continued to cook for Grandmother Wong, and it was up to us children to ferry the food to her in the little Chinese-style stainless-steel canisters. Mum would make sure there was rice, soup, vegetables and a meat dish and I would have to take the food to my grandmother. I remember I had to knock on the door and say who I was. Then she would open the door and she say, 'Just wait', and then she would take the food away and come back with a lolly—a Chinese sweet, preserved plum that seemed big in my child hand. I don't remember ever being invited in.

When she died, I remember being terribly frightened. My dad made us follow Chinese custom—we had to touch the face of the dead person. I think I was about seven or eight years old. I have images in my mind of me being at that funeral but not really understanding what was going on. After my grandmother died, I used to dread going into the back room of our house where she had slept, which was now our storeroom. When mum said, 'Go get me a tin of something', I would first open the door and lean in to see if what Mum asked me to get was in reaching distance, so I would not actually have to enter the room by myself. I was terrified of my grandmother's ghost because I had heard so many ghost stories. On my mother's side, her mother being a Melanesian, there were many stories of sorcery and spirits and all that kind of stuff, which used to freak me out.

I think that in marrying my mother, my father went against the expectations of his family. My father's siblings all married Chinese spouses that were already living in PNG, except for one brother, who moved to Sydney and was a confirmed bachelor. My mother's mother was full Melanesian, from New Ireland Province. We are still trying to ascertain the exact location. My maternal grandfather's name was Leong Yee Kai. He was from Kaiping County, which is in the Guangdong Province of China. He would have travelled by ship to search for work. He would have landed in Rabaul and then gone over to New Ireland for work, potentially, encouraged to go to there by other Chinese he knew or people he met from his own county or province. They may have said, 'Come over; there is work over here'. I know he worked on a plantation. I am not exactly sure what he was doing though; I am still trying to find out. He would have met my grandmother there. She has only one name that we know of, which is Matiram. We don't have a surname for her, or anything like that, but my mother paid tribute to her by naming one of her *haus kai kai* 'Matiram'.

Matiram, as far as I can gather, died early. She was not around in 1966 when I was born; only my first two older siblings remember her. My eldest brother, John, remembers that she was very kind. My maternal grandparents, Leong Yee Kai and Matiram, had three children together. There was Kathleen, then Patrick and then my mum, Winifred. Aunty Kathleen was given away at an early age to the German Mission in Kokopo—Vunapope—to the nuns, so she barely spoke Chinese. However, she was quite fluent in German and Unserdeutsch (Rabaul Creole German) (see Aikhenvald, Chapter 8 in this volume). My uncle Patrick and my Mum could both speak Chinese. The reason Mum could speak Chinese fluently was that she was adopted out at the age of four to a Chinese family. My mother and her sister would have been given away for economic reasons. They may have been adopted out for the sake of a better life. In Chinese families, boys were more highly valued than girls, so my uncle Patrick was kept, and the girls were given away.

The interesting thing is that while Mum could speak Chinese, she was unable to read or write the language. She could not read or write English, either; she was illiterate. However, she was very good at cooking, cleaning and sewing. One can only assume from this that she was never sent to school by her adoptive family. She was never formally educated. She would have been raised as the help—as part of the family, but as the help. The other members of that family can read and write in both English and Chinese; Chinese characters and all. There were three adoptive sisters and an adoptive brother. We knew that our mother had a hard life growing up. She never spoke about it, but it did not make sense to me that she wasn't formally educated. As a result, it was extremely important to her that we were given every opportunity.

When we were little, we were all given Chinese names. I used to wonder why we would go over to this specific lady's place to get our Chinese names. It turns out she was Mum's adoptive sister. She worked out the appropriate and befitting name for each of us.

So, interestingly, in my mother's birth family there was one sibling who grew up speaking German, and two speaking Chinese, but for different reasons (on languages spoken among PNG Chinese see Aikhenvald, Chapter 8, this volume).

I don't know if my Mum and her sister Kathleen were ever allowed to visit or maintain contact with their mother, Matiram. What I do know is that one time when my mother was little, she accompanied her adoptive family to the hospital at Vunapope, where my aunt was at school. The hospital was attached to the school. Mum was playing in the grounds, so the story goes, when another little girl said, 'Hey you need to come down here. There is a little girl who looks like you.' So that was the first time the sisters, Winifred and Kathleen, laid eyes on each other. Over the years they kept in touch, and we used to travel up to Vunapope to visit my aunt Kathleen. She was married to a mixed German man, Gerhard Gangloff. The trips from Rabaul to Vunapope were always fun as we caught up with our 'German' cousins.

My mother's brother, Patrick, was that favourite uncle who took us children out to the community clubs, the Ambonese Club, Rabaul Yacht Club and so on. He would register us as his children so we would get a Christmas gift. He was a very generous, kind and loving man in that respect. He and my mother were quite close. He lived in Rabaul town like us and worked for a company called Coconut Products Limited as a foreman. He married late in life and his oldest child is younger than me. I remember Mum saying that her brother was one of the first Chinese Papua New Guineans to get a visa to go to Hong Kong. The story goes that he went to Hong Kong to visit relatives. We think that my maternal grandfather Leong Yee Kai may have been married before he came to PNG and that my uncle Patrick possibly visited half-siblings in Hong Kong.

At the time my parents were married in 1950, the full Chinese and the mixed-race Chinese in Rabaul did not really mix, but as the years rolled on there was more mingling. By the time my generation was around from the mid-1970s, there were hardly any differences. Everybody got on well and we proudly called each other cousin. If somebody were to fight our cousins, then we would stand up for them.

My mother was brown in complexion, which extended to some of my siblings and myself. She met my father at 'housie-housie' (bingo). He used to call the numbers. They married but I have no information on their wedding and no photos. They may have been too poor to get photos taken. My mother would have been eighteen or nineteen years old when they met. My father was eight years older and had been married previously to a full Chinese woman, but it had ended.

It was only when I was already in my twenties that I became aware of the attitudes of the Chinese towards mixed-race Chinese and the racism to which my mother had been subjected. I think that by the time I was born, as in by the time they had their ninth child, tensions had settled down and my father's family had accepted Mum. It would have been a shock for his family when he chose to marry Mum, as all his brothers had married Chinese women and his sister had also married a Chinese. Something my Mum said to me later in her life is revealing of what she experienced. By this time my parents and my father's sister and family were living in Brisbane. My father's sister would call out a greeting to Mum if she saw her in the shopping centre. The way they address each other is 'sister-in-law' and then usually there is a number, so if you had four sisters-in-law, then you would say 'number four sister-in-law' in Cantonese. My aunt waved at Mum to say hello one day but my mother mumbled to me, 'Funny, isn't it. She is now calling out to me. She never used to.' Another time she commented, 'She didn't want to know me then, but she really wants to know me now.'

After they began to establish themselves in New Guinea, the Chinese community formed several social and political clubs. I remember going to events at the Kuomintang Club. My parents would go to the Double 10 Ball—on the 10th day of the 10th month—celebrating the National Day of Taiwan. This Double 10 Ball was a big thing.

There is another club called Kwong Yick Club. That club was quite interesting because it was a group of labourers. Most of the labourers, like my maternal grandfather, worked on plantations and then came into town when they had their break. But when they came into town, they did not have any money to stay anywhere. They were not allowed to join other Chinese clubs that were in existence at the time. There were Chinese who came to New Guinea who were quite well off already—they were traders and were the ones that built shops and hotels and that kind of thing—but my grandfather and his cohort were not as economically well-resourced. They would have come into town and had nowhere to stay. If they stayed the night, they would just sleep in a shop alcove. Eventually a group of them started to say, 'We need to get a place', so they put some money together and saved and eventually they bought a house for themselves and their family members to stay in when they came to town. Basically, their aim was to look after themselves and to make sure that everybody had a place to stay when they came into town on their breaks. Eventually it became a bigger club and one of its core missions was to do charitable work to help families and others. If a family had lost the main breadwinner, or that sort of thing, they'd make sure they were looked after and supported to go back to China or to stay. The club was eventually granted some land to support an old age home.

Although most members had passed on, or had moved onto Sydney or Brisbane, it stayed active until 2017. I have been advised that it is currently dormant. There are documents in existence listing the members and all their descendants. The main committee members were from Sydney and Brisbane. It is very interesting to see the connections of the different Chinese families listed, to know that at one point our grandfathers established this club, and through them we are all connected.

Of course, the English and the Australians had their own clubs. You had the New Guinea Club that was strictly 'whites only'. The swimming pool was also 'whites only'. I have seen some photos with signs to that effect. My brother has told me stories of how he and other Chinese boys would throw things over the fence into the pool area because they weren't allowed in. Social exclusion based on the colour of one's skin led people to form their own clubs, such as the Ralum Club (at Kokopo), which still exists. Membership of the Ralum Club was originally predominantly mixed-raced German New Guineans, but it eventually opened to all. Other clubs closer to where we lived in Rabaul were the Ambonese Club and the Kombiu Club. Both were known to be mixed-raced clubs. Later, there was the Taiping Club, which was more accepting of both mixed-race and full Chinese membership. Earlier Chinese clubs had originally excluded mixed-race Chinese.

My first school was Sacred Heart School in Rabaul, which had originated as a Chinese school. My dad and all my siblings and cousins went to that school. It's a Catholic school, different to the Methodist school. A lot of Chinese were Methodist. It is interesting that we were Catholic. I am pretty sure that everyone I knew was Catholic. It could have something to do with the social group. It was not until recently that I realised that a lot of Chinese were Methodist and that this could have been based on economic or class distinctions. I think most of the higher-class Chinese were Methodist. There were some Chinese who came to PNG with some sort of wealth behind them. They came to set up trade stores and other businesses. There are also self-made Chinese businesspeople who came with nothing but have accumulated much wealth in property and hotels.

Most of our siblings were sent to boarding school in Australia for secondary education, except for one of my brothers, who refused to go. He went to Rabaul High School. Some of my siblings went to Rabaul High School first, I am not sure why, before they were sent to Australia. Interestingly, I know a lot of other mixed-raced people, mixed with German or other non-Australians, who went to Rabaul High School instead of boarding in Australia.

By the time we were sent to secondary school in Australia, my mother's adoptive family had moved from Rabaul to Port Moresby, and it was expected that whenever we travelled through to Brisbane for boarding school, or anywhere else, we would stop with this family in Port Moresby on the way. I could never understand why; they didn't look like us, but they welcomed us warmly. It wasn't until I grew older that I realised they were my mother's adoptive family.

All the members of my family became Australian citizens, although one of my siblings renounced his Australian citizenship for Papua New Guinea. My father began the application for naturalisation on 10 June 1958. The fee was one pound. His application was supported by two Australians who were living in Rabaul.

A letter dated 19 March 1959 from the Department of the Administrator in Port Moresby to The Secretary Department of Immigration in Canberra, the subject heading of which was 'Naturalisation of Asians', shows my father's name listed among others as having been presented his Certificate of Naturalisation at Rabaul on 16 March 1959.

It was wonderful seeing my father's signature on the application (regarding citizenship issues, see Wood and Backhaus, Chapter 3 in this volume). One of my father's Australian friends convinced him to apply for Australian citizenship. A key benefit my father saw in becoming Australian was the education that would be available for his children. Before Independence, schooling in Australia for Australian children living in PNG was subsidised by the Australian government.

My father was unusual because he didn't just socialise with the Chinese community. He had an outgoing personality. He would mix with all different people and had very good friends amongst the Matupit Islanders in East New Britain, the Japanese community and the English. We sometimes used to billet English people. From this, Mum told me that she had learned that English people don't wash enough!

Dad mixed with a lot of people from different religions, too. It didn't surprise me then, but it surprises me now. He had friends that were of the Bahai faith and all sorts of other religions. I didn't think this was unusual until I arrived in Australia. I didn't know that people in Australia can be very prejudiced against others because of their religion, or that someone from one religion might not necessarily like another person because of their religion. I never understood that. As a child I just thought everybody was the same.

When my father applied for Australian citizenship in 1958, the application included my mother and all their children at that time. I was born in 1966, before Independence in 1975. Just before Independence everyone was given a choice to renounce our Australian citizenship and become Papua New Guinean, but Dad's Australian friends told him, 'Whatever you do, just stick with Australia', so he did.

Our family being granted Australian citizenship has something to do with the way the territory of New Guinea was different to Papua. There were different rules there. At one point the Chinese were not allowed to go to the Territory of Papua. It was only after a certain Australian Government rule came in that the Chinese started to go to Papua and begin businesses there (see Wood and Backhaus, Chapter 3 in this volume).

I used to wonder how my parents knew all these Chinese people that lived over in Papua. At boarding school, I met a Chinese girl from Port Moresby and when we looked at our histories, we were surprised to discover that her parents had been born in Rabaul; in fact, they had lived near my house. I thought that was amazing. I said, 'Really, your parents came from my hometown?' And then when I talked to my parents, they said, 'Yes, we know her parents.' Some people say that certain Chinese families are from Port Moresby, but we know they are originally from Rabaul. Most of the Chinese first came to Rabaul, East New Britain, and only later started to branch out.

Today, most of my family lives in Australia. Dad's siblings and their families are either in Brisbane or Sydney. Some of my cousins are in Port Moresby. Two of my brothers remained in Rabaul and died there, but everyone else is here in Australia. My parents initially bought a small fibro house and land in Brisbane and later sold it to buy a better house. No one was handed anything on a platter in our family. We all made our own way in the world. Our parents educated us, but then it was up to us to make our own way.

Recently I have noticed a distinction between the 'old' Chinese and the 'new' Chinese in PNG (on this distinction see Chin, Chapter 4 in this volume). For example, a PNG Chinese man who attended the workshop that led to this volume commented, after listening to Gessler's paper and seeing the accompanying film clip, that the old Chinese do not barter with Melanesian market sellers like the new Chinese do (see Gessler, Chapter 7 in this volume).

4

The rise and rise of China: Contemporary Chinese community in PNG (2010–2020)

James Chin

Introduction

In this chapter, I will be looking at the Chinese community in Papua New Guinea (PNG), with references to the changes during the past decade (2010–2020). It will be based largely on my earlier work (Chin, 2008), which was published in 2008; in a sense, this chapter is an update of the essay. The central argument I make in this chapter is that while China and mainland Chinese were moving into PNG in the early 1990s and early 2000s, in less than two decades the mainland Chinese have become a dominant economic and political force in PNG.[1] The mainland Chinese in PNG have taken a leadership position among the PNG Chinese community and have also become the second most influential external player in PNG politics after Australia. This situation is unlikely to change for the foreseeable future and China's pole position will be tied to the rise of China in the world and China's position in the South Pacific.

---

1   In this chapter, China is used as shorthand for the People's Republic of China (PRC).

Summary of the 2008 article

In my earlier article, I made the distinction between the 'old' and 'new' Chinese. The 'old' Chinese were basically the PNG-born Chinese (PNGBC) who were in PNG at the time of Independence and had lived in PNG for several generations. Their spiritual 'home' was Rabaul, East New Britain Province. Almost all were Christians, and they used English as their primary language—they seldom used dialects, even among themselves. They sent their children to Australia to study, and many took out Australian citizenship in the decade after Independence. At least one member of the family would hold PNG citizenship so that their businesses could be classified as 'national'. They took pride in long-term relationships with nationals and in playing a major role in community affairs (fundraising for charities, church activities, etc.) and fostered close relationships with PNG politicians, who generally saw, and continue to see, them as part of PNG society.

On the other hand, the 'new' Chinese consisted of two key groups: Southeast Asians (mostly Malaysians, Indonesians and Singaporean Chinese) and Northeast Asians (mostly mainland Chinese and a small handful of Taiwanese and Koreans). The most important and influential among the 'new' Chinese were undoubtedly the Malaysian Chinese, with Rimbunan Hijau (RH) as their flag-bearer. Almost all the logging and timber-related businesses in PNG were dominated by RH. RH also began to diversify in the late 1990s and early 2000s into non-timber business, the most prominent being *The National*, an English daily newspaper. The Malaysian Chinese and the Indonesian Chinese dominated the wholesalers/retail network.

The mainland Chinese were not prominent in the late 1990s. Although they had started coming to PNG, their numbers were still relatively small, and they kept a low profile. A greater number began to come in the 2000s, after Chinese state-owned-enterprises (SOE) began to set up operations. It was during this period that the mainland Chinese small traders began to appear in large numbers and started to flood the market with cheap Chinese products. The mainland Chinese were the biggest group setting up illegal businesses in 'reserved' business such as kai bars.[2] Many of these small traders are from mainland China and would be classified as people

---

2 Tok Pisin term meaning a cheap, takeaway food bar. They usually sell other products such as cigarettes and snacks.

from the lower socio-economic strata. As they are already operating an illegal 'reserved' business they are more likely to pay bribes and deploy other illegal methods.

The main observations I made in the 2008 paper were, first, that the PNG Chinese community, both 'old' and 'new', were the biggest beneficiary of the sell-off of white businesses after Independence and after the dramatic fall in the value of the kina in the 1990s. My second observation was that RH was the most influential political player among the 'new' Chinese. They were able to reach the highest echelons of the PNG Government and even influence the appointment of cabinet ministers, essentially via bribery and inducements (see Barnett, 1989; Gabriel & Wood, 2015). They were able to protect the interests of their business because so many PNG politicians were in their pocket. The model of mixing politics and business was nothing new to RH as this was what the Tiong family, who owned RH, had done for decades in their home state of Sarawak in Malaysia. For years, members of the family held positions as members of the Malaysian Parliament and senators (Chin, 2006). My third observation was that the 'new' Chinese had become the biggest investors outside the oil and gas sectors. Without them, the PNG economy would have very limited investment outside the oil and gas sectors. Fourth, I observed that most of the 'old' PNGBC do not see a future in PNG. The volatile politics, law and order issues, depreciation of the kina and the reluctance of the younger generation to take over the family business caused many to take the attitude that PNG was a place to make money to support their families in Australia. My final observation was that, generally, the PNGBC and the Southeast Asian Chinese do not like the mainland Chinese. They see them as competition but more seriously, they see the mainland Chinese as destroying the long established friendly 'PNG Chinese national' social networks and relationships.

The 2020 scoreboard

If I were to present a succinct summary of the Chinese community in the past decade (2010–2020) and compare it to my 2008 study, it would look something like Table 4.1.[3]

---

3   Like my earlier study, getting precise, or official figures, is close to impossible. The data and analysis presented in this chapter are gathered through a combination of interviews, informal chats, personal communication and observations of online chats, and from my extensive personal contacts among the PNGBC, Southeast Asian Chinese, Mainland Chinese and knowledgeable nationals. I have also spoken to several long-term PNG-based Australian professionals. I have tried to verify the information given and will only include data that I believe to be true or that were collaborated by more than one source.

Table 4.1 Scoreboard

Big winners	Mainland Chinese
Holding pattern with some growth	Malaysian and PNG-born Chinese
Holding pattern	Southeast Asian Chinese (mostly Indonesian and Singaporeans)
Newcomers	South Asians (mostly Indo-Fijians and Bangladesh)

Source: Compiled by author.

The big winners are the mainland Chinese. They have now cemented their position as the most influential group among the Chinse community in PNG, both in politics and the economy. Almost all the big deals have their input, including government projects. They are actively aided and directed by the Chinese Embassy in Port Moresby.

The second group managed to hold on to their business and experienced some growth in the past decade. These are mainly Malaysian Chinese businesspeople and the PNGBC community. They have been in PNG for decades and, as much as possible, have refused to sell out to the mainland Chinese.

The third group consists of those who managed to hold on to their assets but have not really expanded their businesses in the past decade. This is true for the Indonesian Chinese and especially true for the Singaporean Chinese. The main reasons for this are the intense competition from the mainland Chinese and because they have not made any new investments.

One interesting, and unstudied group, that is making a mark on the local PNG economy is South Indians. Although they are not Chinese, I have added them here for the simple reason that they are part of the larger Asian diaspora. In the past decade, they have made their presence known in Chinese business circles. They are mainly Bangladeshis and Indo-Fijians.

I develop my discussion regarding the Chinese community in PNG below. Section 1 deals with the mainland Chinese and Section 2 deals with the other Chinese groups.

Section 1: The rise and rise of mainland Chinese

The mainland Chinese, as I argued above, are now the undisputed 'big man' among the Chinese community in PNG. To understand the community, it is best to divide them into two segments—the officials and the non-officials.

The 'official' mainland Chinese

First, the officials are mainlanders who are directly linked to the Government of the People's Republic of China. Here I am referring to staff at the Chinese Embassy and staff at Chinese state-owned enterprises (SOEs) that operate in PNG. Beijing sees SOEs as an extension of the state apparatus under its 'military-civil fusion' and SOEs are required to support China's official policy and goals (Weinstein, 2021). At present there are at least 40 Chinese SOEs operating in PNG. At this official level, most of what they do is based on what Beijing wants from PNG and the wider Pacific. Their role is primarily to expand China's influence via political and economic means and to try to create a dependent economic linkage between these economies and China.

So, what does China seek from PNG? I would argue that China is aiming for the following (in no particular order):

1. *To drive PNG away politically from its traditional ally, Australia.* Given the traditional closeness between PNG and Australia, China sees Australia as a direct competitor and a hindrance to its moves to gain influence in PNG. This is especially true in recent years, with Beijing accusing Australia of 'anti-China' hysteria and of promoting 'anti-China' sentiments worldwide ('Beijing Accuses Australia of "Whipping up Anti-China Sentiment"' 2019; Johnson & Detsch, 2021). Beijing is especially unhappy with Australia constantly telling the PNG political class that China cannot be trusted, and Australia's increased aid to PNG is seen as a countermeasure to stop PNG from getting close to China (McIlroy, 2019). China is also unhappy that Australia claims PNG as 'our patch'.

2. *To bring PNG under China's orbit, especially in the economic arena.* China wants PNG to be under its influence in the medium term and, in the long term, seeks PNG dependence on China in the economic arena, which it thinks will translate into political influence. In the past decade,

China has been in competition with the US, New Zealand and Australia to see who can sway the small Pacific states (Köllner, 2021). China sees PNG as a big diplomatic prize as it is the largest and most influential Melanesian country and can indirectly influence the rest of the South Pacific. In fact, China sees the entire South Pacific as a low-risk, high-yield opportunity in terms of diplomatic votes in the international arena (Barker Gale, 2019).

3. *To block Taiwan's interests in PNG*. Blocking Taiwan from making any headway in PNG and the wider Pacific is a long-term Chinese goal. Beijing has always been unhappy with Taiwan's move to seek recognition as an independent state via diplomatic moves around the world and has spent enormous resources to isolate Taiwan diplomatically (Zhang, 2019/20). In PNG's case, the Chinese are worried about PNG's volatile political climate. In the 1990s, PNG contemplated changing its diplomatic recognition from Beijing to Taipei in return for economic aid and direct bribes to senior PNG politicians. In 1999, a serious attempt was made by Prime Minister Bill Skate to diplomatically recognise Taipei as the government of China.[4] It was reversed quickly by the next prime minister, Sir Mekere Morauta. Nearly a decade later in 2008, Taiwan spent close to US$30 million trying to lure PNG into recognising Taipei. When this was exposed, Taiwan's foreign minister, James Huang, Deputy Premier Chiou I-jen and Vice Défense Minister Ko Cheng-heng were forced to resign. The money was never recovered ('Taiwanese Officials Resign over Papua New Guinea Scandal', 2008). It is widely believed in Port Moresby circles that in both these attempts, Taiwanese businessmen and PNG fixers were involved and large amounts of money were paid in bribes. Taiwan has maintained an active trade office in Port Moresby since the 1980s and, for many years, the Taiwan representative and the Chinese Embassy have been involved in childish diplomatic games. For example, on the 'double ten' (October 10), both the Taiwanese and the Chinese Embassy will hold formal gatherings, forcing members of the PNG establishment and the diplomatic community to 'choose' which reception to attend.[5] China knows that PNG can, at any time, turn towards Taipei if a desperate situation arises, or if another leader like Bill Skate comes along and can be easily bought.

---

4   Brissenden, Michael. (1999, July 7). Skate announces resignation in wake of diplomatic deal. *ABC Radio National*. web.archive.org/web/20170512150620/www.abc.net.au/pm/stories/s34383.htm
5   October 10 is the date of the Taiwanese National Day.

4. *To make sure Bougainville is China-friendly.* China is watching the Bougainville independence process carefully. They want to ensure that, if Bougainville becomes independent, it will be China-friendly from day one and follow the 'one China' policy. The strong push to ensure that Bougainville is on China's side is also linked to the fear that if China does not take an active role, Taiwan may step in and gain diplomatic recognition.

5. *Security and military interests.* Part of China's push into PNG is driven by security and military interests. China wants to replicate the US model of having a chain of military bases around the world and PNG offers plenty of opportunity due to its strategic location. PNG lies just north of Australia and the strategic planners in Beijing see Australia as part of the Western bloc that is inherently hostile towards the rise of China. Over the long term, if China can secure PNG, then PNG can act as a natural buffer to any Australian/US military operations in the South Pacific. Australia (and the US) already have access to the Lombrum base on Manus Island and Australia maintains intelligence listening posts in PNG (Dorling, 2013).

6. *Implementation of China's Belt and Road Initiative.* Although the original Belt and Road Initiative (BRI) did not include the South Pacific, this was quickly changed, and China is signing up nations from the South Pacific for Xi Jinping's signature policy. Peter O'Neill signed up for the BRI in Beijing in 2018, which officially made PNG the second Pacific nation to sign up after East Timor. Thus far, ten South Pacific nations have signed up for the BRI, much to the discomfort of Australia. Australia's consistent narrative to small Pacific states is that the BRI can lead to a 'debt trap', a narrative that Beijing obviously does not like (Rajah et al., 2019).

To ensure that these goals are met in practice, the Chinese are involved in a major drive to win PNG infrastructure projects. For example, all the main contracts for the Magi Highway project, funded by the World Bank and Asian Development Bank, and rehabilitation and improvement of the existing highway link were won by Chinese companies. The Metallurgical Corporation of China (MCC) is building the first stretch of the highway, while China Wu Yi is building the second section and China Harbour Engineering Company (CHEC) is building the third. The major expansion and upgrade project at Momote Airport on Manus Island was won by CHEC. All these companies are Chinese SOEs. According to a recent analysis, three-quarters of all contracts have gone to Chinese companies, most notably the China Railway Construction and Engineering Group, an SOE (Wall, 2020). Chinese SOEs are offering to open Bougainville mines in the future, while Chinese SOEs already operate the largest mine operation in PNG, the Ramu project. The Ramu project, due for expansion, is operated by the MCC.

A big push is also underway in the fisheries sector. In December 2020, the Fujian Zhonghong Fishery Company, a Chinese SOE, signed a memorandum of understanding with the Papua New Guinea Government to build a US$204 million 'comprehensive multi-functional fishery industrial park' on the island of Daru under its BRI. Daru is in the Torres Strait and shares a porous border with Northern Australia (Cluff, 2020). In the financial sector, in August 2020, the Bank of China established a representative office in PNG, allowing the Chinese a direct entry into PNG's financial system, although the Bank has been in the country since 2019 (Kenneth, 2019).

The rise of China and competition with Australia also means that the Chinese Ambassador to PNG is behaving more aggressively when it comes to blatantly pushing for Chinese interests. Part of it is public diplomacy to show the community that China is capable of upstaging Australia but, more importantly, the Ambassador is sending a clear signal that China's move to bring PNG under its influence is working. I will give several examples of such behaviour.

In July 2020, the UN Human Rights Council voted on a resolution on China's crackdown in Hong Kong. To the surprise of many, including the US, the UK and Australia, PNG joined 52 other countries in supporting the resolution that effectively endorsed China's position on limited free speech and freedom of assembly in Hong Kong. Even some in the PNG Foreign Ministry were surprised by the vote. It was revealed only later that the Chinese Ambassador had directly lobbied Patrick Pruaitch, PNG's foreign minister. The foreign minister decided to support China without deferring to the rest of the government (personal communication, October, 2020).

During the 2020 Independence Day celebrations, the Chinese Ambassador purposely did not attend one official function because he was unhappy that the PNG Government was too slow in approving the permit for the Ramu 2 project, which will benefit Chinese SOEs and further cement the Chinese role in the mining industry. During the inauguration of Ishmael Toroama, Bougainville's newly elected president in October 2020, the Chinese Ambassador forced his way into a meeting with Toroama despite earlier advice that it was against protocol (personal communication, October, 2020).

In the 2018 Asia-Pacific Economic Cooperation (APEC) meeting held in Port Moresby, China showed its diplomatic power when it ensured that APEC was unable to issue the usual joint communiqué (Dziedzic & Whiting, 2018a, 2018b). PNG, as the host, was put under tremendous pressure to not allow the joint communiqué and instead was pushed into issuing a 'chairman's statement' by the Chinese side. Anyone attending the summit would have had no doubt that it was the Chinese who were running the 'show'.[6] This was the first APEC meeting where a common communiqué was not issued; a highly significant event. The dominance of the Chinese in the APEC meeting was unmistakable. A Chinese arch was built in front of The Stanley Hotel, the most prestigious hotel in the country, and the entire lobby of the hotel was decorated with Chinese lanterns. Delegates from other countries staying at the hotel were left in no doubt about which country was the most important player at the summit.

In the past decade, China has also consistently offered the PNG Government capital and technology. The PNG Government finds it difficult to turn down some of these offers as their traditional ally, Australia, often cannot match the Chinese offers ('PNG Ignores Australia', 2019).

The ultimate aim of the Chinese in PNG is to secure PNG natural resources and to ensure that PNG is diplomatically on the Chinese side on major issues. The Chinese see PNG and Fiji as the two most important countries in the South Pacific to influence as they perceive these two countries as the main thought-leaders for the South Pacific Forum and the Melanesian Spearhead Group.

One potential problem for China over the long term is when the Chinese economy slows down and China no longer has the excess financial resources to be generous with PNG and other Pacific states. There may be other competing regions for China's influence, such as Africa and Latin America, that may redirect some Chinese financial aid. How this will impact China's relationship with PNG and the Pacific remains unclear.

---

6   Due to the Chinese decorations and adornments, it was suggested that some observers might have been mistaken that it was a PNG–China meeting rather than an APEC summit (personal communication from a PNG businessman who attended the summit, October 2020; see also Katharine Murphy (2018).

The 'non-official' mainland Chinese

Here I am referring to the thousands of mainland Chinese who are permanent residents in PNG.[7] Some are legal (holding proper employment permits) while others are not (holding non-employment permits or having overstayed). The overwhelming number in this group are small traders who came to PNG to seek their fortune. The majority come from Fujian Province.

They are mostly migrants who had limited or no English language ability when they arrived in PNG, who have little capital and, perhaps most importantly, are willing to break the laws on business and employment. PNG 'reserved business' law restricts small businesses, such as kai bars and sundry shops, to PNG nationals. These small-time Chinese traders will often run these reserved businesses using the name of a PNG national who actually holds the licence and other paperwork. On top of this, many such Chinese traders regularly cheat on their goods and services tax commitments, and some deal with stolen or pirated goods.[8]

Although they are not part of the official group, they are generally in agreement with the Chinese Embassy when it comes to the aims described above. They are proud of China's status as a rising superpower and want to see PNG under the influence of China. They see Xi Jinping's China Dream as the way forward for a better world. They buy the argument that PNG's long-term interests lie in closer ties with China rather than with Australia, New Zealand and the West.[9]

Generally, they see PNG as an easy place to make money. Many of them hold the view that PNG offers a lot of opportunities because there are 'so much natural resources' and there is limited or no competition from the PNG business class. They think their biggest advantage in doing business in PNG is the informal Chinese 'ecosystem' where everything can be done internally with other mainland Chinese (see also Hayes, this volume). This includes procurement, short-term business loans, bureaucratic

---

7   It is impossible to get precise figures but several of my informers tell me there are at least 15–20K mainland Chinese in PNG. Some are legal, others are illegal.

8   This was told to me by many businessmen who dealt with these small Chinese traders. To be fair, the other Chinese businesses, such as the Southeast Asian Chinese and PNGBC, also cheat on their GST and minimise their tax, but not as blatantly as the mainland Chinese.

9   This section of the chapter is based on conversations with several Chinese traders in PNG and Southeast Asian Chinese traders who deal with them.

approvals and sometimes mediation if there is a conflict. In other words, this ecosystem is designed to shut out non-Chinese traders by default. An example is the following message in a private PNG Chinese WhatsApp group, which demonstrates the concerns raised by other traders over such practices (see Figure 4.1).[10]

Most of you are not running a business and don't know PNG has lost retail to Chinese immigrants already.

They are 100% in reserved businesses but we don't enforce the existing laws.

PNG hands out citizenship to them too easily. Just look at what they really contribute back once they become citizens or still sending their profits to their original home.

How can any PNG SME compete against the Chinese "family" network?

Just last week one of them came to my office and asked for a deal on biscuits. He had K1.5million in CASH to pay.

K1.5million cash which is not banked or captured by IRC.

I said he never brought that amount before and he would just take business away from the existing loyal wholesalers.

He said all the other Chinese shops will support him because they are "family". The dragon is growing and there is no solution on how to fix it.

Over to you PNG Government! [pers. comm. 27 October 2020].

Figure 4.1 Message from the 'On Transformation PNG' WhatsApp group
Source: James Chin.

Many of these mainland Chinese traders do not intend to live in PNG for the long term but rather plan to use PNG as a transit point to move elsewhere if they can make enough money. Their preferred destination is North America with Australia and New Zealand as the second choice.

Worldviews

I would argue that the world view of official and non-official Chinese based in PNG, regarding the country and its nationals, is mostly negative and often racist. The same is true of their views about PNG's traditional links with Australia. They see PNG and the wider Pacific as 'uncivilised' peoples who were deliberately 'underdeveloped' by Australia and the West. In their world view, China offers a better model of development; some referenced China's development aid to Africa as an example of failed Western development that is being corrected by the Chinese model.

When asked what the biggest hindrance to PNG's development is, some expressed the view that PNG does not really understand capital and the capitalist system. They find it astonishing that only three per cent of PNG's land is made available for commercial use[10] and do not understand why the government does not change the system to allow more land to be used as capital and commercialised.[11]

One interesting aspect is how official and non-official Chinese explain racism and anti-Chinese sentiment in PNG. They blame anti-Chinese rhetoric on Australian influence in PNG and 'misunderstanding' by PNG nationals. In their view, Australians living in PNG cannot survive the competition from Chinese traders and thus are encouraging these anti-Chinese sentiments (Braddock, 2020). They think cultural differences and miscommunication are to blame for the PNG nationals' hostility. One mentioned that the differences are due to PNG nationals' 'work ethic', which leads to hostility towards the Chinese.[12] They also hold the view that anti-Chinese sentiment will decrease once PNG understands that only China can bring development to the country and that Australia is unwilling or unable to subsidise PNG over the long term.

Projections of soft power

In the past decade, the Chinese have tried hard to boost their public profile in PNG. Many of these efforts are co-ordinated by the Chinese Embassy. The 'soft' approach is undertaken by two organisations that actively promote China–PNG ties: the PNG-China Friendship Association and the PNG Chinese Association.

The PNG Chinese Association is led by Lady Ni Yumei Cragnolini, a controversial Chinese woman who has lived in PNG for several decades. She was married to Sir Luciano Cragnolini, who runs a successful construction business in PNG. She is known to be very close to former prime minister Peter O'Neill and was appointed by him to the National

---

10   Approximately 97 per cent of land in PNG is held under customary principles of landownership. This means it is not titled and cannot be sold or leased to an investor. If a businessperson wants to access customary land, it is generally the government that is required to arrange a lease from its traditional owners. Identifying who are the traditional owners is a big issue that can stop or delay development and key infrastructure projects in PNG (see Gosarevski, Hughes & Windybank, 2004).

11   Strictly speaking, the figure is likely to be slightly higher than three per cent because of special agricultural and business leases (SABLs). A commission of inquiry into the SABLs in 2013 found almost all to be illegal (see Filer & Numapo, 2017).

12   I constantly hear that PNG nationals are 'lazy' when it comes to work and do not show initiative.

Gaming Control Board (Bagshaw, 2020). There are persistent rumours among the business community that she is intimately involved with O'Neill and a proxy for his extensive private businesses. She was the gatekeeper for the mainland Chinese who wanted to meet the then prime minister O'Neill and she normally charged fees for access. She was also very good at arranging for Chinese businesses to buy tables at fundraising dinners for O'Neill's party, the People's National Congress (PNC), often at K50,000 for a table of ten. Most of the tables were purchased by Chinese businesses, with the remaining ones bought by PNG SOEs.[13]

The PNG-China Friendship Association is led by Lin Huanong. Unlike the PNG Chinese Association, this organisation is part of the Chinese Communist Party's United Front Work, established by Beijing to promote China around the world. Thus, it has 'status' with the Chinese Embassy in Port Moresby. Many small traders joined this organisation because of this and one of its senior members is known to have triad ties.[14] Senior Embassy staff attend almost all of its functions and even provide funding to the organisation. Hence, the organisation was in a position to donate K1.3 million to help with earthquake relief in 2018. Befitting his status, the Embassy's deputy, Yao Ming, rather than the president of the organisation, handed the cheque to Peter O'Neill (Keneqa, 2018).

Therefore, one way of looking at these two organisations is that the PNG-China Association is led by the more established mainland Chinese who have lived in PNG for a long time, while the PNG-China Friendship Association is led by the more recent arrivals and those with less wealth. As a United Front organisation, it is certain that the PNG-China Friendship Association takes its orders directly from the Embassy. Nevertheless, many mainland Chinese are members of both organisations. PNG nationals and others are also welcomed as members of the PNG-China Friendship Association, while membership of the PNG Chinese Association is mainly confined to ethnic Chinese.

---

13 Personal communication from both Chinese and PNG sources, September to October 2020. See also Connolly (2020).
14 Personal communication, September to October, 2020. I was told this person offers 'protection' to small traders, especially when it comes to issues relating to the police where he can act as the interlocutor. Apparently, the name he used in PNG is not the name he used in China (see Kumbon, 2019; 'Chinese "Triad" Mobsters Arrested In PNG', 2008; 'PNG warned about Asian gangs', 2010).

Schools and scholarships

Another area where soft power is projected is in education. China provides more than 50 fully funded scholarships to PNG students to study in China's tertiary institutions. These scholarships are given directly to the central and provincial governments. Many of the scholarships also include language training.[15]

The most public display of soft power using education is the Butuka Academy, a high school in Port Moresby. It was built by China Construction Steel Structure Corp, an SOE. President Xi officially opened the school during the 2018 APEC Summit (Bagshaw, 2020). It was supposed to offer high quality education to the local population, given the poor state of public education in PNG. Previously, the only other choice was international schools where the fees are prohibitive—often more than the annual salary of a PNG worker. Another key feature of the school was the availability of Chinese Mandarin classes, taught by teachers from China ('Port Moresby School to Teach Chinese Language', 2020). Three years on, the school is no longer in a good shape due to poor maintenance after the fall of the O'Neill government. It was seen as an O'Neill project and the present government does not really want to be associated with the school. Lady Ni Yumei Cragnolini, who is directly connected to Peter O'Neill, remains the chairperson of the school board.

Chinese triads

One of the issues I identified in my 2008 article was the inevitable presence of Chinese triads once the mainland Chinese community became large enough to support their activities. Unfortunately, this prediction has come true.[16] One of the key triad leaders holds a leadership position in the PNG-China Friendship Association and masquerades as a Chinese businessman.

---

15 I have been told that many of the scholarships were not taken up for various reasons. Personal communication from a civil servant, October 2020.

16 There are scholars who disagree with my analysis of the triad. They argue these are just 'stories' and 'perceptions' (see Filer, 2013; Smith, 2013). I take a different view. Too many of my informants tell me they exist and are able to tell me in some detail what they do, and the very nature of their operation is hidden deep within the Chinese community. In Southeast Asian countries with sizeable Chinese populations, they also operate in the shadows. The reason it is so hard to document their presence is largely that they also operate legitimate businesses on top of the illicit businesses. A senior PNG writer agreed with my views. See Kumbon, D. (2019, July 5) Asian triads undermining security, *The National.* www.thenational.com.pg/asian-triads-undermining-security/

There is no way the PNG police can deal with this problem because, for the most part, the triad has confined their criminal activities to members of the Chinese community, including non-mainland Chinese such the Southeast Asian Chinese. Key to understanding the triads is to acknowledge that they are not one hundred per cent criminal enterprises. While they do offer the traditional 'protection' system, they also help the Chinese community by acting as the middlemen if there is a problem with the PNG police or bureaucracy. If there is any violence involved, it is most likely to be confined to the Chinese community. The unwritten modus operandi appears to be 'working in the shadows'. This modus operandi is consistent with the way triads work in other countries.

The PNG-based triads are probably involved in smuggling of goods, including narcotics and cigarettes, and operating private unlicensed casinos and brothels. These premises mostly serve the expatriate community and the PNG elite, and thus have no contact with ordinary PNG nationals ('Chinese Hitmen Connected to Deported Mob Boss', 2010).

The Chinese triads have kept an even lower profile since two particular incidents. The first was the attempted assassination of Jason Tan, a Malaysian Chinese businessman with extensive links to the mainland Chinese. He was, in fact, the honorary chair of the PNG-China Friendship Association ('Chinese-PNG Friendship Association Condemns Murder Attempt', 2010). The two Chinese mainlanders, from Fujian, who were arrested for the attempted assassination were subsequently bailed and promptly 'disappeared' from PNG ('What has happened to the Chinese suspects in Tan shooting?', 2010).

The second is the interview given by William Kapris, a well-known leader of one of the most successful *raskol* gangs. His speciality was bank robberies and escaping from prisons.[17] He claimed that more than a dozen candidates in the 2012 PNG elections were sponsored by Asian gangs ('PNG Warned About Asian Gangs', 2010).[18] While this may sound fanciful, he is probably correct that Asian businesspeople donate cash and materials to many PNG candidates. However, many of these Asian businesspeople are not triad members. What is probable is that the triads will support one of two candidates in the bigger towns such as Madang, Lae or Port Moresby.

---

17   William Kapris was murdered in 2013 by a former policeman. See Zarriga (2017).
18   The video of Kapris' interview with the police where he made the allegations are widely available on PNG Facebook pages.

It is almost certain that these candidates are not aware that their 'Chinese friends' are triad members.[19] The triads are always trying to widen their circle of influence.

Section 2: The other Chinese

In this section, I will update the status of the PNGBC, the Southeast Asian Chinese and the new Asians.

PNG-born Chinese (PNGBC)

In my 2008 article, I wrote that the PNGBC were almost a dying breed, with the younger generation refusing to take over the family businesses, preferring to live in Australia and pursuing other careers. This has largely been vindicated. My interviews with PNGBC over the past decade reveal that many of the younger generation are still refusing to come back to PNG. In many cases, the family holdings amount to millions in real estate, but they still refuse to return to PNG. Their first option is always to sell, followed by being an absentee landlord. For the older generation still running their business, the process of consolidating their holdings is still happening while others are quietly selling out after accepting the reality that their children will never come back to live in PNG.

Most of the PNG Chinese businesses are holding on, while others have experienced some expansion, building on foundations that were formed prior to the large influx of mainland Chinese. Many of these family-run businesses were started even before Independence in 1975. One clear example of a PNG Chinese family-run business that managed to expand is the Chow family, originating in Rabaul and led by the late Sir Henry Chow.[20] Their name is synonymous with the Lae Biscuit Company. What is not widely known is that, in the past decade, their biscuit factory has become the largest in the South Pacific and they control a sizeable share of the biscuit market in both PNG and the Solomon Islands. Another long-term family business is Coastal Shipping. In the past decade they have

---

19   I have tried, without success, to ascertain with certainty who were the 2012 candidates directly supported by the triads. I have been provided several names of those alleged to have been supported by the triads.

20   The history of the Chow family business is typical of many PNG Chinese family-run trading houses. See Jackson (2017) for an obituary of Henry Chow.

also tried to move into plantations and expand their shipping business. The family has survived because they are constantly trying new businesses and restructuring their existing businesses.

Another successful PNG Chinese business that managed to expand is JJS Holdings, owned by the Seeto family. The company underwent a restructuring, led by Irene Seeto, a daughter-in-law from mainland China. The Seetos maintain their dominance of the wholesale trade in Kokopo.

An example of a PNG Chinese trying to sell off their business is Martin Tsang, owner of MST Wholesale, who operates the oldest supermarket in Madang. Martin has been trying to sell his business for the past few years, but the only willing buyers are mainland Chinese.

In my 2008 essay, I wrote the following:

> The group that the PNG Chinese detest most is the mainland Chinese, whom they characterise as 'con men' and 'uncivilised', which is the greatest insult in PNG. The main reasons people give for this is that mainland Chinese have spoiled the previously good relationship between the Chinese community and PNG nationals. People say that before the coming of mainland Chinese PNG nationals never killed ethnic Chinese over business affairs, but now they are stirring up trouble by competing with nationals in small businesses like kai bars and small retail stores. People also complain that the mainland Chinese are corrupting the system because they are involved in too much smuggling and have set up a market in stolen goods. (Chin 2008, p. 125)

This remains the case. The only difference is that the PNGBC think that the mainland Chinese cannot be stopped on their way to the top, and that eventually, even the 'big boys' (Australian-owned businesses) will be overtaken by the mainland Chinese. For them, it's just a matter of time.

PNGBC contacts also complained that it is virtually impossible for PNGBC or other Chinese to compete with the mainland Chinese because they do not rely on conventional finance. They claim the mainland Chinese have their own financial network, closed to outsiders, and prefer group buys. What they are probably referring to are Chinese SOEs who operate based on decisions made by Beijing and the Chinese Embassy. These Chinese SOEs are big enough to bypass all the financial and customs barriers enacted by the PNG authorities.

On the other hand, the PNGBC will go into joint venture with the mainland Chinese because they know the mainland Chinese have access to better pricing and services in China. But the level of trust is much lower compared to joint ventures with, say, Malaysian or Indonesian Chinese.

Overall, the PNGBC are even more pessimistic about their presence in PNG compared to the 2008 survey. This was made clear to me when one of them expressed the following: 'In the future, the PNGBC, if lucky, will be the landlord but the business will be run by the mainland Chinese' (personal communication, October 2020).

Southeast Asian Chinese: Malaysians

The biggest and the most influential Chinese business in PNG for most of the 1980s and 1990s was Rimbunan Hijau (RH), a Malaysian conglomerate with extensive timber-related businesses in PNG and the rest of the Pacific (Gabriel & Wood, 2015). Politically they were active as well, setting up *The National.* There is enough evidence to suggest that they directly and indirectly control at least half of all the timber operations in PNG. Until recently, they were the owners of Kina Securities, which operates a bank and, according to the company's website, is: 'the largest wealth management business in PNG with over K8 billion funds under management; the largest fund administrator, administering accounts on behalf of more than 850,000 beneficiaries whose funds total almost K14 billion; and the leading stockbroking company'.

Because of their sheer size and deep political connections, RH has survived and thrived in the past decade. In the 2010s, they developed Vision City, a development that includes PNG's largest shopping centre, cinema, convention centre, The Stanley Hotel (reputed to be the best hotel in the country) and private apartments (Vision City Mega Mall, n.d.).

RH remains a key player in the timber industry, but they have significantly expanded their non-timber operations in the past decade. One could argue they are found in most sectors of the PNG economy including retail, accommodation, construction, food and beverage, financial services, pharmacy, shipping, media and IT services. Again, because of their size, they are always on the lookout for new business opportunities. In the past decade, the company has spent a significant amount to rebrand itself as a good corporate citizen of the country and try to whitewash its history as an outlaw timber baron (Moussea, 2018).

One interesting aspect of the Malaysian community in PNG is that almost all of them come from a specific Malaysian state: Sarawak. Sarawak is located on the island of Borneo and there were about 8,000 Malaysians of Sarawak origin living and working in PNG in 2022. RH and all the Malaysian businessmen mentioned in this section come from Sarawak. RH was already a timber powerhouse in Sarawak before it ventured into PNG.

The number of new Malaysian businesspeople arriving in the past decade has dwindled to a trickle compared to the 1990s. Many find PNG too hard, especially if they have to compete with the mainland Chinese. The same is true for Singaporean and Indonesian Chinese businesspeople. Hardly any new Singaporean businesspeople came to PNG in the past decade; in fact, the reverse has happened. Many Singaporean businesspeople have left PNG in the past decade. Most Singapore-owned holdings in PNG now are capital investments.

Most of the Indonesian Chinese businesses in PNG, such as Papindo Trading and Super Value Stores, are the same ones I described in my 2008 essay. They have been able to hold on to their share of the wholesale market and even expand into new areas.

One Malaysian Chinese businessman who went against the general trend is Martin Poh of Borneo Pacific Pharmaceuticals (BPP). His real name is Sang Chung Poh and he comes from Kuching, Sarawak, Malaysia. His case is unusual. Unlike most of the successful Malaysian Chinese businesspeople in PNG who come from the Foochow dialect group, Martin is from the Heng Hua dialect group, but his ancestors come from Fujian.[21] He holds PNG citizenship even though Malaysia does not allow dual citizenship. He was even given a knighthood in 2007 by the PNG Government.

BPP really took off in 2013 when Poh managed to secure an exclusive multi-million dollar pharmaceutical contract to supply the entire country. An investigation later revealed that most of the drugs supplied were substandard and overpriced (Cochrane, 2013; Transparency International, n.d.). Martin Poh has a very close relationship with Peter O'Neill and was awarded an exclusive contract worth millions to supply educational

---

21   The Foochow are the most dynamic business segment of the Malaysian Chinese community. They dominate business in Sarawak. Rimbunan Hijau and WTK, another major Malaysian Chinese timber company operating in PNG, are both owned and operated by Foochows.

materials for the entire country. He is also involved in business ventures with Lady Yumei Ni Cragnolini, another well-known O'Neill proxy (see 'Profiting from Sickness', 2017).

Another interesting case relating to Malaysian Chinese is that of Huang Tiong Sii. Sii, like Poh, comes from Sarawak but he is a Foochow, like the RH group. Normally, Foochow Chinese businesspeople in PNG will keep a low profile back in Sarawak but this is not the case with Sii. Sii, who is involved in the PNG timber business and has links with Peter O'Neill, used his considerable wealth generated from PNG to get elected as a state assemblyman in his home state of Sarawak. He was elected in 2016 in the Report State Constituency. In the 2022 Malaysian general elections, he became an MP (member of Parliament) as well when he won the Sarikei seat. Two weeks later, he was appointed as Malaysian Deputy Federal Minister of Natural Resources, Environment and Climate Change (see 'BN's Timber Tycoon', 2016).

Another Malaysian Chinese worth mentioning is Simon Sia, the owner of Bintangor Trading (Bintangor is a small town in Sarawak, where Sia comes from). Sia first came to PNG in the 1980s to work before setting up Bintangor Trading. In the 2012 elections, Sia stood as a candidate for the Eastern Highlands Regional Seat after securing PNG citizenship in May 2012.[22] This is highly significant given that had he won, he would have automatically become the Governor of Eastern Highlands. Sia lost in 2012 but he stood again for the Eastern Highlands Regional Seat in the 2022 election, under the PNC party. This time he won, and he became the first PNG MP from a Malaysian background.

South Asian

One interesting development in the past decade is the emergence of South Indians as a new component of the Asian business community in PNG. They were not prominent when I wrote my 2008 essay. Back then, the small number of Bangladeshis and Indo-Fijians were mostly workers and not business owners. Since 2010, they have become more prominent as business owners. For example, Gerehu in Port Moresby is a notorious suburb for crime and *raskol* activities. Because of the high risks, very few

---

22   It is interesting to note that Malaysia does not allow dual citizenship, although this did not stop Sia from getting PNG citizenship. For more of his background see Sia: Do things right, give back. (2019, January 3). *The National*. www.thenational.com.pg/sia-do-things-right-give-back/

businesspeople are willing to set up shops in Gerehu. New trade stores in Gerehu and several petrol stations were established by Bangladeshis. The Bangladeshis are also thought to be involved in people smuggling, using PNG as a transit point to Australia (for example see EMTV Online, 2013). The Indo-Fijians have established themselves in the pharmacy sector and telecommunications. These Indians tend to keep to themselves and do not have much business contact with the Chinese community. At the time of writing, they are not seen as a business threat by the Chinese community.

Observation and discussion

While most of the observations I made in the 2008 essay remain valid today, there are some significant changes to the contemporary Chinese community in PNG. The biggest change, and the focus of this essay, is the massive increase in influence (politically, economically and socially) of China and mainland Chinese in PNG. Mainland Chinese have taken a leadership position among the PNG Chinese community and have also become the second most influential external player in PNG politics. Australia and its allies, New Zealand and the US, remain the most influential but the consensus among the PNG Chinese community is that the clock is ticking. They think, sooner or later, China will replace Australia as the most influential external actor in PNG politics.

While the economic boom in PNG in the later part of 2010s, generated by the gas pipeline, was beneficial to the entire PNG economy, the mainland Chinese companies, especially the Chinese SOEs, were the major beneficiaries. In general, the entire Chinese business community benefited but the mainland Chinese SOEs were probably the biggest legatee among Chinese businesses.

In my opinion, it is almost impossible to stop the rise of China in PNG because the official and non-official groups, as described above, operate as a single entity with a common aim. Their work is either directly or indirectly co-ordinated by the Chinese Embassy in Port Moresby. The Chinese Ambassador and his staff are unusually aggressive when it comes to pushing China's interest in PNG. As mentioned earlier, China sees PNG and Fiji as the two most important countries in the South Pacific, which must therefore be brought under China's influence. It is also interesting that China's main competitor for influence in both countries is Australia.

I was partly wrong in my 2008 paper about the mainland Chinese taking over from Malaysian Chinese. In fact, RH and selected Malaysian Chinese businesspeople, such as Martin Poh and Huan Tiong Sii, have continued to thrive in PNG. However, all three are not new arrivals; they have been operating in PNG for many years. There have been few new arrivals since 2010. The business environment has become competitive with the arrival of mainland Chinese.

It is my view that the 'old' PNGBC do not know how to handle the mainland Chinese. Their relationship is complex and ambiguous. They see the mainland Chinese as both an opportunity and a threat. They know that in the long run they might be eclipsed by the mainland Chinese but at the same time they know that only the mainland Chinese have the capital to buy them out. There are some who think a genuine joint venture with mainland Chinese is possible, although there are no prominent examples yet. Some even hold the view that the rise of the mainland Chinese is a good thing overall as the PNGBC suffered under racism in the past and it is time for Australians and other 'whites' to experience 'reverse' racism. It is very likely that the PNGBC numbers will dwindle even further in the coming years and that eventually they may have to sell out. However, one part of their holdings that they will not sell is real estate. The rental return in PNG is probably the highest in the region and is at least seven or eight times what they can get in Australia. Hence, the default thinking is that if they eventually move south to Australia, they can depend on rental income from PNG.

PNG national attitudes

The final part of this chapter will deal with the attitudes of nationals towards the rise of China.[23] While some PNG elites, especially those in the upper class, hold sentimental attachments to Australia, and to the West generally, they also see the rise of China in the region as inevitable. They are widely read and well educated and thus know the risks of dealing with China. However, they are of the view that dealing with China is almost like dealing with Australia—both countries try to influence the direction of the country and place PNG under their sphere of influence. The difference is that the

---

23   Most of this section is based on conversations with senior PNG officials and PNGBC, September to October 2020.

Chinese are 'flexible' and do not react negatively when issues of malpractice or corruption surface. For these elites, corruption exists because of PNG's volatile political system and low levels of development.[24]

Most of the PNG elite think that the best option is for PNG to play China against Australia and vice versa to gain maximum benefits for the country. Most PNG national elites are of the view that Australia would grant fewer concessions and less aid to PNG if not for the threat from China.[25]

My guess is that over the long term PNG will probably move politically closer to China but remain culturally with Australia. The reason is that many of these elites send their children to Australian schools and those with disposable wealth almost always buy real estate in Queensland and place their family members there.[26] In January 2023, PNG–Australia ties were enhanced with the signing of a bilateral security treaty. There is little doubt this treaty was signed because of concerns over Chinese influence in the Pacific.

Conclusion

In summary, in a period of one decade (2010–2020), the power balance among the Chinese community in PNG has shifted significantly from the PNGBC and the Southeast Asian Chinese to mainland Chinese. The speed of this transition has been remarkable. However, the trend in PNG is consistent with global trends where the rapid rise of China has totally changed the environment that is familiar to the West.[27] The West can expect to be challenged not only on the world stage but also in many individual developing countries such as PNG.

24　See Crocombe (2007).

25　For example, see Smith & Wesley-Smith (2021) and Zhang (2022).

26　One constant joke I hear is that the real estate market in Cairns will collapse if PNG nationals are banned from buying real estate in Australia.

27　An excellent example of this was the first high-level meeting between the new Biden Administration and China in Alaska in March 2021. China turned the tables on the US by lecturing them on decline. See 'China's Warning to Biden', 2021).

References

Bagshaw, E. (2020, August 16). How a school in Australia's closest neighbour became a diplomatic weapon for China. *Sydney Morning Herald.* www.smh.com.au/world/asia/how-a-school-in-australia-s-closest-neighbour-became-a-diplomatic-weapon-for-china-20200811-p55kqj.html

Barker Gale. J. (2019, August 15). *Competition and cooperation in the South Pacific.* The National Bureau of Asian Research. www.nbr.org/publication/competition-and-cooperation-in-the-south-pacific/

Barnett, T. E. (1989). *Commission of Inquiry into the Forestry Industry in PNG.* www.pngforests.com/barnett-inquiry-3/

Beijing accuses Australia of 'whipping up anti-China sentiment' after foreign interference accusations. (2019, September 16). *SBS World News.* www.sbs.com.au/news/beijing-accuses-australia-of-whipping-up-anti-china-sentiment-after-foreign-interference-accusations

BN's Timber tycoon candidate for Repok illegally plundered Baram–Expose. (2016, May 1). *Sarawak Report.* www.sarawakreport.org/2016/05/bns-candidate-for-repok-plundered-timber-from-baram-expose/

Braddock, J. (2020, August 27). Australian media stokes fears over Papua New Guinea-China links. *WSWS.Org.* www.wsws.org/en/articles/2020/08/27/pnga-a27.html

Chin, J. (2008). Contemporary Chinese Community in Papua-New Guinea: Old money versus new migrants. *Chinese Southern Diaspora Studies*, 2, pp. 117–26.

Chin, U. H. (2006). *Chinese politics in Sarawak.* Oxford University Press.

China's Warning to Biden. (2021, March 21). *Wall Street Journal.* www.wsj.com/articles/chinas-warning-to-biden-11616360915

Chinese 'Triad' mobsters arrested in PNG. (2008, September 1). *The National.*

Chinese hitmen connected to deported mob boss. (2010, January 5). *The Post Courier.*

Chinese-PNG Friendship Association condemns murder attempt on Tan. (2010, January 6). *The National.* www.thenational.com.pg/chinese-png-friendship-association-condemns-murder-attempt-on-tan/

Cluff, R. (2020, December 15). China's plan to build a fish processing facility in the Torres Strait raises alarm over-fishing, border security. *ABC News*. www.abc.net.au/news/2020-12-15/trepidation-as-china-prepares-to-move-into-the-torres-strait/12985504

Cochrane, L. (2013, December 26). Australia withdraws funding from Papua New Guinea health programs over corruption, fake drug concerns. *ABC News*. www.abc.net.au/news/2013-12-26/an-australia-cuts-funding-of-png-medical-kits/5174992

Connolly, P. (2020). The belt and road comes to Papua New Guinea. *Security Challenges*, 16(4), pp. 41–64. www.jstor.org/stable/26976257

Crocombe, Ron. (2007). *Asia in the Pacific Islands: Replacing the West*. University of South Pacific Publications.

Dorling, P. (2013). Revealed: How Australia spies on its neighbours. *Sydney Morning Herald*. www.smh.com.au/politics/federal/revealed-how-australia-spies-on-its-neighbours-20131030-2whpg.html

Dziedzic S., & Whiting, N. (2018a, November 18). APEC 2018: Regional meeting ends in disarray as leaders fail to reach consensus on communique. *ABC News*. www.abc.net.au/news/2018-11-18/apec-leaders-fail-to-agree-on-communique-wording/10508974

Dziedzic S., & Whiting, N. (2018b, November 18). APEC 2018: Chinese officials barge into PNG Foreign Minister's office after being denied meeting. *ABC News*. www.abc.net.au/news/2018-11-18/chinese-officials-create-diplomatic-storm-at-apec/10508812

EMTV Online. (2013). 22 Bangladeshi Arrested in Lae – Illegal Immigration [video]. *YouTube*. www.youtube.com/watch?v=7cdXCiTrZFM

Filer, C. (2013). Asian investment in the rural industries of Papua New Guinea: What's new and what's not? *Pacific Affairs*, 86(2), pp. 305–25. doi.org/10.5509/2013862305

Filer C., & Numapo, J. (2017). The Political Ramifications of Papua New Guinea's Commission of Inquiry. In S. McDonnel, M. Allen & C. Filer (Eds.), *Kastom, property and ideology land transformations in Melanesia* (pp. 251–82). ANU Press. doi.org/10.22459/kpi.03.2017.08

Gabriel, J., & Wood, M. (2015). The Rimbunan Hijau Group in the forests of Papua New Guinea. *The Journal of Pacific History*, 50(3), pp. 322–43. doi.org/10.1080/00223344.2015.1060925

Gosarevski, S., Hughes, H., & Windybank, S. (2004). Is Papua New Guinea viable with customary land ownership? *Pacific Economic Bulletin*, 19(3), pp. 133–36. openresearch-repository.anu.edu.au/bitstream/1885/157725/1/193_papua.pdf

Jackson, K. (2017, January 23). Death of businessman & philanthropist Sir Henry Chow. *PNG Attitude*. www.pngattitude.com/2017/01/death-of-businessman-philanthropist-sir-henry-chow-.html

Johnson, K., & Detsch, J. (2021, May 4). Australia draws a line on China. *Foreign Policy*. www.foreignpolicy.com/2021/05/04/australia-china-defense-tariffs-policy-taiwan-us/

Keneqa, L. (2018, March 6). China PNG Friendship Association presents K1.3 million towards victims of earthquake. *EMTV*. www.emtv.com.pg/china-png-friendship-association-presents-k1-3-million-towards-victims-of-earthquake/

Kenneth, G. (2019, April 29). Bank of China to open office. *The Post Courier*. www.postcourier.com.pg/bank-china-open-of%EF%AC%81-ce-png/

Köllner, P. (2021). Australia and New Zealand recalibrate their China policies: Convergence and divergence. *The Pacific Review*, 34(3), pp. 405–36. doi.org/10.1080/09512748.2019.1683598

McIlroy, T. (2019, November 23). Australia to loan PNG $US300m to counter rising China. *Australian Financial Review*. www.afr.com/policy/foreign-affairs/australia-to-loan-png-us300m-to-counter-rising-china-20191122-p53d7d

Mousseau, F. (2018). The Great Timber Heist-Continued: Tax Evasion and Illegal Logging in Papua New Guinea. *The Oakland Institute*. www.oaklandinstitute.org/sites/oaklandinstitute.org/files/great_timber_heist_cont.pdf

Murphy, Katharine. (2018, Nov 19). Apec leaders unable to agree on communique amid US-China trade tensions. *The Guardian*. www.theguardian.com/world/2018/nov/19/apec-leaders-unable-to-agree-on-communique-amid-us-china-trade-tensions

PNG ignores Australia, asks China to refinance US$7.8 billion national debt. (2019, August 7). *South China Morning Post*. www.scmp.com/news/asia/australasia/article/3021734/papua-new-guinea-asks-china-refinance-its-national-debt

PNG warned about Asian gangs. (2010, March 25). *Sydney Morning Herald*. www.smh.com.au/world/png-warned-about-asian-gangs-20100324-qwuq.html

Port Moresby school to teach Chinese language. (2020, September 24). *The National*. www.thenational.com.pg/port-moresby-school-to-teach-chinese-language/

Profiting from sickness: The dark economy of public health in PNG part II. (2017, October 10). *PNGi Investigates*. www.pngicentral.org/reports/profiting-from-sickness-the-dark-economy-of-public-health-in-png-part-iii#sang-chung-poh

Rajah, R., Dayant. A., & Pryke, J. (2019, October 21). Ocean of debt? Belt and road and debt diplomacy in the Pacific. *Lowy Institute Analyses*. www.lowyinstitute.org/publications/ocean-debt-belt-and-road-and-debt-diplomacy-pacific

Smith, G. (2013). Beijing's orphans? New Chinese investors in Papua New Guinea. *Pacific Affairs*, 86(2), pp. 327–49. doi.org/10.5509/2013862327

Smith, G., & Wesley-Smith, T. (Ed). (2021). *The China Alternative: Changing Regional Order in the Pacific Islands*. ANU Press. doi.org/10.22459/ca.2021

Taiwanese Officials resign over Papua New Guinea scandal. (2008, May 6). *Wall Street Journal*. www.wsj.com/articles/SB121012909623773089

Transparency International (PNG). Borneo Pharmaceuticals. www.transparencypng.org.pg/borneo-pharmaceuticals/

Vision City Mega Mall. www.visioncitypng.com/

Wall. J. (2020, September 30). Australia must demand answers on Asian Development Bank funding in Papua New Guinea. *The Strategist*. www.aspistrategist.org.au/australia-must-demand-answers-on-asian-development-bank-funding-in-papua-new-guinea/

Weinstein, E. (2021, February 5). Don't underestimate China's military-civil fusion efforts. *Foreign Policy*. www.foreignpolicy.com/2021/02/05/dont-underestimate-chinas-military-civil-fusion-efforts/

What has happened to the Chinese suspects in Tan shooting? (2010, March 31). *Crime and Corruption in PNG*. www.crimeandcorruptionpng.wordpress.com/category/tan-attempted-murder/

Zarriga, M. (2017, September 13). Man alleged to have killed William Kapris Charged. *The Post Courier*. www.postcourier.com.pg/man-alleged-killed-william-kapris-charged/

Zhang, D. (2019/20). *Comparing China's and Taiwan's Aid to the Pacific. Department of Pacific Affairs in brief series*. devpolicy.org/comparing-chinas-and-taiwans-aid-to-the-pacific-20200120/

Zhang, D. (2022). China's influence and local perceptions: the case of Pacific island countries. *Australian Journal of International Affairs*, 76(5), pp. 575–95. doi.org/10.1080/10357718.2022.2112145

Section 2:
The Chinese as transformers of PNG and its political economy

5

Growing Chinese dominance of the bêche-de-mer trade: A Papua New Guinean resource sector characterised by paradox

Simon Foale, Cathy Hair and Jeff Kinch

Introduction

The export commodity market for bêche-de-mer in Papua New Guinea (PNG) is unique and fascinating. Bêche-de-mer is the cooked, gutted and dried body wall of sea cucumbers. There are over 25 species of sea cucumbers that are processed into bêche-de-mer in PNG, most of which can be hand collected without scuba or compressors (though these can make it easier to harvest some species). The market price varies significantly among species, with three species typically fetching prices above K200/kg if properly processed. It costs relatively little to produce and can be easily stored. Once dried, bêche-de-mer can remain in good condition without refrigeration for months while awaiting suitable transport to take it to market, which makes it a particularly suitable commodity for producers in remote locations such as small islands where transport is infrequent. The equipment required to harvest and process sea cucumbers is relatively simple (the freshly harvested sea cucumber must be boiled, gutted and dried, either by sun or over a low fire) and within financial reach of most rural coastal and island people in PNG. As such, it represents one of the most evenly distributed sources of substantial income for these rural coastal and island people. While the benefit can be distributed relatively evenly in space, it has mostly been sporadically distributed over time as sea cucumber fisheries are prone to series of 'boom and bust' cycles, which have been the topic of commentary in fisheries management circles for many years (Hair et al., 2016; Kinch et al., 2008; Preston, 1993). This has significant implications for the various economic, social and cultural impacts of the fishery. For example, when coastal families derive substantial pulses of income from the sale of a large quantity of bêche-de-mer, they may significantly reduce labour inputs to subsistence gardens because they can buy imported foods such as rice and flour (Foale, 2005; Hair et al., 2019). The risk of loss of traditional agricultural knowledge as a result is real and could potentially impact on food security over the long term (Kinch, 2020; Macintyre & Foale, 2010; Macintyre & Foale, 2013).

For PNG, the bêche-de-mer market represents a complex and analytically challenging intersection of value systems, which can be examined from four perspectives. First, the commodity is marketed predominantly into China, Southeast Asia and countries with a Chinese diaspora, where people believe it has great health benefits (Fabinyi & Liu, 2014; Fabinyi et al., 2012). By contrast, most coastal Papua New Guineans do not seek it out as a valuable food (indeed, many see it as 'rubbish' [Tok Pisin: *pipia*] and are bemused by the Chinese predilection for it), though some species of sea cucumbers have been traditionally consumed for special purposes in some parts of the country (Kinch et al., 2008).

Second, the very high unit value as a tradable commodity combined with the low subsistence value means that marine resource owners think about this fishery differently to many others. As a result, community-based management of this fishery has generally been a failure, and the only management that has had any level of success to date has been government intervention, primarily in the form of moratoria (i.e., a total shut-down of the fishery for a specified period, typically on the scale of one to several years) (Foale, 2007; Kinch et al., 2008; Lee et al., 2020). Even the moratoria have only been partially successful, as they are supposed to be tied to a provincial quota system, which is routinely exceeded. We discuss this further in the section below on sea cucumbers as a fishery management conundrum.

Third, despite the importance of the fishery as a generator of cash for coastal and island people, it has been largely ignored by the conservation non-governmental organisation (NGO) community until quite recently, resulting in the listing of white teatfish (*Holothuria fuscogilva*) and black teatfish (*H. nobilis* and *H. whitmaei*) on Appendix II of the Convention on the Trade of Endangered Species (CITES) (FAO, 2019; Gisawa et al., 2020; Shedrawi et al., 2019). In late 2022, the three sea cucumber species in the genus *Thelenota* were also listed in Appendix II in CITES despite being assessed by the Food and Agriculture Organization as not meeting the criteria for listing (FAO, 2022). This is despite the ongoing popularity of the 'conservation-and-development' formula, a key component of which is the fostering of 'alternative livelihoods'; bêche-de-mer is clearly a locally appropriate example of alternative livelihoods, given its importance as a source of income.

Finally, the highly dynamic encounter between two very culturally distinct groups of people—Melanesian coastal and island resource owners (the producers) and Chinese merchant capitalists (the buyers and traders)—in a mutually beneficial market exchange exposes several highly charged cultural tensions. The producers usually seek a form of rent from their resources, which they utilise according to a very different set of economic values to those held by the buyers, while the latter seek to maximise the value they can extract from the encounter, often using manipulative tactics and violation of regulations. Both parties routinely break management rules associated with the fishery, particularly minimum size limits.

In this chapter we elaborate on these four perspectives on the sea cucumber fishery and bêche-de-mer trade and discuss the extent to which the sector is changing as direct Chinese control of the market chain increases.

1. The food value of bêche-de-mer

The protein content and nutritional value of the meat from the body wall of sea cucumbers are understood by the scientific community to be very high (Bordbar et al., 2011; Ram et al., 2017; Wen et al., 2010). Despite this, sea cucumbers are rarely consumed in PNG (Kinch et al., 2008), and although most coastal languages have a generic name for them (e.g., '*puol*' in Lihir and '*pula*' in the Tigak Islands, New Ireland Province; and '*pisi*' or '*buyoki*' in the Misima and Tubetube languages respectively of the Milne Bay Province), specific names matching scientific taxa are uncommon. A small number of groups, however, do use them for specialised (typically ritual) purposes. At Mali Island in the Lihir group, for example, women with infants often ate the (white) flesh of certain species of sea cucumbers, after scraping off the pigmented skin, in the belief that this food would help with lactation. The relatively low desirability, coupled with comparatively low human population densities along most of PNG's coastlines and islands mean that if all the sea cucumbers suddenly disappeared, few people would see this as a problem for subsistence food security as other types of marine protein remain abundant in most places (Foale et al., 2011). However, sea cucumbers are extremely valuable as a marketable commodity, once they have been cooked, gutted, smoked and dried to make bêche-de-mer.

The Chinese value bêche-de-mer very highly and pay exorbitant prices for well-processed, top-grade species. Bêche-de-mer qualifies as a '*Bu*' food (Fabinyi & Liu, 2014), which means it is believed to impart a high level of vitality to the consumer. The dramatically expanded engagement the Chinese Community Party has fostered with global markets since the late 1970s has meant that there is now a much larger 'middle class' who seek to elevate their status through consuming '*Bu*' foods such as bêche-de-mer. Consequently demand, and with it, prices, have risen steadily over the past three decades.

2. Sea cucumbers: A fishery management conundrum

A lot has been written about the role, realised and potential, of customary prohibitions, particularly local marine tenure systems and taboos, for the management of coastal subsistence and commodity fisheries (Almany et al., 2013; Cohen & Foale, 2013; Foale et al., 2011; Govan et al., 2009). There is some evidence that trochus, a relatively low-value commodity fishery, has been successfully managed in a small number of locations where communities have partnered with either governments or NGOs to implement serial closure-based management regimes (a type of 'hybrid' management based partly on traditional taboos) (Nash et al., 1995; Pakoa et al., 2008). However, we have seen limited evidence of any successful community-scale management of sea cucumber fisheries in PNG (or indeed beyond) to date.

While some have claimed there is evidence that supposedly representative samples of coastal and island communities in PNG possess the social and cultural attributes to collectively and intentionally manage marine fisheries sustainably (Cinner et al., 2012), not only are these claims contestable, but there are compelling examples of local social and cultural institutions being completely inadequate for managing coastal fisheries successfully, especially where there is any significant level of population or market pressure (Foale et al., 2011; Friedman et al., 2009; Hair et al., 2020; Hair et al., 2016; Kinch, 2020). Moreover, recent ethnographic and other social data from a community in New Ireland Province shows that despite a long period of negotiation and provision of support to a local community for management of a sea cucumber 'ranching' project, communal management of this high-value species can collapse very quickly, resulting in premature harvesting of 'protected' areas (Hair et al., 2020) and potentially an extended recovery time for the fishery (Bell et al., 2008; Cohen & Foale, 2013; Foale et al., 2011). In Milne Bay Province, declining sea cucumber stocks and escalating prices led to the rise of heated disputes over resource areas, several of which required State intervention through the legal system (Fabinyi et al., 2015; Kinch, 2020).

The combination of the high commodity value of sea cucumbers with the kinds of political divisions that typically exist in most Melanesian communities (Filer, 1990) means that community-scale management of this resource is very challenging, if not impossible. For this reason, the only successful form of management that has been observed to date has been government moratoria (Foale, 2007; Hair et al., 2016). A large part of the government's success is due to the fact that the product must pass through a small number of market bottlenecks (points of sale) in PNG because it must be containerised before it is exported. This significantly reduces the time and cost for government officers to monitor and regulate the market at these points. A fishery with a more dispersed marketing system, such as reef fish, cannot be subjected to the same level of scrutiny and control. Improvements on the current system could be achieved by limiting the number of exporter licences, controlling intra-provincial transfers and policing the export ports (Barclay et al., 2019; Barclay et al., 2016). This would significantly reduce the time and costs of monitoring, control and surveillance operations for the National Fisheries Authority (NFA) and provincial fisheries officers.

While the PNG NFA has in recent years been able to exert some measure of control over the bêche-de-mer market, this control is somewhat tenuous (Hair et al., 2020). Part of the reason for this appears to be both an increase in the number of buyer licences issued by the NFA and a change in the behaviour of Chinese buyers, who in some instances are now travelling out to remote island communities themselves where they know there are significant stocks of sea cucumbers (to compete for access to the product), and who are offering high prices for partly processed (such as fresh or simply boiled) sea cucumbers (because processing by fishers is often sub-standard and results in lower-value product). This greatly complicates the task of monitoring and regulation for the government. We have also directly observed large volumes of (illegally) undersized bêche-de-mer that were seized by police and NFA officers in Kavieng. The seized catch was very unlikely to represent all the illegally marketed product for that season. There is also evidence that staff at various levels within provincial and national fisheries agencies have become aligned with corporate and political interests within the sector.

3. Conservation NGOs arriving late to the bêche-de-mer party

The 'conservation-and-development' model has been used by international conservation NGOs in PNG and the Pacific since it become popular in the 1990s, following the 1992 Rio Convention, and the poor performance of NGOs in relation to the 'development' side of the equation has been critiqued for almost as long (Filer, 2000, 2004; Foale, 2001; Van Helden, 1998; West, 2006). Ecotourism, bioprospecting and small-scale 'eco-timber' have been the preferred sustainable development options among conservation NGOs for a long time, but these options have seen very limited success over the past two decades. At the same time, the sea cucumber fishery has seen significant returns accruing to coastal and island communities (Hair et al., 2019; Kinch, 2007, 2020; Kinch et al., 2008) but the sector has mostly been ignored by the NGO community until relatively recently (Mangubhai et al., 2017).

It will be interesting to watch how the NGO community proceed with their new interest in bêche-de-mer as a livelihood option given the antipathy that many environmental NGOs have traditionally displayed toward governments (Foale, 2007; West, 2006), particularly given NGOs' perennial emphasis on community-scale resource management, and what we have argued in Section 2 above. Some environmental NGOs now appear to be forging more productive collaborations with governments, though how this will play out in PNG's bêche-de-mer sector remains to be seen, particularly given the recent listing of some of the higher value species on Appendix II of CITES, as outlined above, and the likelihood of other sea cucumber species being added to this list in the near future.

4. Melanesian resource sovereigns meet Chinese merchant capitalists

Traditional Melanesian economic personhood is geared to deliver elevated social and political status primarily through *redistribution*, not accumulation, of economic surplus (typically horticultural) (Gregory, 1982). The more someone can give away, generally at a traditional mortuary ritual or perhaps a marriage feast, the bigger their 'name' (or political capital) becomes. Personal material possessions may not change at all, and culturally Papua New Guineans are stereotypically not predisposed to 'making a profit' (Curry, 1999; Curry et al., 2015). Most people in this cultural region are strongly influenced by pressure from kin and extended family to share monetary surpluses generated by small businesses such as trade stores. State-enshrined customary land (and marine) tenure and relatively low human population densities have in part facilitated the survival of this cultural and economic system in PNG. Expatriate Asians, by contrast, like the early colonial traders of European extraction, are dependent entirely on their capacity to produce, and accumulate, profit from trading. They are highly skilled at it, and thus tend to dominate in the business sector (Smith, 2013, 2016). With the exception of a small number of European traders in the early phases of the colonial period, Chinese have always dominated the bêche-de-mer market in the Pacific Islands region, including PNG. They control the entire bêche-de-mer market chain all the way from the local buyer (who is legally supposed to be a Papua New Guinean, but who is often financed by a Chinese 'businessman') to the end consumer in China. Language, and capacity to establish a mutual trade relationship, is a fundamental barrier to participation and scrutiny from any non-Chinese players (Barclay et al., 2016).

While it is illegal for foreign nationals to be involved in the bêche-de-mer industry it is no secret that they bankroll it. Very few PNG nationals have the cash backing to buy bêche-de-mer or the contacts in Chinese markets. Indigenous Papua New Guinean buyers often have Chinese financial backing. So, from the start, Chinese are integral to the trade. The influx of new, more aggressive, mainland Chinese into the trade can be seen in the rise in numbers of licensed buyers in recent years since the reopening of the fishery in 2017.[1] As a result of this influx, many of the older, established

---

1   This was the first time the sea cucumber fishery had been reopened since 2009; it has been closed and opened several times since 2017.

buyers (including members of the so-called 'old Chinese' families, as well as several expatriates of European descent) are exiting the sector (see similar accounts in various other sectors identified by Chin in this volume).

The relationship between 'propertied' bêche-de-mer producers and (often landless) Asian buyers and merchants is far from cordial or trusting but is nevertheless important, and productively transactional for both parties. The Chinese buyers in Kavieng appear to have become somewhat more manipulative and aggressive during the 2018 open season, and for the first time came out in boats to remote islands in the Tigak group to try to get access to unprocessed or partially processed product so they could process it themselves to a standard they preferred (Hair et al., 2020). They exchanged food stuffs (including foods brought from town such as chicken) for fresh sea cucumbers and already processed bêche-de-mer instead of paying cash.

Some bêche-de-mer producers are resentful about the level of control of the market by Asians, including Chinese, though most are happy with the significant returns they get for their catches, which represent a relatively large percentage of the ultimate market value of the product (Barclay et al., 2016). The Nature Conservancy's (TNC's) Manus Island branch obtained an export licence from the NFA in 2018 and succeeded in selling bêche-de-mer made from one of the high-value sea cucumber species directly to Hong Kong, through a subsidiary contact who knew the market there, and managed to obtain significantly higher prices for the producers (Rick Hamilton, personal communication, 2016), but this activity did not result in an ongoing, alternative market chain. This may have been to do with difficulties TNC had with banking arrangements, delaying the return of funds to PNG. Since then, it appears that fishers prefer the immediacy of returns from selling product directly to local buyers (cf. Rasmussen, 2015). Most of the bêche-de-mer continues to become essentially invisible to non-Chinese observers once it is acquired by buyers in PNG. The extent of oversight of the market by the PNG NFA has also become increasingly difficult to gauge in recent years, but it appears that costs of monitoring and regulating the trade are increasing, with likely negative impacts on the prevention of capital flight from the sector. Ineffective management, which permits illegal activities to continue in the sea cucumber fishery and bêche-de-mer trade, undermines not only the livelihood benefits to coastal and island communities, but also the national revenue and foreign exchange earnings that are vital to the development of Papua New Guineans.

Conclusion

There are some parallels to this picture of heavy Asian, and increasingly Chinese, dominance of a commodity chain between PNG and China—timber is the most obvious example (Filer, 1997). The key differences are that the monetary benefits from bêche-de-mer remain fairly (though not perfectly) evenly distributed; apart from occasionally significant thinning or clearing of littoral vegetation (including mangroves) for firewood, there is relatively little environmental damage caused by the fishery. There are sometimes negative social impacts due to jealousies and disputes over access to stocks in some areas (Kinch, 2020), sustainable management and benefit distribution (Barclay & Kinch, 2013; Barclay et al., 2016; Hair et al., 2020; Hair et al., 2019; Hair et al., 2016; Kinch, 2020), though these are not on the same scale as are commonly observed in association with logging.

We offer this vignette as an example of a commodity market that brings together people with radically different world views and modes of economic personhood. It reveals the power of a high-value commodity to change local economies and cultures, raising questions about the extent to which the market facilitates both economic and human development, and it highlights the difficulty of managing a high-value marine resource at multiple scales (Barclay et al., 2019). In a country such as PNG, with persistent, pressing needs for dramatic improvements in human development and basic service delivery, the financial transparency and effective governance of a market as lucrative *and* widely beneficial as bêche-de-mer remains a major development priority.

References

Almany, G. R., Hamilton, R. J., Bode, M., Matawai, M., Potuku, T., Saenz-Agudelo, P., Planes, S., Berumen, M. L., Rhodes, K. L., Thorrold, S. R., Russ, G. R., & Jones, G. P. (2013). Dispersal of Grouper Larvae Drives Local Resource Sharing in a Coral Reef Fishery. *Current Biology, 23*(7), 626–30. doi.org/10.1016/j.cub.2013.03.006

Barclay, K., Fabinyi, M., Kinch, J., & Foale, S. (2019). Governability of High-Value Fisheries in Low-Income Contexts: A Case Study of the Sea Cucumber Fishery in Papua New Guinea. *Human Ecology, 47*(3), 381–96. doi.org/10.1007/s10745-019-00078-8

Barclay, K., & Kinch, J. (2013). Local Capitalisms and Sustainability in Coastal Fisheries: Cases from Papua New Guinea and the Solomon Islands. In F. McCormack & K. Barclay (Eds.), *Engaging with Capitalism: Cases from Oceania* (pp. 107–38). Emerald. doi.org/10.1108/s0190-1281(2013)0000033007

Barclay, K., Kinch, J., Fabinyi, M., NSW, E., Waddell, S., Smith, G, Sharma, S., Kichawen, P., Foale, S., & Hamilton, R. (2016). *Interactive Governance Analysis of the Beche-de-mer 'Fish Chain' from Papua New Guinea to Asian Markets.* University of Technology Sydney.

Bell, J. D., Purcell, S. W., & Nash, W. J. (2008). Restoring small-scale fisheries for tropical sea-cucumbers. *Oceans & Coastal Management, 51*, 589–93. doi.org/ 10.1016/j.ocecoaman.2008.06.011

Bordbar, S., Anwar, F., & Saari, N. (2011). High-value components and bioactives from sea cucumbers for functional foods—a review. *Marine Drugs, 9*(10), 1761–805. doi.org/10.3390/md9101761

Cinner, J. E., McClanahan, T. R., MacNeil, M. A., Graham, N. A. J., Daw, T. M., Mukminin, A., Feary, D. A., Rabearisoa, A. L., Wamukota, A., Jissawi, N., Campbell, S. J., Baird, A. H., Januchowski-Hartley, F. A., Hamed, S., Lahari, R., Morove, T., & Kuange, J. (2012). Comanagement of coral reef social-ecological systems. *Proceedings of the National Academy of Sciences of the United States of America, 109*(14), 5219–22. doi.org/10.1073/pnas.1121215109

Cohen, P. J., & Foale, S. J. (2013). Sustaining small-scale fisheries with periodically harvested marine reserves. *Marine Policy, 37*(1), 278–87. doi.org/10.1016/ j.marpol.2012.05.010

Curry, G.N. (1999). Markets, social embeddedness and precapitalist societies: the case of village trade stores in Papua New Guinea. *Geoforum, 30*, 285–98. doi.org/ 10.1016/s0016-7185(99)00020-2

Curry, G. N., Koczberski, G., Lummani, J., Nailine, R., Peter, E., McNally, G., & Kuaimba, O. (2015). A bridge too far? The influence of socio-cultural values on the adaptation responses of smallholders to a devastating pest outbreak in cocoa. *Global Environmental Change, 35*, 1–11. doi.org/10.1016/j.gloenvcha. 2015.07.012

Fabinyi, M., Foale, S., & Macintyre, M. (2015). Managing inequality or managing stocks? An ethnographic perspective on the governance of small-scale fisheries. *Fish and Fisheries, 16*, 471–85. doi.org/10.1111/faf.12069

Fabinyi, M., & Liu, N. (2014). Seafood Banquets in Beijing: Consumer Perspectives and Implications for Environmental Sustainability. *Conservation & Society, 12*(2), 218–28. doi.org/10.4103/0972-4923.138423

Fabinyi, M., Pido, M., Harani, B., Caceres, J., Uyami-Bitara, A., De las Alas, A., Buenconsejo, J., & Ponce de Leon, E. M. (2012). Luxury seafood consumption in China and the intensification of coastal livelihoods in Southeast Asia: The live reef fish for food trade in Balabac, Philippines. *Asia Pacific Viewpoint, 53*(2), 118–32. doi.org/10.1111/j.1467-8373.2012.01483.x

FAO. (2019). *Report of the sixth FAO Expert Advisory Panel for the Assessment of Proposals to Amend Appendices I and II of CITES Concerning Commercially-exploited Aquatic Species, Rome, 21–25 January 2019. FAO Fisheries and Aquaculture Report, No. 1255.* FAO.

FAO. (2022). *Report of the seventh FAO Expert Advisory Panel for the Assessment of Proposals to Amend Appendices I and II of CITES Concerning Commercially-exploited Aquatic Species, Rome, 18–22 July 2022. FAO Fisheries and Aquaculture Report, No. 1389.* FAO. doi.org/10.4060/cc1931en

Filer, C. (1990). The Bougainville rebellion, the mining industry and the process of social disintegration in Papua New Guinea. In R. J. May & M. Spriggs (Eds.), *The Bougainville Crisis.* Crawford House Press. doi.org/10.1080/03149099009508487

Filer, C. (Ed.). (1997). *The Political Economy of Forest Management in Papua New Guinea.* NRI, IIED, PNG Biodiversity Conservation and Resource Management Programme and the Resource Management in Asia-Pacific Project.

Filer, C. (2000). *How can Western conservationists talk to Melanesian landowners about indigenous knowledge* (Resource Management in Asia-Pacific Working Paper No. 27, Issue. ANU Resource Management in Asia-Pacific Project.

Filer, C. (2004). The knowledge of indigenous desire: Disintegrating conservation and development in Papua New Guinea. In A. Bicker, P. Sillitoe, & J. Pottier (Eds.), *Development and Local Knowledge: New approaches to issues in natural resources management, conservation and agriculture* (pp. 64–92). Routledge. doi.org/10.4324/9780203606445-9

Foale, S., Cohen, P., Januchowski, S., Wenger, A., & Macintyre, M. (2011). Tenure and taboos: origins and implications for fisheries in the Pacific. *Fish and Fisheries, 12*(4), 357–69. doi.org/10.1111/j.1467-2979.2010.00395.x

Foale, S. J. (2001). 'Where's our development?' Landowner aspirations and environmentalist agendas in Western Solomon Islands. *The Asia Pacific Journal of Anthropology, 2*(2), 44–67. doi.org/10.1080/14442210110001706105

Foale, S. J. (2005). *Sharks, sea slugs and skirmishes: managing marine and agricultural resources on small, overpopulated islands in Milne Bay, PNG.* [RMAP Working Paper]. taxpolicy.crawford.anu.edu.au/rmap/pdf/_docs/rmap_wp64.pdf

Foale, S. J. (2007, July 5–7). Acknowledging the importance and potential of governments in managing marine resources in Melanesia. People and the Sea IV: Who Owns the Coast? MARE Conference, Amsterdam.

Friedman, K., Kronen, M., Pinca, S., Magron, F. Boblin, P., Pakoa, K., Awira, R., & Chapman, L. (2009). *Papua New Guinea Country Report: Profiles and Results from Survey Work at Andra, Tsoilaunung, Sidea and Panapompom*. Secretariat of the Pacific Community. pacificdata.org/data/dataset/oai-www-spc-int-91e3a4c7-5b7e-438d-9e64-32f6ccb12472

Gisawa, L., Kinch, J., Ugufa, J., Lis, R., & Pakop, N. (2020). *Non-Detriment Finding (NDF) for two teatfish species Holothuria witmaei and Holothuria fuscogilva in Papua New Guinea*. N. F. Authority.

Govan, H., Tawake, A., Tabunakawai, K., Jenkins, A., Lasgorceix, A., Techera, E., Tafea, H., Kinch, J., Feehely, J., Ifopo, P., Hills, R., Alefaio, S., Meo, S., Troniak, S., Malimali, S. a., George, S., Tauaefa, T., & Obed, T. (2009), *Community Conserved Areas: A Review of Status and Needs in Melanesia and Polynesia*.

Gregory, C. A. (1982). *Gifts and Commodities*. Academic Press.

Hair, C., Foale, S., Daniels, N., Minimulu, P., Aini, J., & Southgate, P. C. (2020). Social and economic challenges to community-based sea cucumber mariculture development in new Ireland province, Papua New Guinea. *Marine Policy, 117*, 103940. doi.org/10.1016/j.marpol.2020.103940

Hair, C., Foale, S., Kinch, J., Frijlink, S., Lindsay, D., & Southgate, P. C. (2019). Socioeconomic impacts of a sea cucumber fishery in Papua New Guinea: Is there an opportunity for mariculture? *Ocean & Coastal Management, 179*, 104826. doi.org/10.1016/j.ocecoaman.2019.104826

Hair, C., Foale, S., Kinch, J., Yaman, L., & Southgate, P. C. (2016). Beyond book, bust and ban: The sandfish (Holothuria scabra) fishery in the Tigak Islands, Papua New Guinea. *Regional Studies in Marine Science, 5*, 69–79. doi.org/10.1016/j.rsma.2016.02.001

Kinch, J. (2007). *Socio-economic Assessment of the* Beche-de-mer *Fishery: Western, Central and Manus Provinces, PNG*. National Fisheries Authority, PNG.

Kinch, J. (2020). *Changing Lives and Livelihoods: Culture, Capitalism and Contestation over Marine Resources in Island Melanesia* [PhD, Australian National University].

Kinch, J., Purcell, S., Uthicke, S., & Friedman, K. (2008). Papua New Guinea: a hot spot of sea cucumber fisheries in the Western Central Pacific. FAO Fisheries and Aquaculture Technical Paper No. 516. In V. Toral-Granda, A. Lovatelli, & M. Vasconcellos (Eds.), *Sea cucumbers: A global review of fisheries and trade* (pp. 57–77). FAO (2). doi.org/10.1111/j.1467-2979.2011.00443.x

Lee, S., Govan, H., Bertram, I., & Kinch, J. (2020). A comparison of sea cucumber fishery management plans and implications for governance in Pacific Island Countries. *SPC Fisheries Newsletter, 161,* 34–39.

Macintyre, M., & Foale, S. (2010). Mining and Cultural Loss: Assessing and Mitigating Impacts in Papua New Guinea. In L. Maffi & E. Woodley (Eds.), *Biocultural Diversity Conservation: A Global Sourcebook* (pp. 68–9). Earthscan.

Macintyre, M. A., & Foale, S. J. (2013). Science, traditional ecological knowledge and anthropology: managing the impacts of mining in Papua New Guinea. *Collaborative Research, 6,* 399–418. doi.org/10.1353/cla.2013.0024

Mangubhai, S., Lalavanua, W., & Purcell, S. W. (Eds.). (2017) *Fiji's Sea Cucumber Fishery: Advances in Science for Improved Management. Report No. 01/17.* Wildlife Conservation Society.

Nash, W., Adams., T., Tuara, P., Terekia, O., Munro, D., Amos, M., Leqata, J., Mataiti, N., Teopenga, M., & Whitford, J. (1995). *The Aitutaki Trochus Fishery: A Case Study.* South Pacific Commission.

Pakoa, K., Friedman, K., Tardy, E., Lasi, F., Kronen, M., & Vunisea, A. (2008). *Status of Trochus Fisheries in the Pacific Islands* [Poster].

Preston, G. l. (1993). Beche-de-mer. In A. Wright & L. Hill (Eds.), *Nearshore Marine Resources of the South Pacific: Information for Fisheries Development and Management* (pp. 371–407). Forum Fisheries Agency.

Ram, R., Chand, R. V., Forrest, A., & Southgate, P. C. (2017). Effect of processing method on quality, texture, collagen and amino acid composition of sandfish (Holothuria scabra). *Lwt-Food Science and Technology, 86,* 261–9. doi.org/ 10.1016/j.lwt.2017.08.003

Rasmussen, A. E. (2015). *In the Absence of the Gift: New Forms of Value and Personhood in a Papua New Guinea Community.* Berghahn. doi.org/10.2307/j.ctt9qdb0f

Shedrawi, G., Kinch, J., Halford, A. R. Bertram, I., Molai, C., & Friedman, K. J. (2019). CITES listing of sea cucumber species from class Holothuroidea provides opportunities to improve management of the beche-de-mer trade. *SPC Fisheries Newsletter, 159,* 6–8.

Smith, G. (2013). Beijing's Orphans? New Chinese Investors in Papua New Guinea. *Pacific Affairs, 86*(2), 327–49. doi.org/10.5509/2013862327

Smith, G. (2016). The Drivers of Current Chinese Business Migration to the South Pacific. In M. Powles (Ed.), *China and the Pacific: The View from Oceania* (pp. 144–9). Victoria University Press.

Van Helden, F. (1998). *Between cash and conviction. The social context of the Bismark-ramu Integrated Conservation and Development Project.* National Research Institute.

Wen, J., Hu, C., & Fan, S. (2010). Chemical composition and nutritional quality of sea cucumbers. *Journal of the Science of Food and Agriculture, 90*(14), 2469–74. doi.org/10.5509/2013862327

West, P. (2006). *Conservation is Our Government Now: The Politics of Ecology in Papua New Guinea.* Duke University Press. doi.org/10.5380/cam.v10i1.18585

6

Manufacturing compromise: Labour process analysis of a Chinese refinery site in Papua New Guinea

I-Chang Kuo

Introduction

This chapter investigates labour relations at the Basamuk refinery, a Chinese nickel and cobalt processing plant in Madang Province, Papua New Guinea (PNG) (see Map 6.1). The refinery, around 50 kilometres southeast of Madang town, is owned and managed by a Chinese multinational corporation (CMC) called the Metallurgical Corporation of China (MCC) in collaboration with Canadian and PNG shareholders.[1] The Basamuk refinery is the site of the Ramu Nickel mine's refining operations, whereas the Kurumbukari mine is the site of the mine's mining and beneficiation operations. Construction was finished in late 2012 and the refinery is now in production, with MCC serving as the primary operator. As a result of this transition, present employment relations at the refinery are markedly

---

1   MCC owns 85 per cent as a shareholder, Canadian company CaConic Metal owns 8.56 per cent and the PNG Government and landowners respectively own 2.50 per cent and 3.94 per cent.

different from those during the construction phase, when provincial-based Chinese contractors oversaw various work locations, and language barriers hampered collaboration and relationship building (Smith, 2013).[2]

This chapter emphasises the acid leach production phase to demonstrate changing work relations in the refinery. I chose this option because high-pressure acid leach processing was critical to the mine's economic profitability. This processing method was also a driving factor in the construction of the Basamuk processing plant (Ramu Nickel Joint Venture, 1999). Additionally, the refinery employs the largest number of employees in the Ramu Nickel mine. Of the approximately 900 employees working across seventeen departments, one-third were Chinese and two-thirds were Papua New Guineans.[3] These factors show that the acid leach production phase is an excellent example to study changing work relations.

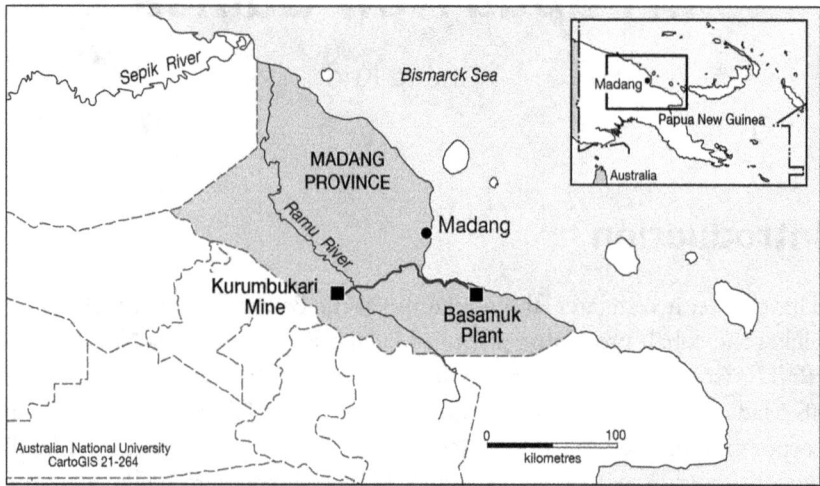

Map 6.1 The Ramu Nickel mine
Source: ANU CartoGIS.

2   This finding is like the observation of Bunkenborg, Pedersen and Nielsen (2022) regarding a Chinese mining enclave in the Gobi Desert, where Chinese and Mongolian personnel perceived one another as quite different and hence difficult to comprehend.

3   These departments are high-pressure acid leach; acid plant; counter current decantation (CCD); lime plant; mobile equipment; instrumentation; fixed equipment; training; admin; warehouse (wharf); water pump; power plant; safety; maintenance; lab; human resources departments; and community affairs (CA). According to Smith (2013), there were around two-thirds Chinese and one-third PNG employees during the construction phase. The proportion of Chinese employees compared to PNG employees is thus reversed throughout the production phase.

Figure 6.1 A meeting in Enekwai after the 2014 strike
Source: Photo by the author.

My interest in labour relations began in 2014 when I conducted preliminary fieldwork in Enekwai, a displaced village near the Kurumbukari mine. A week before I left Madang, a group of armed young men from Enekwai assaulted the mine, setting fire to nine excavators, one fuel tank and one lighting vehicle, injuring five Chinese employees. This strike, precipitated by villagers' dissatisfaction with MCC's employment policy, inspired me to research labour relations. Following that, I frequently encountered PNG interlocutors who talked about previous strikes between PNG and Chinese workers during three months of fieldwork in 2017 and between December 2018 and October 2019 near the refinery (see Figure 6.1). One account detailed a 2009 strike that they claimed was precipitated by PNG workers' complaints about workplace issues, including salary, training and working conditions. The strike was subsequently resolved with the intervention of mediators from both sides during a meeting in the old camp attended by PNG and Chinese personnel. Due to the ferocity of the 2009 strike, some Chinese interlocutors refer to it as the '8th May incident'. While these previous confrontations appear to be unresolved, they serve as a constant reminder to PNG workers to fight for their rights and as a reminder to Chinese employees to understand the critical nature of adhering to rules in PNG and appreciating PNG workers' benefits and workplace safety.

Rather than emphasising workers' strikes, this chapter explains how work relations changed after these early disputes. According to interview responses, most Papuan New Guinean interlocutors reported increased job opportunities at the refinery. The Ramu NiCo Allied Workers' Union was critical in negotiating for worker benefits and training within the refinery regarding job creation. According to its chair, the union spent six months in Madang meeting with MCC and a representative from the Labour Department to finalise an industrial award in early 2018. This example is noteworthy because it demonstrates how PNG workers used the trade union to advocate for their rights when the PNG state was not involved in the refinery's operation but was present during the industrial relations agreement negotiation.

The recruitment of the trade unions and the non-intervention of the state effectively institutionalised a tripartite (employer, trade union and the state) industrial relations system that had originated in PNG during the Australian colonial period. According to Imbun's (2016) labour market study and Hess's (1992) unionisation study, this tripartite structure represents the transition from a coercive indentured labour system to a modernised Australian-style industrial system that arose in PNG during the 1960s. Imbun (2008) adds that work relations in PNG shifted from antagonistic to collaborative during the same transitional period, requiring cooperation between employers and workers in remote mining areas. Due to the inability of the PNG Government to closely monitor activities, the state's involvement in negotiations between foreign employers and PNG employees becomes an absent presence that deepens the cooperation between the two parties (Bainton & Macintyre, 2021). Imbun (2007) notes that foreign employers and PNG workers should view one another as significant others to meet their mutual needs—the former requires organised labour's agreement to operate the production, while the latter requires job opportunities and services offered by the company. For foreign companies, including MCC, Imbun (2017) emphasises that they must meet the needs of PNG workers because the PNG Government supports their right to form unions.

This chapter is divided into three sections. The first is a literature review on capital–labour relations in Chinese firms operating within and outside the People's Republic of China (PRC). The second portrays the experiences of PNG workers as they learn a Chinese work ethic and a workplace language. The third section discusses Chinese employees' concessions to Australian management and the growing role of PNG managers in ensuring workplace safety. Finally, this chapter explains why the refinery's work relations correspond to Przeworski's (1985) conception of a class compromise theory and Wright's (2000) definition of negative compromise.

CMCs' concession in the workplace

Capital–labour relations in the PRC have long been a vibrant academic topic in labour process studies, following the acceleration of reform and opening up during the 1990s.[4] In order to protect labour welfare, the Chinese government enacted a slew of new laws, including the Labour Contract Law of the People's Republic of China in 2007 and the Social Insurance Law of the People's Republic of China in 2010.[5] To counteract increased labour mobility in the workplace, researchers have documented how Chinese state-owned enterprises (SOEs) enhance labour control through the use of subcontractors, paternalistic dormitories and migrant labour (Pun & Smith, 2007; Jia, 2016; Smith & Zheng, 2016; Zhang, 2008). Additionally, the Chinese government has a substantial role in controlling the workplace union, the party factory committee and SOEs' management principles and structure to resolve labour conflicts. Based on Burawoy's (1985) ideas, previous research has demonstrated that hegemonic labour consent is generated in the PRC by Chinese managers' increasing power, decisive state interference and the insignificance of trade unions (Lu, 2016; Zhang, 2008).

With the PRC's growing global engagement, labour process academics have suggested a new framework for examining capital–labour relations in CMCs (Burawoy, 2014). This advocacy is motivated by two primary objectives. To begin, the Chinese government and the Communist Party branch have little involvement in directing CMCs' overseas operations (Smith, 2008; Andrijasevic & Sacchetto, 2016). Second, rather than a transfer of domestic practice and belief from the PRC, CMCs' behaviour is better seen as being influenced by local institutions and societies (Smith & Zheng, 2016). Notably, there is research demonstrating CMCs' proclivity for negotiation and concession. For example, Miriam Driessen's

---

4   Reform and opening up began in the late 1970s and accelerated in the 1990s after Bill Clinton's administration granted the PRC the most-favourable-nation status and membership in the World Trade Organization.
5   In this chapter, the Chinese Government refers to the Chinese state government. Similarly, the PNG Government refers to the national government of Papua New Guinea.

(2019) research on Chinese construction companies in Ethiopia reveals why Chinese management frequently made concessions to Ethiopian employees due to their coalition with local residents, collective labour withdrawal and strikes (14–15). In addition, Lee's (2017) study on a CMC in Zambia's Copperbelt identifies three factors contributing to CMCs' willingness to make concessions. To begin, the Chinese Government was in many ways absent from the company's terms and conditions negotiations, although long-term copper supply is critical to the PRC's national resource security. Second, the Zambian Government supported the right of Zambian workers to unionise. Third, the acute militancy of local employees worked as a check on CMCs' tendency to unilaterally set their employees' working conditions (Lee, 2009, 2017). These considerations help characterise some of the complicated, even contradictory, political contexts surrounding CMCs' agreements and relations with states and labourers in other developing countries such as PNG.

This chapter expands on Lee's findings by demonstrating compromises made by Chinese employees and PNG workers. This two-way concession procedure is partially a result of the PNG Government's relative lack of precision as a regulator and the mutual incomprehension of Chinese employees and PNG workers (Bainton, 2021).[6] Due to a lack of corporate expertise in PNG mining regulations, Chinese managers must negotiate with and concede to PNG employees. Chinese managers were subjected to new forms of control in PNG when they adapted by working with PNG staff, despite owning the manufacturing know-how and machinery (Wright, 2011). Even if the Chinese work ethic and communication limitations posed challenges, PNG workers had to negotiate with and concede to Chinese employees.[7] Although the training method is based on Australian standards, PNG staff were reliant on the evaluation of Chinese supervisors. By showing how the two parties could learn to co-operate, this chapter demonstrates how PNG workers and Chinese employees can interact through mutual compromises rather than permanently remaining in fundamentally adversarial positions.

---

6   According to Bainton (2021), mutual incomprehension refers to the foreign mining company's lack of awareness about the landownership ideology in PNG and the local community's lack of information about corporate practices such as corporate social responsibility. Mutual incomprehension is used in this chapter to refer to MCC's ignorance of PNG mining regulations and PNG employees' inexperience of working with and interacting with Chinese employees.

7   This chapter defines work ethic as the value placed on labour by those who perform it. By executing work in this manner, labour can accomplish a personal objective, while the manager can maximise productivity from the workforce (Scott, 2015).

PNG workers' adaptation to working in a Chinese mine

This chapter is based on interviews with refinery workers and corporate documentation gathered during fieldwork in an impacted village, Duman, near the refinery (see Map 6.2). Although participant observation was not permitted within the refinery, I had numerous opportunities to interview PNG employees in the local market and communities. When describing work relations with Chinese personnel, PNG interlocutors frequently stated that they needed to adapt to a new system by understanding how Chinese employees worked and communicated in a workplace pidgin. In this section, I utilise PNG workers' stories to illustrate how they learned to work alongside Chinese employees.

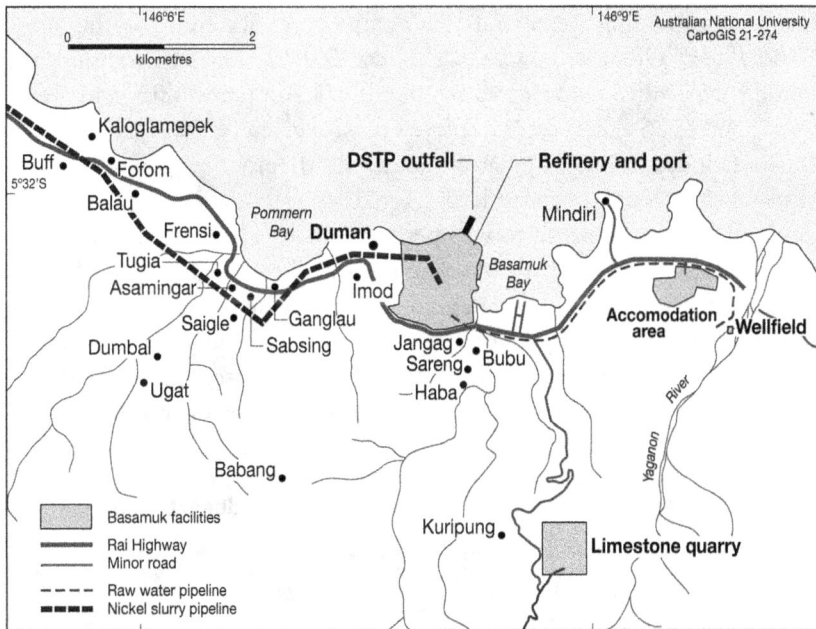

Map 6.2 Duman village and the Basamuk refinery
Source: ANU CartoGIS.

Learning Chinese work ethics

The first story is about Nathan, a PNG worker in his late twenties.[8] Nathan obtained a university degree and worked in the acid leach department's control room. Nathan stated that he became aware of MCC's distinctions when looking for a position with the company. As a recent university graduate, Nathan expected to perform accounting-related employment consistent with his skill set and understanding of Australian corporate culture. After receiving word of job acceptance, the human resources department inquired whether he might work in another department due to the lack of accounting-related employment openings. Nathan was surprised by this arrangement but accepted the job offer to develop his talents and build on the knowledge he gained at the university.

After being assigned to the acid leach department, Nathan was introduced to a specific training system for PNG employees. According to the *Ramu Nickel Project Operations Industrial Award 2018 (Basamuk overview)*, the training system was governed by the PNG Apprenticeship and Trade Testing Act 1986. There were five levels of workers in Nathan's department, which included trainee operator (grades 2–3), process operator level 1 (grades 4–5), process operator level 2 (grades 6–8), process operator level 3 (grades 9–10) and control room operator (grades 11–12) (see Table 6.1). Staff pay rates would rise if they were promoted to a higher level. Nathan had started in grade 2 and was in grade 10 or 11 when I met him, based on his completion of training courses in machinery and equipment operation, sulphur handling and steam production. Nathan's case demonstrates that PNG workers had a formal and quite effective process for improving their skills, levels and pay rates.

Table 6.1 Workers' grades and levels in the acid leach department

Classification & grades															
Schedule 1. Classification and wage grades															
Work area & pay grades	1	2	3	4	5	6	7	8	9	10	11	12	13	14	15
Acid plant															
Trainee operator		X	X												
Process operator level 1				X	X										
Process operator level 2						X	X	X							

---

8   All names in this chapter are fictitious to protect the identities of interlocutors.

Classification & grades														
Schedule 1. Classification and wage grades														
Work area & pay grades	1	2	3	4	5	6	7	8	9	10	11	12	13	14	15
Process operator level 3									X	X					
Control room operator											X	X			
Trainee room operator															
Trainee assayer			X	X	X										
Assayer						X	X	X							
Boiler operator					X	X	X	X	X						

HR Grade	Title	Points	K
2	Trainee 0.1	0 to 4	3.65
3	Trainee 0.2	5 to 9	3.80
4	Level 1.1	10 to 14	4.16
5	Level 1.2	15 to 19	4.92
6	Level 2.1	20 to 24	5.74
7	Level 2.2	25 to 29	6.56
8	Level 2.3	30 to 34	7.38
9	Level 3.1	35 to 39	8.2
10	Level 3.2	40 to 44	9.02
11	Level 3.3	45 to 49	9.84

Reproduced by the author from Ramu Nickel Project Operations Industrial Award 2018. Basamuk overview.

Along with the PNG-defined training system, Nathan received on-the-job instruction using more distinctly Chinese methods. Nathan and other PNG personnel learned numerous technical skills (such as welding, grinding and scaffolding) from Chinese staff while they were trainee operators. While training on the job was available in other mines in PNG, the Chinese team's engagement brought a training system unique to early Chinese SOEs— *chuanbangdai* ('transferring, assisting and leading'). As in an apprenticeship, new employees were assigned to a 'master' who instructed them on specific tasks and kept tabs on their overall attitude and performance. In addition, MCC provided a formal definition of this training approach in an internal corporate document:

> Transferring entails conveying the concepts of eating bitterness and working hard. Assisting involves passing on knowledge. Senior Chinese personnel with solid security awareness would be partnered

with new PNG colleagues to help them develop their abilities. Leading entails encouraging work ethics, including abstaining from betel nuts and tobacco, working diligently, and being devoted to working.[9]

This explanation demonstrates that MCC intended to use *chuanbangdai* to teach PNG personnel skills and the Chinese work ethic—eating bitterness ('enduring adversity and working hard').

Nathan encountered some tensions and contradictions between the two systems due to his participation in two different training methods, particularly in terms of workplace safety. During his Health, Safety and Emergency training as a trainee operator, Nathan was told by a PNG trainer about the importance of workplace safety. Nathan should stop working if he considered the working conditions unsafe, according to the PNG trainer. During on-the-job training, Nathan observed some Chinese employees' devotion to work that he deemed unsafe, such as working on rainy days when the sulphur dust and steam would be brought by the rain to the ground rather than evaporate in the sky. Nathan was initially hesitant to assist the Chinese staff due to the PNG trainer's instructions. However, after attempting to assist them a few times, he realised how Chinese employees understood and practised hard work ethics to maintain consistent production. Nathan gained this idea during a pre-start meeting the next day after arriving on the job site. During the meeting, Chinese supervisors discussed the performance of PNG workers based on whether they aided Chinese employees in their work. '[In a] Chinese company, you have to work very, very hard,' Nathan stated to explain his realisation. 'It is rain or sun, whatsoever. You must work. And then they will know that you are [a] hard-working guy.' Confronted with divergent perspectives from PNG trainers and Chinese supervisors, Nathan chose to work 'very hard' since he was aware that the Chinese supervisors' evaluations were a significant component in evaluating his work performance on the performance sheets used for the job promotion (see Figure 6.2).

9   This paragraph is a verbatim quote from the corporate document. The original language of this paragraph is Mandarin Chinese and is translated into English by the author.

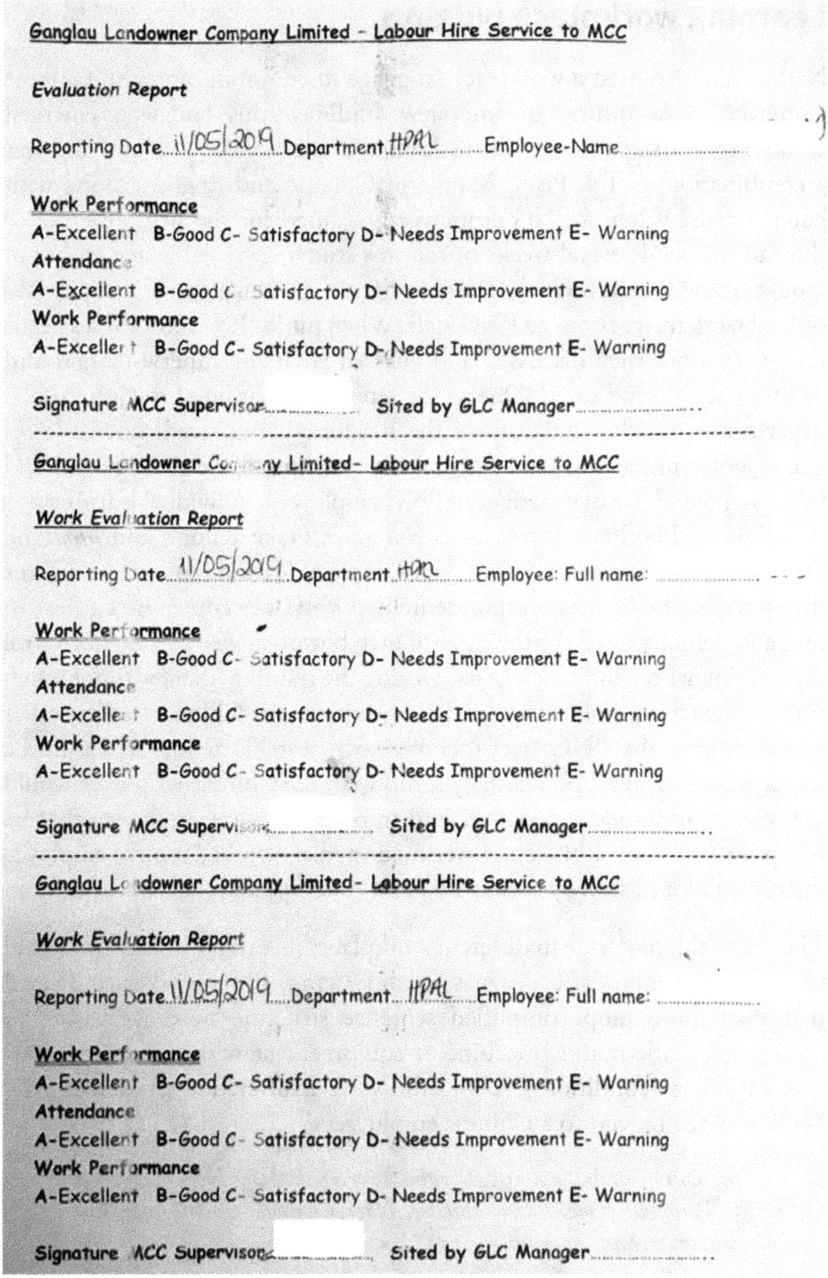

Ganglau Landowner Company Limited – Labour Hire Service to MCC

Evaluation Report

Reporting Date...11/05/2019..Department..HPAL.....Employee-Name.................

Work Performance
A-Excellent B-Good C- Satisfactory D- Needs Improvement E- Warning
Attendance
A-Excellent B-Good C Satisfactory D- Needs Improvement E- Warning
Work Performance
A-Excellent B-Good C- Satisfactory D- Needs Improvement E- Warning

Signature MCC Supervisor............. Sited by GLC Manager...............

Ganglau Landowner Company Limited- Labour Hire Service to MCC

Work Evaluation Report

Reporting Date...11/05/2019..Department..HPAL.....Employee: Full name:...........

Work Performance
A-Excellent B-Good C- Satisfactory D- Needs Improvement E- Warning
Attendance
A-Excellent B-Good C- Satisfactory D- Needs Improvement E- Warning
Work Performance
A-Excellent B-Good C- Satisfactory D- Needs Improvement E- Warning

Signature MCC Supervisor............. Sited by GLC Manager...............

Ganglau Landowner Company Limited- Labour Hire Service to MCC

Work Evaluation Report

Reporting Date..11/05/2019....Department...HPAL...Employee: Full name:...........

Work Performance
A-Excellent B-Good C- Satisfactory D- Needs Improvement E- Warning
Attendance
A-Excellent B-Good C- Satisfactory D- Needs Improvement E- Warning
Work Performance
A-Excellent B-Good C- Satisfactory D- Needs Improvement E- Warning

Signature MCC Supervisor............. Sited by GLC Manager...............

Figure 6.2 An example of PNG workers' performance assessment sheet
Source: Photo by the author.

Learning workplace pidgin

Nathan also acquired a workplace language to communicate with Chinese employees.[10] According to interview findings, this language emerged because of years of collaboration between Chinese and PNG staff and was a combination of Tok Pisin, Mandarin Chinese and English, along with hand signals. When a PNG employee was hired for the first time, he or she had to spend several weeks or months studying the language, either in groups or individually. Group learning occurred when a Chinese supervisor offered work instructions to PNG staff. When junior PNG employees heard the instruction, they discussed and guessed what the supervisor said and what his actions indicated. Due to the repetitious nature of the job in each department and the similarity of the machinery employed, novice PNG employees could acquire this language by working for a given period and following the advice of experienced PNG employees. Individual learning was described by PNG employees as *wokim aksen* ('take action') and *bihainim aksen* ('follow the action'). Using the example of learning to operate a Terex dump truck, the Chinese employee invited PNG newcomers to sit next to him and demonstrated the function of each button as well as how to control the steering wheel and block gears. During the training, there was not much verbal interaction. Following the demonstration, the Chinese staff member would request the PNG staff member to repeat his action to ensure he understood it. If the PNG employee did well, the Chinese employee would say, 'okela ' or 'Good, good' and inform other Chinese employees that he had passed. When a PNG employee made a mistake, the Chinese employee instructed him to stop by saying 'no good' and repeated the demonstration.

The use of this language in different workplaces reveals both similarities and variances. For Chinese colleagues to understand, PNG workers indicated that they must adopt simplified sentence structure by emphasising or repeating specific nouns (machine or equipment names), verbs (activities) and adjectives (conditions). Using the valve malfunction as an example, Nathan stated he said to a Chinese employee:

> *Poroman* [friends], *nage* [that] *valve no good ah. Nage broken, no good ah. Poroman come, stand, and see. Nage no good, we talk talk and maintenance ah, come ah, fix.*

---

10   Chinese interlocutors indicated that they were required to acquire this specific workplace language. As a result, this industrial dialect is not exclusive to PNG employees.

(Friends, the valve is not operating correctly. Friends, come, stand here and check the valve. The valve has a problem. Let us have a discussion and inform the maintenance team to come and fix the valve.)

This example demonstrates how Nathan communicated the valve's malfunction to Chinese colleagues by emphasising and repeating the noun '*nage*' ('that' or 'the valve') and the adjective 'no good' to convey that additional action was required.

Additional instances of this workplace pidgin were used in the acid leach department. '*Poroman* ('friends') *gut* ('good') morning ah,' a PNG employee would say after distributing tasks to Chinese colleagues in the morning. '*Mi* ('I') *wok* ('work') *wok* with you, *mi wok wok* with you. Today *mi wok wok* with you ah.' (Good morning, friends. I collaborate with you. I am working with you today). In this scenario, the PNG employee repeated the verb '*wok*' ('work') to inform his Chinese colleagues that they were working together today. 'Okay, you stay, *poroman* ('friends'),' a PNG employee would respond when he or she received gifts (such as salt, cigarettes, biscuits or noodles) from Chinese colleagues. '*Mi* ('I') go home la. Mushroom, lemon *kam* ('come') give you.' (All right, my friend, you can stay here. I am going home to get some mushrooms and lemon to offer to you.) The PNG employee emphasised the nouns mushroom and lemon since they were familiar with how Chinese employees used them when cooking in the dorms. Finally, PNG staff were taught common Mandarin Chinese terms to describe labour or machine situations, such as *nage* ('that one'), *you* ('have'), *meiyou* ('do not have'), *hao* ('good'), *huaile* ('broken') and *alibaba* ('stealing or thief').

The use of this workplace pidgin varied according to the names of various machines and equipment in various departments. During on-the-job training with Chinese supervisors, for example, PNG employees learned different Mandarin Chinese machine names, such as *chaiyou* ('diesel fuel') and *yaoshi* ('key') in the limestone mill; *pidai* ('conveyor belt'), *bangpu* ('pump') and *qiumoji* ('ball mill') in the limestone processing plant; and *banshou* ('spanner'), *dahuoji* ('lighter') and *shoutao* ('gloves') in the instrumentation department. Nathan said he used onomatopoeia to write the machine name's pronunciation without tone to remember these terms. When employees used this workplace pidgin, it was not easy to tell if they spoke English or Mandarin Chinese. A more accurate description is that it reflected a situation in which two groups of workers did not share a common language and interacted by employing limited vocabulary derived from Tok Pisin, English and Mandarin Chinese.

Finally, the requirement to learn this language made PNG workers who had not completed college or university education more equivalent to those with such qualifications. Learning this language did not necessitate formal academic qualifications. The ability to speak this language also provided PNG employees with the opportunity to learn how to operate machinery and other relevant technical skills, particularly in welding, grinding and scaffolding. A few PNG workers with official higher education credentials indicated they were being pushed to downgrade their linguistic abilities. When people spoke this language, they had the impression that they were speaking in a childlike manner or simplifying things. They expressed frustration at their inability to speak at an average rate and perform tasks rapidly. Additionally, some workers said that their capacity to communicate in this language affected their job promotion. Owen, a PNG worker at the limestone plant, said that his brother was promoted to team leader because of his ability to converse with Chinese people. In contrast, Owen's inability to communicate in this language frustrated him and affected his relationships with other employees who spoke it fluently.[11]

This section's demonstration of worker training and workplace language reflects a situation similar to Lee's (2017) discussion of Zambian mineworkers' changing attitudes towards the Chinese work ethic. Nathan's participation in training shows that implementing a new training system does not negate the Chinese system or values. Instead, PNG workers' emphasis on the Chinese work ethic and workplace pidgin indicates that Chinese management retains some power in evaluating and promoting PNG workers. After realising the situation, Nathan's participation reflects a compromise between opposing ideas and a concession to Chinese management. Based on these findings, I argue that implementing the new training system in the refinery creates a situation in which workplace labour mobility increases. At the same time, Chinese managers retain some degree of control. This story demonstrates the importance of comprehending

---

11   There were still PNG employees with university or college degrees who could communicate in this workplace pidgin. Nathan, for example, expressed no apprehension about communicating in this language with Chinese colleagues. Owen was hesitant to use this language because he stressed that he had completed training in Australia and possessed the necessary skills and experiences to perform his job. As a result, Owen may have been hesitant to learn this language because he perceived it as a threat to his competence.

employees' experiences in addition to the concession reached between the company and the union. In a similar vein, the following section discusses the experiences of Chinese and PNG managers to illustrate another facet of work and power relations associated with CMCs' concession.

Chinese employees' subordination to the Australian administrative system

When I lived in Duman, I occasionally spoke with Chinese workers working outside the refinery or visiting the local market and villages. PNG staff also helped me contact some Chinese workers to conduct phone interviews. Based on these findings, this section explains how Chinese employees adapt to PNG mining regulations and why PNG managers were critical for MCC.

According to Clint, a white PNG national who was a former chair of Raibus Limited, Chinese employees were initially ignorant of PNG regulations based on Australian and New Zealand standards (e.g. AS/NZS 4801).[12] During the first meeting with MCC staff, Clint's presence, as a white man, surprised Chinese managers. Clint believed the Chinese employees thought signing an agreement with the Michael Somare government gave them the approval to direct the operation of this mine. This story corresponds with that of an Australian employee named Horace, previously working with MCC. Situated in between Chinese and PNG employees, Horace's experience of educating Chinese workers regarding mining regulations in PNG included three stages: first, understanding that Chinese staff had a different way of working; second, realising the PNG Government's limited capability to police rules and regulations; and third, persuading Chinese staff they must adhere to laws and rules in PNG to avoid severe punishment (such as shutdown). Horace noted that the absence of the PNG state in the mine's operation forces MCC to self-govern when complying with regulations in PNG. Following Horace's view, this section shows how MCC's self-governance is achieved by Chinese managers making concessions given the increasing influence of PNG managers.

---

12   Raibus Limited is a landowners' company with subsidiaries such as engineering, security, housekeeping and a national catering service. Clint is an Australian who worked as a patrol officer during the Australian administration. Following Papua New Guinea's independence in 1975, he obtained PNG citizenship and began managing businesses in Madang. In addition, AS/NZS 4801 is a standard that specifies how a mining business should manage occupational health and safety in the workplace.

The first story is about a Chinese manager named Mr. Xiang, who worked at the acid leach department. Mr. Xiang's family had been working for MCC for three generations. Describing himself as a *zidi* ('son') of MCC, he started to work for the company at the age of twenty. Since then he had worked in many jobs as a car repairer, machine operator, driver, manager of the vehicle garage and material storage room, and now, aged over fifty, he worked as a safety manager. Mr. Xiang noted that he gained many experiences through the training method called *chuanbangdai* discussed above. Mr. Xiang also said that MCC has a unique work culture that developed during the PRC's planned economy era, when there was no formal training and employees faced hard working conditions and low wages. The prior grim situation, according to Mr. Xiang, resulted in MCC's emphasis on following supervisors' orders and sustaining continuous production.

Working in the refinery for more than a decade, Mr. Xiang learned the workplace pidgin and some PNG culture through visiting local villages (Kuo, 2022, 2023). He also became aware of the different views of workplace safety held by personnel from Chinese SOEs and other foreigners. In Chinese SOEs' culture, Mr. Xiang said the focus was on a top–down managerial system based on detailed rules accompanied by rewards and punishments. Supervisors played a critical role in managing workplace safety compared to workers' relative insignificance within this system. For non-Chinese managers, in contrast, the focus was on sufficient training for workers and adequate safety equipment to achieve workers' self-safety management—workers assessed the situation and decided whether to work. Encountering these contradictory ideologies, Mr. Xiang noted this was unavoidable when MCC operated in PNG. The necessity was to adjust Chinese senior employees' attitudes and behaviour inherited from the Chinese SOEs' culture. After years of negotiation with non-Chinese managers on work safety, Mr. Xiang said the situation in the acid leach department became a combination of some Chinese managerial methods and the importance of obeying occupational health and safety regulations in PNG. Using his experience as an example, Mr. Xiang accompanied PNG workers to decide whether the workplace was safe. He also participated in health, safety and emergency training with PNG employees to update his knowledge and ensure that their work follows the Golden Rules based on the Australian understanding of workplace safety and PNG mining regulations (see Table 6.2).

Table 6.2 Ramu Nickel's 'The Golden Rules'

I Pledge to Follow the 8 Golden Rules:	
1	I will report hazards and incidents immediately.
2	I will asses [sic] risks and ensure safety.
3	I will only operate equipment if qualified and authorized.
4	I will always work with a permit as required.
5	I will drive safely.
6	I will work safely at heights.
7	I will keep clear of suspended loads.
8	I will manage my fitness for duty.

Note: Adapted from a photo taken by the author.

Finally, different understandings of workplace safety also affected operations in the acid leach department. Describing how Chinese staff worked as *kaobenneng* ('by instinct'), Mr. Xiang said most senior Chinese workers were experienced operators, so they knew the standard operating procedures and could run the operation. However, there were situations when Chinese operators must negotiate with Australian managers regarding workplace safety. For instance, some Chinese operators might take shortcuts or breach the rules to achieve a higher production rate. These behaviours were unacceptable to non-Chinese, including Australian managers, who required that Chinese employees always adhere to safety regulations in PNG. Additionally, Chinese workers placed a strong focus on continuous production ahead of their best efforts to ensure safety. For non-Chinese managers, the primary priority was to ensure their safety before moving to production. When confronted with these opposing viewpoints, Mr. Xiang stated that Chinese employees must negotiate with and frequently make concessions to Australian managers.

The critical role of PNG managers

PNG managers also play an essential role in monitoring workplace safety. According to Horace, five to six foreigners worked in the Ramu Nickel mine in 2021 compared to ten to fifteen at the peak. He said the difficulty of communication with Chinese employees was one reason for the decrease in foreigners. PNG managers, especially those educated at Chinese universities, played an increasingly important role because of the declining number of non-Chinese foreign managers and their understandings of PNG mining regulations and Chinese culture and language.

Luke, a previous safety trainer manager at MCC, was one illustration of this transition. Luke was hired by a private Chinese company to teach younger Chinese personnel business English and project management. The company also financed his study at a Chinese university. MCC hired him as a training manager after he graduated from university to teach Chinese and PNG staff about workplace safety because he spoke Mandarin Chinese and Tok Pisin. He provided safety training and inspected work locations for senior Chinese workers. He also constantly advised PNG employees to say no to their Chinese supervisors when they accompanied Chinese supervisors to work and perceived the work environment to be unsafe. His reminders reflect Australia's influences on his knowledge of the mining safety regulations in PNG. 'Even Chinese (employees) they have the capability to manage their own operation,' Luke said, based on his observations in the refinery. 'Just like all the mining companies in PNG, they [Chinese managers] have to report to MRA [Mineral Resources Authority of Papua New Guinea].' This instance demonstrates Luke's critical role in educating PNG and Chinese employees about the importance of workplace safety and assisting MCC in understanding and complying with PNG's mining rules.

Finally, Luke's position allowed him to bargain with Chinese employees. Luke's power to do this was based on his understanding of mining regulations in PNG and his knowledge of some Chinese workers' violations of safety practices. Previous research has shown how such claims to authority could increase a supervisor's ability to intervene. For example, in Burawoy's (1985) study of a tractor plant in Soviet Hungary, the Red Star, workers' violations of rules in search of higher output rates underwrote the foreman's ability to police the regulations and alter workers' rates. Burawoy also explains in another chapter how applying the 'safety first' programme in Zambia's Copperbelt empowered supervisors to monitor workplace safety in the dangerous underground mine. Given that working in the acid leach department was a high-risk job, Luke's knowledge of mining rules in PNG and his managerial position gave him the ability to influence Chinese employees.

In this section, Mr. Xiang's and Luke's stories demonstrate MCC's concession in incorporating Australian and New Zealand workplace safety management. Chinese management must negotiate with and concede to Australian or PNG managers to understand PNG regulations when implementing this safety system. This demonstrates that, while Chinese employees continue to wield power based on production know-how and machinery ownership, PNG managers' power is growing due to their understanding of western managerial culture and regulations in PNG. This balance of power is similar to that shown in the previous section, in which PNG employees' mobility in improving grades and levels at work is increasing. At the same time, Chinese managers still have some control over that mobility. I argue that Chinese employees have limited control over workplace safety. Non-Chinese foreigners and PNG managers can use safety regulations to counteract Chinese management. This situation demonstrates the institutional embeddedness of CMCs' mining activities in PNG, quite distinct from the mere presence of the mineral deposit. This finding is comparable to Driessen's (2019, p. 177) study on the embeddedness of Chinese construction companies' activities in Ethiopia due to the challenges posed by Ethiopian staff.

Conclusion

This chapter explains how Chinese employees and PNG staff collaborate despite workplace conflict. I suggest that studies of employment relations in the PRC based on Burawoy's theories cannot completely account for shifting work relations in the refinery. As demonstrated here, the Chinese and PNG states are both physically absent but visible from afar. The engagement of the PNG trade union also ensures the existence of a system for defending PNG employees' benefits and resolving workplace problems. Finally, because Chinese managers lack an understanding of PNG's safety norms and laws, they are forced to negotiate with and concede to non-Chinese foreigners and PNG managers. These three elements demonstrate that the situation at the refinery is distinct from that in the domestic PRC, where the Chinese state intervenes, the trade union fails to represent employees' interests, and employers' control grows because of their allegiance to the state and the trade union.

Based on these findings, I argue that a compromise theory can help us better understand shifting employment relations in the refinery. Przeworski (1985) lays the groundwork for a labour process compromise theory based on Gramsci's (1971) discussion on establishing hegemony between the state and its citizenry. According to Przeworski, capitalist production relations can be adequately coordinated by considering the material interests of employers and employees. To that end, he asserts that a class compromise is possible through employees' willingness to participate in the labour process to meet material demands and employers' investment in a mechanism that secures employees' salary increases. Przeworski emphasises that the state's role is critical in fostering an institutional framework conducive to compromises between companies and employees. Following Przeworski's approach, this chapter has demonstrated how Chinese and PNG refinery workers reach compromises where the state is absent from the workplace but present during the process of negotiating an industrial relations agreement.

Additionally, this chapter argues that PNG employees' engagement is critical in reaching compromises at the refinery, conforming with Wright's (2000) discussion of how employees' power influences the formation of workplace class compromises. Based on Przeworski's work, Wright (2000, pp. 957–8) demonstrates how conflictual employment relations devolve into a situation akin to a combat stalemate when two parties recognise the need to halt mutual harm in exchange for concessions from both sides. According to Wright, different stages of capital–labour relations are determined by workers' associational power (such as founding a trade union or a labour party) and structural power (such as employees' critical position in the workplace).[13] Considering the refinery's current circumstances, the trade union's endeavour to implement the training system illustrates PNG workers' growing associational power in bargaining with Chinese management. During MCC's implementation of Australia's and New Zealand's safety regulations, PNG managers' knowledge and important positions become their structural power against Chinese employees. These examples demonstrate that work relations in the refinery might sometimes resemble Wright's notion of the negative compromise—two parties retain divergent and frequently clashing beliefs but recognise they cannot progress without negotiating with and conceding to the other party. These examples also indicate that MCC must alter its behaviour and adapt to the demands of PNG personnel if it is to maintain the stage of negative compromise; otherwise, the situation may revert to conflict.

Finally, in terms of workplace language, I argue that the material in this chapter demonstrates how workplace compromises are about more than just the material interests of capital and labour, as discussed in Wright (2000)

13　Wright's (2000) theory of class compromise has three stages: an illusion, the negative compromise and the positive compromise. According to Wright, the first stage refers to a situation in which employees strike for benefits and rights because employers retain (or try to retain) complete control over workers. The second stage refers to a situation in which two parties' relations are akin to a stalemate on the battlefield after years of conflicts. The third stage denotes a situation in which two parties' stable cooperation is achieved, and the employer can no longer control wage increases and working conditions unilaterally.

and Moodie (2010). Regarding workplace language development and communication about safety management, we discover that language plays a critical role in realising the concession between two parties and improving work relations. In other words, language development, in this case, is more than just a representation of compromise; rather, the development of the workplace pidgin and the effectiveness of communication (between Chinese and PNG managers) affects the situation of compromise in this inter-cultural work situation (Brewer, 2018). By focusing on the language dimension of mining, this research enables us to examine capital–labour interactions and CMCs' growing involvement in the mining industry in developing nations from new perspectives (Cornips & Muysken, 2019; Gillespie, 2014). Given the refinery's predominantly male workforce, additional research is needed to evaluate whether this workplace language is gendered, rather than drawing judgments merely because language users are primarily male.

Acknowledgements

An earlier version of this chapter was presented at the annual conference of Taiwan society for anthropology and ethnology in September 2020, and the 'Re-visualising the Past, Imagining the Future: Race, Governance and Development in PNG' workshop organised by the Cairns Institute and the College of Arts, Society and Education, James Cook University in November 2020. I thank the organisers for inviting me to present this chapter and reviewers' valuable ideas, and Merran Laver, Jennifer Dawes and Jean Kennedy for proofreading and editing the chapter. I also thank the Anthropology PhD Thesis Writing Workshop at The Australian National University (ANU) for stimulating discussions on this chapter. I want to express my special gratitude to Jean Kennedy, Sinclair Dinnen, Colin Filer and Kuntala Lahiri-Dutt at ANU for developing this chapter's intellectual insights and guidance. Last but not least, I am grateful to Michael Wood for offering me invaluable inspiration in formulating this chapter and to Alexandra Aikhenvald and Anna Hayes for their precious comments. Any errors or misinterpretations are, of course, solely my responsibility.

References

Andrijasevic, R. & Sacchetto, D. (2016). Foxconn beyond China: capital labour relations as co-determinants of internationalization. In M. Liu & C. Smith (Eds.), *China at Work: Labour Process Perspective on the Transformation of Work and Employment in China* (pp. 337–60). Red Globe Press. doi.org/10.5040/9781350394643.ch-014

Bainton, N. A. (2021). Menacing the Mine: Double Asymmetry and Mutual Incomprehension in Lihir. In N. Bainton, D. McDougall, K. Alexeyeff & J. Cox (Eds.), *Unequal Lives: Gender, Race and Class in the Western Pacific* (pp. 401–38). ANU Press. doi.org/10.2307/j.ctv1h45mj4.18

Bainton, N. A. & MacIntyre, M. (2021). Being Like a State: How Large-Scale Mining Companies Assume Government Roles in Papua New Guinea. In N. Bainton & E. Skrzypek (Eds.), *The Absent Presence of the State in Large-Scale Resource Extraction Projects* (pp. 107–40). ANU Press. doi.org/10.2307/j.ctv1zcm2sp.10

Brewer, J. D. (2018). Towards a Sociology of Compromise. In J. D. Brewer (Ed.), *The Sociology of Compromise after Conflict* (pp. 201–23) Palgrave Macmillan. doi.org/10.1007/978-3-319-78744-2_1

Bunkenborg, M., Pedersen, M. A. & M. Nielsen. (2022). *Collaborative Damage: An Experimental Ethnography of Chinese Globalization.* Cornell University Press. doi.org/10.1515/9781501759819

Burawoy, M. (1985). *The Politics of Production: Factory Regimes Under Capitalism and Socialism*, Verso Books.

Burawoy, M. (2014). The Colour of Class Revisited: Four Decades of Postcolonialism in Zambia. *Journal of Southern African Studies, 40*, pp. 961–79. doi.org/10.1080/03057070.2014.946213

Cornips, L. & Muysken, P. (2019). Introduction: Language in the mines. *International Journal of the Sociology of Language*, 2019, pp. 1–11. doi.org/10.1515/ijsl-2019-2026

Driessen, M. (2019). *Tales of Hope, Tastes of Bitterness: Chinese Road Builders in Ethiopia.* Hong Kong University Press.

Gillespie, K. (2014). Mining and language change in the Lihir Islands. *Language & Linguistics in Melanesia, 32*, pp.110–7.

Gramsci, A. (1971). *Selections from the Prison Notebooks*, Lawrence and Wishart.

Hess, M. (1992). *Unions Under Economic Development: Private Sector Unions in Papua New Guinea*, Oxford University Press.

Imbun, B. Y. (2007). Cannot Manage without The 'Significant Other': Mining, Corporate Social Responsibility and Local Communities in Papua New Guinea. *Journal of Business Ethics, 73*, pp. 177–92. doi.org/10.1007/s10551-006-9189-z

Imbun, B. Y. (2008). Making sense of an imposed industrial relations system in Papua New Guinea: a review of literature. *Journal of South Pacific Law, 12*, pp. 1–14.

Imbun, B. Y. (2016). The Genesis and Performance of an Australian Wage-Fixing System in Papua New Guinea. *Labour History, 110*, pp. 143–60. doi.org/10.5263/labourhistory.110.0143

Imbun, B. Y. (2017). The Chinese, Political CSR, and a Nickel Mine in Papua New Guinea. In A. Verbos, H. Ella & A Peredo, (Eds.), *Indigenous Aspirations and Rights: The Case for Responsible Business and Management* (pp. 47–59). Routledge.

Jia, W. (2016). The making of a dualistic labour regime: changing labour process and power relations in a Chinese state-owned enterprises under globalization. In M. Liu & C. Smith (Eds.), *China at Work: A Labour Process Perspective on the Transformation of Work and Employment in China* (pp. 76–97). Red Globe Press. doi.org/10.5040/9781350394643.ch-004

Kuo, I.-C. (2022). *Manufacturing Compromise: A Study of Gendered Labour Processes at a Chinese Nickel Refinery in Papua New Guinea*. PhD diss., The Australian National University.

Kuo, I.-C. (2023). Kamapim gutpela man: Papua New Guinean and Chinese refinery workers' changing understandings of becoming a man. *Oceania, 93*(1), pp. 2–22. doi.org/10.1002/ocea.5359

Lee, C. K. (2009). Raw Encounters: Chinese Managers, African Workers and the Politics of Casualization in Africa's Chinese Enclaves. *The China Quarterly, 199*, pp. 647–66. doi.org/10.1017/s0305741009990142

Lee, C. K. (2017). *The Specter of Global China: Politics, Labor, and Foreign Investment in Africa*. The University of Chicago Press. doi.org/10.7208/chicago/9780226340975.001.0001

Lu, M. (2016). Control and consent in the process of employee participation in Chinese state owned enterprise—A field research in BZ Iron and Steel Company. In M. Liu & C. Smith (Eds.) *China at Work: A Labour Process Perspective on the Transformation of Work and Employment in China* (pp. 31–55). Red Globe Press. doi.org/10.5040/9781350394643.ch-002

Moodie, T. D. (2010). Comprehending Class Compromise in the History of Class Struggle on the South African Gold Mines: Variations and Vicissitudes of Class Power. *South African Review of Sociology, 41*, pp. 99–116. doi.org/10.1080/21528586.2010.516130

Przeworski, A. (1985). *Capitalism and Social Democracy,* Cambridge University Press. doi.org/10.1017/cbo9781139171830

Pun, N. & Smith, C. (2007). Putting transnational labour process in its place: the dormitory labour regime in post-socialist China. *Work, Employment and Society, 21*, pp. 27–45. doi.org/10.1177/0950017007073611

Ramu Nico Joint Venture. (1999). Ramu Nickel Project Environmental Plan: Volume A: Executive Summary Victoria, Australia: NSR Environmental Consultants Pty Ltd.

Scott, J. (2015). *A Dictionary of Sociology [electronic resource],* Oxford University Press.

Smith, C. (2008). Work organisation within a dynamic globalising context: A critique of national institutional analysis of the international firm and an alternative perspective. In C. Smith, B. McSweeney, & R. Fitzgerald, (Eds.), *Remaking Management: Between Global and Local* (pp. 25–60). Cambridge University Press. doi.org/10.1017/cbo9780511753800.003

Smith, C. & Zheng, Y. (2016). Chinese MNCs' globalization, work and employment. In R. Drahokopoupil, R. Andrijasevic & D. Sacchetto, (Eds.), *Flexible Workforces and Low Profit Margins: Electronics Assembly between Europe and China* (pp. 67–92). ETUI Printshop. www.etui.org/sites/default/files/Chapter%203_2.pdf

Smith, G. (2013). Nupela Masta? Local and Expatriate Labour in a Chinese-Run Nickel Mine in Papua New Guinea. *Asian Studies Review, 37*, pp. 178–95. doi.org/10.1080/10357823.2013.768598

Wright, C. (2011). Historical Interpretations of the Labour Process: Retrospect and Future Research Directions. *Labour History, 100*, pp. 19–32. doi.org/10.5263/labourhistory.100.0019

Wright, E. O. (2000). Working-Class Power, Capitalist-Class Interests, and Class Compromisel. *American Journal of Sociology, 105*, pp. 957–1002. doi.org/10.1086/210397

Zhang, L. (2008). Lean Production and Labor Controls in the Chinese Automobile Industry in an Age of Globalisation. *International Labor and Working-Class History, 73*, pp. 24–44. doi.org/10.1017/s0147547908000033

7

'Money face': Haggling Chinese and foreigner talk at a PNG mining market-place

Shaun Gessler

> The technical rules are more or less given by the situation and thus are essentially universal, the same in Haiti or Oaxaca as in Nigeria or Morocco. 'A tug of war between seller and buyer,' bargaining as a formal procedure consists in a series of alternating, stepwise approaches toward an agreed price from separated initial offers. (Geertz, 1979, p. 225)

Introduction

This chapter examines the 'tug of war between seller and buyer' among local female fish and vegetable sellers and the predominantly male Chinese expatriate refinery workers at the Marmar (Tok Pisin: 'raintree') informal rural roadside market-place, located underneath a large raintree beside the Chinese majority-run Ramu Nickel Cobalt Project refinery in Basamuk, on the Rai Coast of Madang Province, Papua New Guinea (PNG).

In other recent research on market-places in Melanesia, Busse and Sharp (2019) claim that markets play important social functions. First, markets are critical to the livelihoods of rural Papua New Guineans by providing a vital source of income, especially for women, and second, markets are key to the redistribution of wealth among PNG's majority rural population. Similarly, the Marmar market-place acts as a significant income redistributor for local women who are generally excluded from employment opportunities in the highly masculinised refinery workforce. While previous ethnographic research conducted specifically at the Marmar market examines the market's impacts on economic inflation among Rai Coast communities (see Leach, 2011), this chapter examines the market from different perspectives.

My interest in the Marmar market is partly socio-linguistic in that Chinese-speaking expatriate workers communicate and trade with Tok Pisin-speaking PNG national women, even though these two groups do not share a common language. Through ethnographic vignettes and conversational analysis of the linguistic interactions between buyers and sellers, I show evidence of the PNG women speaking in a special register of Tok Pisin to trade with the Chinese buyers. The women sellers use both a simplified form of Tok Pisin and hand gestures, and they mimic words used by the Chinese buyers. Linguists define this form of simplification and mimicry as 'foreigner talk' (Ferguson, 1975; Velupillai, 2015, p. 17), which is technically more than jargon but not yet a pidgin.

Second, the market-place interactions between Chinese men and PNG national women demonstrate a degree of cultural friction and gendered tension between the two groups. Expatriate Chinese men engage in competitive market practices such as haggling and bartering. While these competitive marketing practices may be culturally accepted at local markets in China (Orr, 2007), the PNG women sellers disdain the practice, which they regard as socially unacceptable in the context of informal rural PNG markets (Schram, 2016). I argue that this cultural friction ultimately boils down to differing attitudes regarding the role of building social relationships in PNG market-places compared to local Chinese markets. Whereas rural markets in Melanesia are strongly centred around building social relationships (Busse & Sharp, 2019), bargaining in local markets in China constitutes what Orr (2007, pp. 75–6) describes as a primary genre (Bakhtin, Holquist & Emerson, 1986) that has the tightly circumscribed communicative purpose of commodity exchange, rather than building social relations. There is a clash of values at the Marmar market. While developing social relations and mutual obligations is central to the Melanesian market-place, Chinese expatriate workers engage in competitive practices to seek the best price for a commodity and not build social relations. In Tok Pisin, this emphasis on commodity exchange over building relationships is loosely translated as 'money face' (*mani pes*).

This chapter begins with a review of literature concerning market-places and morality in Melanesia. A discussion of the importance of relationship building at market-places in Melanesia is then followed by a brief discussion of the Chinese presence in PNG, followed by an introduction to the details of the Ramu Nickel Cobalt Project. Ethnographic vignettes and conversational analysis display the market-place interactions I recorded between local women sellers and Chinese expatriate men, which illustrate just how the Chinese workers' practice of haggling and bartering undermines the local women sellers' expectations at the market. This is shown in the local women sellers' learning of the Chinese names for coin denominations and items that are sold. The women sellers have learned the Chinese names to specify a price from the Chinese buyers and to emphasise their interest in money and not bargaining.

I argue that the practice of haggling not only prevents complex trade relationships or a moral economy from developing between the Chinese expatriates and PNG nationals, but that the local women sellers have come to perceive the differences between themselves and the *Sainaman* (Chinese) as incommensurable. By this, I mean that while the Chinese haggle and barter at the Marmar market, locals are unable to behave similarly at either the market-place or the Chinese-run trade stores in town and must follow strict market norms that convey equality and respect.

Markets in Melanesia

According to an official Metallurgical Corporation of China (MCC) company press release circulated in a PNG newspaper, the Marmar market has been touted as an 'ideal business spinoff' and a 'wonderful source of income' for rural women (Kila, 2017). My field work, however, found a less benign situation at the market-place, one which reveals the challenges that local Papua New Guineans face when interacting with Chinese expatriate refinery workers. Busse and Sharp (2019) argue that it is the process of forming and maintaining relationships that is critical to aspects of market-place interactions in Melanesia.

> In Melanesia, exchange is central to identity and relationship with others. People are created and sustained through exchange, and they remain entangled within networks of obligation and reciprocity. While discussions of markets in the West frequently background the role of social relations, Melanesians are certain that relationships are central. (Busse & Sharp, 2019, p. 212)

On any given day, the Marmar market-place comprises between twenty and thirty vendors sitting underneath the raintree on patches of bare earth near the roadside. However, unlike the many markets situated across PNG rural villages, the Marmar market-place is different in that PNG women sellers trade with between fifty and one hundred Chinese expatriate workers on a daily basis. Roughly half of the women sellers come from Mindere village, which is approximately ten minutes walk from the market-place; however, some travel from other nearby hamlets and villages further afield to sell their vegetables at the market-place (see Leach, 2011). Overall, the market is unusual in that it is a place where grassroots Papua New Guineans freely interact with Chinese expatriate workers, who usually do not venture outside the razor wire–encircled mining fence, to exchange seafood and vegetables for money.

In Melanesian markets, different social interactions can define a transactable entity as a gift or a commodity (Busse, 2019). What distinguishes a gift from a commodity is not the object per se, but rather how the object is given and the intentions of the transactors. For example, Busse (2019) documents the practice of 'giving extra' at the Goroka market. This practice is a product-based price reduction that is fully under the control of the women. For example, when a customer buys three onions for one kina (K1), the onion seller may give them an extra onion. When asked, the seller remarks that they are giving the extra onion to thank the person for buying it from them, and to encourage future service. Busse and Sharp (2019) further explain that in this practice of 'giving extra', objects of the same category can be used simultaneously as commodities and gifts. This leads Busse (2019) to remark that just because a market-place exchange appears on the surface to be a transaction between commodities, this does not necessarily mean that people are engaging in mere commodity exchange; beneath the surface there may be greater interpersonal interactions at play. During my field work at the market, several women sellers engaged in this practice of 'giving extra' with me when I bought peanuts or bananas from them; however, I did not observe any women sellers 'giving extra' to the Chinese expatriate workers. Similar to Busse and Sharp's (2019) analysis, I claim that in my case study of the Marmar market-place there are greater interpersonal interactions at play than the mere commodity exchange that appears at the surface.

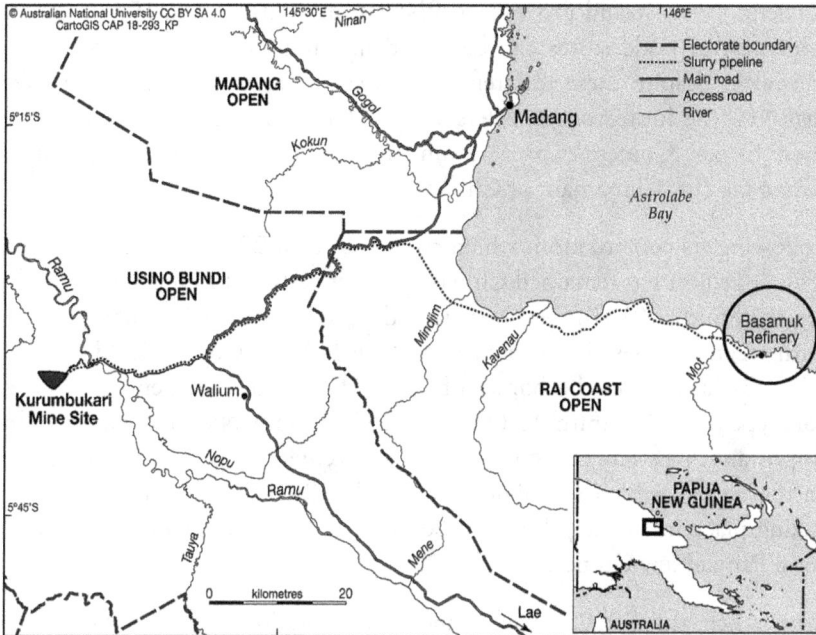

Map 7.1 The Ramu Nickel Project Basamuk refinery (encircled)
Source: ANU CartoGIS.

The Chinese refinery workers that local PNG women interact with at the Marmar market are, in fact, quite different to the Chinese expatriates they usually encounter. Since there are no Chinese-run trade stores at the Ramu Nickel Project's refinery or mine site, local women sellers most commonly interact with Chinese expatriates at trade stores in Madang town, approximately two hours away by dinghy boat. While the Chinese refinery employees are fly-in fly-out workers (with whom I found extreme difficulty communicating with during my field work), Smith (2013b) estimates that the majority of new Chinese investors in the PNG retail sector hail from Fuqing, a coastal community in Fujian Province in China. These Fuqing merchants have now become ubiquitous across both urban and rural PNG; however, there are no Chinese merchants, Fuqing or otherwise, located at either the Ramu Nickel mine site or the refinery community at Basamuk (see Map 7.1). This is because the operator, the MCC, regards these Fujianese migrants as damaging to the reputation of other long-standing Chinese investors in PNG due to their alleged involvement in organised crime (Smith, 2013b, p. 339). Long-standing Chinese communities date back as far as the colonial era of German New Guinea, and their descendants are more commonly found in either Rabaul, West New Britain Province or

Kavieng, New Ireland Province of PNG (Cahill, 2012; Wu, 1982). Today, Chinese-run trade stores can be found in almost every corner of PNG. However, despite these differences between types of Chinese expatriates in PNG, the local women sellers at the Marmar market-place refer to all these diverse Chinese expatriates under the same Tok Pisin group name: *Sainaman* (lit. Chinaman, or Chinese).

Following its construction, which commenced in 2005, the Ramu Nickel Cobalt Project has remained China's largest investment in the South Pacific region (Smith, 2013a). However, this title has the potential to change hands with recent Chinese investment in the Frieda River Copper-Gold Project, which is located on the border of PNG's East and West Sepik provinces (Skrzypek, 2020; Smith & Dinnen, 2015). Ramu Nickel remains as an important case study that symbolises China's emerging geopolitical presence in the region, which is embodied in the localised day-to-day interactions taking place in Madang Province between Chinese expatriate workers and local Papua New Guineans.

Ever since the 1960s when minerals exploration commenced in the Bundi region of Madang Province, local landowner expectations for a mining development have been high (Zimmer-Tamakoshi, 1997, 2001). During the 2002 election campaign, PNG's political 'father of the nation' Sir Michael Somare promised that, if elected, his National Alliance Party would find a developer for the project. After winning the election, then Prime Minister Somare invited the Chinese government to appoint its state-owned enterprise, the MCC, as majority (85 per cent) developer of the project. A raft of government-to-government agreements were subsequently signed between China and PNG (Matbob, 2014, p. 60).

The Ramu Nickel Cobalt Project comprises three main sites in Madang Province: the company headquarters located in Madang town, a mine located in Usino-Bundi District, and a refinery located in Rai Coast District. At the mine site, a relatively low-grade 0.5 per cent nickel laterite ore is strip mined from the Kurumbukari plateau, located at roughly 800 m elevation above the Ramu valley. From the Kurumbukari mine site, nickel and cobalt ore is pumped as slurry through a 135-kilometre pipeline. Breakages in the pipeline have been known to occur, causing slurry to burst along the Ramu highway and cause concern for roadside communities (*PNG Today*, 2016). Once the slurry reaches the Basamuk refinery on the Rai Coast, it is processed in one of three autoclaves in a procedure called high-pressure acid leaching. The refined nickel/cobalt intermediary is then shipped to China for further processing, and the remaining slurry waste is controversially dumped into an underwater canyon 150 metres below the ocean's surface in a process called deep sea tailings placement (DSTP). This method of mine waste disposal came into question during the construction phase of the project, when Rai Coast landowners placed a temporary, but ultimately unsuccessful, court injunction on construction of the DSTP facility (Coumans, 2018). The project has faced regular criticism, with worker riots in 2014, mining accidents in 2015 and accidental ocean spillages (Fox, 2019).

Sunrise at Marmar

It is sunrise as I walk along the dusty limestone road from Mindere village to the main gate entrance of the Ramu NiCo Basamuk refinery workers' accommodation site. The warm orange tropical sun quickly rises above the canopy, bringing first light to the Rai Coast. There are no government services, churches or trade stores located near the accommodation site, and only employees are allowed to enter the razor wire–encircled perimeter. Inside the fence are services available only to employees, including a mess hall, basketball courts and accommodation blocks. While the mess offers both Western and Chinese-style cuisine to cater to the tastes of both expatriate and local employees, the Chinese workers are also known to cook their own food individually in their accommodation blocks. For this reason, and to break the monotony of consuming the same meals at the company mess each day, the Chinese workers frequent the Marmar market-place in search of fresh vegetables and seafood to supplement their diet.

The Marmar market-place is located under a large raintree, about 500 metres from the accommodation site's main entry gate. There are no tables or chairs, so women sellers sit on the ground by their goods, which they arrange neatly. Each morning, Marmar is abuzz with activity as Chinese expatriate workers walk outside the main gate to buy fish and vegetables from local female women sellers. Unlike other rural markets on the Rai Coast, Marmar caters primarily for the majority-Chinese expatriate refinery workers. Each morning I would wake up before dawn to see the market at its busiest, usually during the refinery's shift rotation time between 6 a.m. and 8 a.m. Outside of these hours, Marmar transforms into a small and quiet 'buai' (betelnut) market catering almost exclusively to Papua New Guinean national refinery employees.

Above the hive of activity is the wafting scent of Chinese *Hong He* brand cigarettes . Men in orange and blue hi-vis uniforms stand over the women sellers, inspecting the fish that were caught the evening before by their relatives. Chinese men are holding up smartphones and taking pictures of large fruits and fishes, laughing and cajoling each other to buy items as they amble under the raintree. The women sellers sit, quietly and patiently, waiting for the workers to buy their items. Suddenly a crowd of orange-clad workers swarm around a new woman, who has arrived to sell a bag of fresh fish. Chinese men wave money in her face while picking up and inspecting the fish. Some tap her on the shoulder shouting *'poloman, poloman'* ('friend, friend') to attract the woman's attention. The men grab the fish out of the woman's woven *bilum* bag, hand her money, place the fish into their 'RAMU NICO' branded plastic bags they have obtained from the mess hall, then wander back to their razor wire–encircled accommodation block. Some men try to barter with the women sellers using food from the mess hall, offering sausages, bread rolls and packets of washing powder in return for vegetables. Other workers attempt to barter for food with soap and instant noodles. One local woman openly mocks the Chinese pronunciation of a PNG brand of soap, 'Was Was': *'no wasi wasi, nogat!'* ('no soap, no!'), the woman exclaims using foreigner talk, *'Mi laikim mani lo skul fees'* ('I want money for my child's school fees').

Some women sellers are more direct with their disdain for the Chinese workers. A local woman selling fish attempts to attract the attention of the Chinese workers. They walk past, ignoring her, and she mutters *'Eh bargain lain, idiot!'* loud enough for myself and the other female sellers to hear her and respond with a chuckle. I am unclear whether the women talk like this normally, or if my presence has provoked them to become more openly insulting than usual. Here, the woman uses the term *'bargain lain'* (a person who haggles) in a derogatory sense to refer to the Chinese expatriate workers who practice haggling.

'Sainaman! No cheapey-cheapey!' exclaims another woman, again imitating the Chinese workers' words and pronunciation in an example of foreigner talk. Another woman shouts out with more foreigner talk: *'Yu cheapa-cheapa man kam yu noken toktok!'* ('You cheap man come, you cannot speak!'), and the local women sellers erupt in laughter. The woman seems to be either insulting the Chinese worker for his lack of Tok Pisin proficiency, or instructing the worker not to haggle, or perhaps a combination of the two.

After the workers have returned to their shifts, and the market becomes quiet again, a woman explains to me how some Chinese attempt to barter with the women sellers, and how things were different when a previous Australian minerals exploration company, Highlands Pacific Limited, was developer during the project's pre-construction phase:

> *Em ol waitman ikam, ol boat ship i kam na ol waitman ikam, em ol mama sa holim mani. Ol sa kam baim lo mipla. baim stret na mipla sa holim mani. Ol go aut tasol na Saina kam na nogat. Exchange, kaikai na soap tasol … Em sa hard tru lo go lo haus sik, kampani ino halivim mipela. wokabaout tasol. Em hard tru lo wokabaout … Mipla Mindere nogat wanpla kampani helpim mipela.*

(When the white-men came on boats, us women had money in our pockets. The white-men would buy things from us, and we would have money. They've left now, and the Chinese are here and we don't have money. The Chinese just barter with food and soap … It's hard to go to the aid post, the company doesn't help us. It's hard to walk there. Us people from Mindere don't have a company to help us).

There is a sense of nostalgia in the woman's description of the time when Highlands Pacific Limited, the Australian minerals exploration company, was the developer during the pre-construction phase. The woman equates the presence of white men to a surplus of money in the local community, in contrast to the present when the Chinese are less willing to part with their money among the local women sellers.

Other women sellers explain to me the Chinese tendency to bargain or barter for fruits:

> *Yu lukim Sainaman baim samting. Mipela pickim pineapple ikam putim tri Kina, em ol tok tu Kina … em traim baim wantaim kaikai or kaikai lo mess or Omo.*

(Look at this Chinese buying something. We pick pineapples and sell them for three kina, but he wants them for only two kina … They try to buy things with food, or food from the mess hall, or washing powder).

> *Ol exchange tasol. Ol mama ol needim mani. long skul fees long ol pikinini. klos blong ol Saina. Saina ol kam na ol bagarapim tingting long ol mama. Ol laikim exchange wantaim soap, or kaikai, o disla kain … Samting wanem ol putim lo fridge na kol istap ya na givim na giamanim mama.*

> (They just exchange. Us women need money for our children's school fees, or clothes from the Chinese stores. The Chinese have come and ruined the mindset of us women. They like to barter with soap or food, or these kind of things … They try to give us cold things that have been in the fridge, and cheat us women).

Here, the woman uses a powerful phrase to indicate how the practices of bartering and haggling have changed the mindsets of the local women sellers (*'bagarapim tingting long ol mama'*) and equates the practice of bartering to a form of cheating the women sellers out of earning money. The woman clearly states that she needs money for her children's school fees, or to buy clothes from the Chinese-run stores in town. By referring to the Chinese stores in town (*'klos blong ol Saina'*), the woman is making an indirect link between the Chinese retail workers in town and the Chinese expatriate workers that she engages with at the refinery. She is also making a point about the different rules applying in those stores while also highlighting a commonality between Chinese trade stores and the women sellers' understanding of appropriate behaviours in both the Marmar market and Chinese-run trade stores.

Transcripts of market-place interactions

During my field work at the Marmar market-place, I documented some of the interactions that took place between the Chinese expatriates and local women sellers. The following section outlines some transcripts of anonymised dialogue that illustrate more examples of foreigner talk between the two groups.

Transcript number 1:

'Pis nogudi'

Sainaman	*'Hamas?'*
	(How much?)
PNG	*'Teti kina'*
	(Thirty kina)
Sainaman	*'Seti kina? Pis nogudi'*
	(Thirty kina? This fish is bad)
PNG	*'Ino nogudi, olo man sa hatwok'*
	(It's not bad, those men worked hard)

In this dialogue, the *Sainaman's* focus is on the quality and price of the fish. Declaring that the fish is not good *('pis nogudi')* is a common strategy employed when bargaining in Chinese markets that Orr (2007, p. 85) describes as 'product talk'. When the *Sainaman* questions the price of the fish *('seti kina?')*, this is another example of a common bargaining strategy in Chinese markets called 'price talk' (Orr, 2007, p. 77), which can involve asking about price, naming the price, complaining about the price, justifying the price and so on. In contrast to the *Sainaman's* price talk and product talk, the PNG seller emphasises the degree of labour *('hatwok')* required to catch the fish and bring it to market. This aligns with Busse's (2019) argument that price is reflective of the degree of labour required to produce the good, not the market-driven supply or demand forces. There is a social disconnect between what the price reflects to the producer and what it reflects to the buyer. For the Chinese buyer, price is indicative of the quality of the item, or perhaps also the buyer's skill in bargaining down the price. However, for the PNG female producer–seller, price is indicative of the hard work taken by the seller's kin to catch the fish. There is a broader kinship community of production at work here, where fish are often caught by partners, brothers, in-laws and other members of the household unit the day before and then brought to market by the women sellers. Here, price is directly related to the degree of labour required to produce the item, which is a personal reflection of the seller and her relationship network that assisted her in bringing the fish to market. For the local vendor, an attempt to bargain down the price of the fish is, in a sense, demeaning the woman and her network's collective labour, which has already exerted effort to catch the fish and bring it to the market-place.

Transcript number 2:

'We can't bargain at your stores'

Sainaman	*'Dis seven kina'*
	(This is seven kina)
PNG	*'Seven kina nogat, ten kina wan-wan'*
	(Not seven kina, ten kina each)
Sainaman	…
	(Silent, holds seven kina in front of the woman)
PNG	*'Putim narapla tri kina antap. Mani istap lo bilum'*
	(Add another three kina. The money is in your bag)

Sainaman	...
	(Silent, continues to hold seven kina in front of the woman)
PNG	*'Ol bigpla bigpla man. Bai ol ino nap mekim sem lo yu.*
	Mipela laik go kisim samting lo stoa lo yupla, mipela bai noinap mekim displa kain'
	(You are big men. We cannot behave the same as you.
	When we want to buy something at your trade stores we can't behave like this)

In this example, the *Sainaman* attempts to bargain down the price of goods; however, the PNG vendor notes that they are unable to behave similarly at the Chinese-run trade stores in Madang town. Again, the woman is defining rules by drawing attention to the approved morality of trade store transactions that should also apply to the market. For the PNG sellers, their inability to bargain at Chinese-run trade stores (or at any other stores in Madang town for that matter) draws attention to the unequal power relations inherent in this exchange. PNG sellers are aware that they are engaging in an unequal exchange with the Chinese.

Transcript number 3:

'Okela'

PNG	*'Twenti kina okela'*
	(Twenty kina okela)
Sainaman	*'Ten kina okela'*
PNG	*Faiv, faiv, faiv, faiv'* (points to each individual crab)
	(Five, five, five, five)
Sainaman	*'No! Ten kina okela'* (Holds a ten kina note out in front of the woman)
	(No! Ten kina okela)
PNG	*'OK fiftin kina okela'*
	(Ok, fifteen kina okela)
Sainaman	*'No! No no'*
	(No! No no)

PNG	*'Twenty kina okela'*
	(Twenty kina okela)
Sainaman	*'Okela!'*
	(Okela!)
PNG	*'Twenty kina okela'*
	(Twenty kina okela)
Sainaman	*'Poloman, okela!'*
	(Friend, okela)
PNG	*'Faiv kina more. Twenti kina'*
	(Five kina more. Twenty kina)
Sainaman	…
	(Silent, holds out a K10 note and K2 note)
PNG	*'No! Tri kina moa'*
	(No! Three kina more)
Sainaman	*'Okela!'*
	(Okela!)
PNG	*'Tri kina moa'*
	(Three kina more)
Sainaman	*'Okela! Noguda'* (Points to the bag of seafood)
	(Okela! No good)
PNG	*'Guda! Tri kina moa'*
	(Good! Three kina more)
Sainaman	…
	(Picks up bag, hands K12 to the woman)
PNG	*'OK, go pinis'*
	(OK, now leave) (accepts final offer of twelve kina)

In this example, both the *Sainaman* and the PNG woman imitate each other using the word *'okela'*. It is possible that the Chinese may have misheard the PNG pronunciation of the Tok Pisin word *'olgeta'* (all, every, all together), which they pronounce as *'okela'*. For the Papua New Guineans, they then imitate this new term, *'okela'*, to facilitate communication as an example of foreigner talk. It is also possible that the term *'okela'* stems from the Singapore English phrase *'ok la'*, where *la* is an intensifier. Some Chinese workers may have learned this Singapore English phrase while transiting from China to PNG via Singapore; however, it is more likely to be a Chinese mispronunciation of the Tok Pisin term *'olgeta'*, which is then imitated by PNG sellers in an example of foreigner talk.

Foreigner talk

When a speaker is confronted with someone who is not fluent in their own language, Velupillai (2015) claims that the speaker will intuitively alter their speech. Sometimes likened to baby talk, foreigner talk occurs when a speaker simplifies their own language when speaking with someone with little proficiency in that language. Linguists theorise that foreigner talk may have a possible role in the emergence of pidgin languages, as outlined in the 'foreigner talk theory' (Velupillai, 2015, p. 141). This theory suggests that it is the conscious simplification by speakers when interacting with speakers of other languages that forms the basis for the structure of the new pidgin language.

The examples of foreigner talk that have emerged at Marmar market demonstrate not only the capacity for linguistic creativity but also an attempt by both local women sellers and Chinese expatriates to come together and interact through trade.

Table 7.1 PNG imitation of Chinese coin denominations

Coin denomination	PNG seller says	Chinese say	Chinese character
10 toea	'ee-mo'	Yī máo	一毛 'ten cents'
20 toea	'lay-mo'	Liǎng máo	两毛 'twenty cents'
50 toea	'oo-mo'	Wǔmáo	五毛 'fifty cents'

Source: Table compiled by author. Images copyright V. Gladysh, accessed via: en.numista.com/catalogue.

Attempting to communicate more effectively with Chinese expatriates, some of the local women sellers have learned the terminology for Chinese coin denominations, as shown in Table 7.1 above. This seems to be an attempt by women to negotiate price more effectively and perhaps empower themselves against bargaining. I observed some women sellers communicating nonverbally with hand gestures while indicating one, two or five fingers, to indicate the price associated with their goods. In addition to this, some women sellers have also learned the Chinese names for some items that they sell to the Chinese workers. One word I often heard among women sellers at the market was *'tagozi'*, which is an imperfect imitation of the Chinese word for gas lighter: dǎhuǒjī (打火机).

Second, the local women sellers' attitudes towards Chinese market behaviour, primarily haggling and bartering, shapes the women's perceptions about the contested morality and moral economy of Chinese, or *Sainaman* in Tok Pisin. Many of the conversations are attempts by the women to describe and define the situation and interactions in the market and its rules of (moral) behaviour; as a result, they produce and reproduce stereotypes of the Chinese as a reified group. Further, this research contributes to a growing body of literature concerning markets and morality in PNG (Busse & Sharp, 2019). While Busse and Sharp's research contributes to our understanding of social relations, personhood and gender in PNG market-places, my chapter adds both a linguistic and cross-cultural dimension to this body of knowledge.

A fragmented moral economy?

Stemming from the work of Thompson (1971) and Scott (1976), Carrier (2018, p. 30) defines the term moral economy as the mutual obligations that arise when people transact with each other over time. Moral economic activity occurs in relationships and helps to reproduce those relationships in which the transactors have become obligated to each other because of their past transactions. In their analysis of market-places and morality in PNG, Busse and Sharp (2019, p. 184) discuss moral economy in terms of relationships at Melanesian markets:

> Relationships develop and obligations emerge from a history of interactions, each transaction builds on those before it and provides the base for future transactions, and from this emerges appropriate ways to act and transact. The way people exchange, and their relationships and obligations with one another, are also mutually reinforcing and constituting.

In their description of rural Melanesian market-places such as Marmar, Busse and Sharp (2019) argue that relationship building plays a fundamental role in the moral economy between buyer and seller. However, in contrast to this Melanesian perspective, Orr claims that at Chinese markets the relationships between buyers and sellers are radically different. Orr (2007, p. 93) argues that Chinese buyers and sellers regard each other as outgroup persons (Hofstede, 1980) with whom the normative relationship is dissociative or even competitive (Triandis & Vassilou, 1972). Herein lies the fundamental difference and clash in the approaches towards relationship building at the Marmar market-place. While building relationships of mutual obligation is fundamental to the way Melanesians behave in rural market-places, Orr (2007) claims that buyers and sellers in local Chinese markets regard each other as competitors, who are not members of the same group. Both the local PNG women sellers and the expatriate Chinese men are behaving in ways that they each regard as culturally appropriate for each of their own local market scenarios; however, there is a fundamental clash of values when it comes to the role of relationship building at the markets. This is the source of the cultural friction that occurs at the Marmar market-place.

While it would be tempting to issue a blanket statement that 'all Melanesians do not practice haggling at market-places', evidence suggests otherwise. Unlike Sharp's (2019) research into the moral economy of PNG highlanders who haggle for betelnut with coastal producers, in my case study there are quite limited moral obligations between Chinese expatriate workers who haggle and barter with local women sellers. In this fragmented moral economy, Chinese expatriate workers subvert PNG market-place norms by haggling and bartering, even though this practice is deemed culturally acceptable at local markets in China.

There are several factors inhibiting the development of mutual obligations between buyers and sellers that would constitute a moral economy. First, the extremely limited common language between buyers and sellers inhibits any highly developed trade relationships from forming between the Chinese expatriates and local women sellers. This lack of common language, and the use of foreigner talk, may contribute to the sense of frustration and antagonism that local women sellers feel towards the Chinese refinery workers. The extremely limited lingua franca contributes to the women perceiving the Chinese, or *Sainaman*, as anonymous—as far as the women see, they wear the same orange and blue hi-vis uniform and speak the same unintelligible language. Due to the limited communication between the two groups, and the fact that the Chinese tend to congregate among themselves at the market, there are limited opportunities for ongoing ties to develop between buyer and seller.

Another factor limiting the development of mutual obligations between buyers and sellers is the intermittency of women sellers at the Marmar market. Most women sellers only visit the market-place a couple of times a week—when they have a surplus of vegetables in their gardens. The rest of the week, they work in their gardens or attend to household duties. This means that there is less opportunity for returning or daily buyers and sellers to develop a sense of mutual obligation. These limited mutual obligations between buyers and sellers enable the Chinese to subvert local PNG market customs and conventions and instead impose their own conventions at the market. Likewise, PNG women sellers are attempting to subvert Chinese market conventions by expressing their dislike of bargaining.

These factors contribute to the sense of anonymity at the rural Marmar market-place, which I argue makes it easier for the Chinese to engage in competitive market practices such as haggling and bartering, to the dislike of local women sellers. As mentioned earlier, Orr (2007, p. 93) argues that at Chinese markets, buyers and sellers regard each other as outgroup persons with whom the normative relationship is dissociative or even competitive. If there was more of a common language and returning business among the customers, there would be more opportunities for rapport to develop between the buyers and sellers. In this regard, the market-place is somewhat anonymised, and in the absence of any mutually agreed obligations, both Chinese expatriates and local PNG women sellers behave as they would normally in either Chinese or Melanesian market-places.

Gendered interactions

The majority of market-place interactions took place between local women sellers and Chinese expatriate men; however, there were some rare exceptions to this generalisation. Occasionally, one of the very few Chinese female expatriate employees would visit the Marmar market early in the morning. These women behaved much less aggressively towards the local women sellers, and often kneeled down to engage with the local women sellers at eye level, rather than standing above them. I did not observe Chinese expatriate women haggling or bartering with the local women sellers. This would suggest that Chinese conventions around market haggling at Marmar market-place seem to be gendered.

On a similar note, I did not notice Papua New Guinean men selling fish or vegetables. The men would refer to the market-place as a *'mama market'* (lit. mothers' market). Occasionally, husbands or other members of kin would attend the market to observe the Chinese expatriates, standing a few feet back from the women sellers as if to adjudicate the interactions with Chinese. I did not witness the men intervening in market transactions, or any physical altercations around the market. Many of the men who observed were company employees, simply killing time between their shift breaks. The market seemed for many to be a source of entertainment. Overall, the limited interactions between genders in this environment contributes to a limited moral economy developing between the local women sellers and male Chinese expatriates.

One possible explanation for the reluctance of the Chinese expatriate men to part with their money was the difficulty in obtaining cash on the Rai Coast of Madang Province. Since there are no automatic teller machines (ATMs) located anywhere near the Ramu NiCo Basamuk refinery, Chinese expatriates would have to take all their cash with them from Madang town before travelling for two hours on the company ferry to the refinery. This lack of 'cashflow' was a common complaint expressed to me by both landowners and PNG employees in middle management. One Papua New Guinean middle manager described to me how he had tried for years to encourage the company to install an ATM nearby the refinery but had no success.

This unequal balance of power between Chinese expatriates and local women sellers complements Sharp's (2019) observation of a power imbalance between haggling highland betelnut buyers and lowlands betelnut sellers in PNG. Just like the women sellers at Marmar market, lowland betelnut producers and sellers have negative opinions of the practice of haggling. However, there is an added gendered dimension associated with the power imbalance of haggling and bartering at the Marmar market. The local women seller's antagonism towards the Chinese expatriate men is illustrated in their derogatory and at times mocking language towards *Sainaman*. On top of this, the competitive market practices further reinforce the power imbalances between local women sellers and Chinese expatriate men.

Racial stereotypes at the market

Rather than being a place where a simple commodity exchange takes place, I argue that the Marmar market is a place where local women sellers shape their derogatory stereotypes of *Sainaman*. This chapter takes a similar approach to Busse and Sharp (2019, p. 127), who imagine market-places in PNG not just as gatherings at particular places focused on trade, but as significant social meeting places where people of different cultural backgrounds interact and form new social connections, and also as 'at times a source of anxiety, as people with different moral understandings interact'. The conflict over haggling and bartering at Marmar market-place demonstrates different understandings of exchange and the role of relationship building at market-places between the Chinese expatriate workers and local women sellers.

Through these market-place interactions with Chinese expatriates, local women sellers construct stereotypes and perceptions around what it means to be Chinese or a *Sainaman*. The way *Sainaman* go about their haggling and bartering demonstrates contested moralities of exchange between the Chinese expatriates and local women sellers. These value judgements pertain to the way that Chinese expatriates interact with the local women sellers through negotiating down the price of their goods or attempting to barter with food. Local women-sellers are frustrated with a perceived inequality whereby Chinese can negotiate down the price of vegetables at the market, but the women sellers are not permitted to haggle or barter at the Chinese-run supermarkets or trade stores in Madang town. A common sentiment that local women sellers expressed to me was that *'they bargain with us, yet we can't bargain at their stores'*. Busse and Sharp (2019, p. 145) observed similar negative sentiments at the Kokopo market-place towards Asian customers attempting to negotiate down the price of food:

> In 2017 an Asian woman's attempt to negotiate down the price of some food in the Kokopo market-place was mocked by one vendor, with much laughter from surrounding vendors; 'you try and reduce our prices, but we can't reduce the prices at your [Asian-owned] stores'. The Asian women reportedly did not own a store, but the vendor's comments reflect different cultural expectations about different ways to transact in different places. (Busse & Sharp, 2019, p. 145)

While the Asian woman at Kokopo is assumedly quite different from the Chinese expatriate refinery workers in Basamuk, both the Kokopo and Basamuk local vendors express similar sentiments towards Asians practicing haggling. Both local vendors perceive of their relationship with *Sainaman* as incommensurable—their standards of behaviour in the market-place are not equal. Other common sentiments expressed to me about the Chinese workers were that *'ol Sainaman sa mani pes'* (the Chinese are money face), *'ol Sainaman sa bargain lain'* (Chinese are bargainers), *'ol het pen lain'* (they're obstinate) and *'ol kain olsem brick wall'* (they're stubborn). These sentiments display the Chinese workers' refusal to follow PNG market-place norms and instead practice their own market-place conventions.

Conclusion

This chapter has outlined how rural women sellers on the Rai Coast of PNG perceive of Chinese expatriate workers at the Ramu Nickel Project, through their market-place interactions and primarily through exchange haggling and sometimes bartering. In this sense, it tells only one side of the story, predominantly from the perspective of the local PNG women sellers, and more research is needed into the Chinese expatriate perspective of the Marmar market-place. By building on Busse and Sharp's (2019) research on markets and morality in PNG, I discuss the challenges of cross-cultural communication and price negotiation at an informal rural PNG market-place.

On a socio-linguistic level, I have also outlined examples of foreigner talk at the market-place, and other examples of communication challenges between local women sellers and Chinese expatriate men. Over time, there is the potential for either a Tok Pisin-Chinese pidgin to emerge between PNG nationals and Chinese expatriates at either the Ramu Nickel Project's Kurumbukari mine site, the Basamuk refinery, at the local markets surrounding these communities, or at other locations in PNG such as trade stores or construction sites where Chinese expatriates regularly interact with PNG nationals. A Tok Pisin-Chinese pidgin could take the form of either a trade pidgin or a mine pidgin. The development of pidgin languages is common among multi-lingual workforces at mine sites, with linguists documenting examples in Africa such as Shaba Swahili spoken in the Democratic Republic of Congo, or Fanakalo spoken in South Africa (Velupillai, 2015, pp. 24–9). In sum, rural 'grassroots' Papua New Guineans are more likely to create often derogatory racial stereotypes about *all* Chinese in PNG, labelling them as *Sainaman* and asserting that *'they bargain with us, but we can't bargain at their stores'*. Under this fragmented moral economy between local female fish and vegetable sellers and the predominantly male Chinese expatriate refinery workers, the Marmar market-place will continue to be a site for cross-cultural misunderstandings and tensions.

References

Bakhtin, M. M., Holquist, M., & Emerson, C. (1986). *Speech genres and other late essays* (1st ed. Vol. no. 8). University of Texas Press.

Busse, M. (2019) Morality and the Concept of the Market Seller among Gehamo. *Oceania, 89*(2), pp. 205–19. doi.org/10.1002/ocea.5220

Busse, M., & Sharp, T. L. M. (2019). Marketplaces and Morality in Papua New Guinea: Place, Personhood and Exchange. *Oceania, 89*(2), pp. 126–53. doi.org/10.1002/ocea.5218

Cahill, P. (2012). *Needed but not Wanted: Chinese in Colonial Rabaul 1884–1960.* CopyRight Publishing.

Carrier, J. G. (2018). Moral economy: What's in a name. *Anthropological Theory, 18*(1), pp. 18–35.

Coumans, C. (2018). Into the deep: science, politics and law in conflicts over marine dumping of mine waste. *International Social Science Journal, 68*(229–230), pp. 303–23. doi.org/10.1111/issj.12199

Ferguson, C. A. (1975). Toward a Characterization of English Foreigner Talk. *Anthropological Linguistics, 17*(1), pp. 1–14.

Fox, L. (2019). Chinese-owned Ramu Nickel plant spills 200,000 litres of 'toxic' slurry into the sea. *ABC News.* www.abc.net.au/news/2019-08-30/chinese-owned-mine-in-png-spills-200000-litres-of-toxic-slurry/11464108

Geertz, C. (1979). Suq: The Bazaar Economy in Sefrou. In C. Geertz, H. Geertz, & L. Rosen (Eds.), *Meaning and order in Moroccan society: three essays in cultural analysis* (pp. 123–244). Cambridge University Press.

Hofstede, G. H. (1980). *Culture's consequences: international differences in work-related values.* Sage Publications.

Kila, J. G. (2017, March 3). The Unique 'Marmar' Market. *The National.* www.thenational.com.pg/unique-marmar-market/

Leach, J. (2011). 'Twenty Toea has no power now.' Property, Customary Tenure and Pressure on Land near the Ramu Nickel Project Area, Madang, PNG.' *Pacific Studies, 34*(2/3), pp. 295–322.

Matbob, P. (2014). We are not anti-Asia—just victims of poor governance: a media perspective. In P. D'Arcy, P. Matbob, & L. Crowl (Eds.), *Pacific-Asia Partnerships in Resource Development* (pp. 59–71). DWU Press.

Orr, W. W. F. (2007). The bargaining genre: A study of retail encounters in traditional Chinese local markets. *Language in Society, 36*(1), pp. 73–103. doi.org/10.1017/s0047404507070042

PNG Today. (2016, March 7). Slurry pipeline leakage is not 'disaster': Ramu Nico. news.pngfacts.com/2016/03/slurry-pipeline-leakage-is-not-disaster.html

Schram, R. (2016). Indecorous, Too Hasty, Incorrect: Market and Moral Imagination in Auhelawa, Papua New Guinea. *Anthropological Quarterly, 89*(2), pp. 515–37. doi.org/10.1353/anq.2016.0041

Scott, J. C. (1976). *The moral economy of the peasant: rebellion and subsistence in Southeast Asia.* Yale University Press.

Sharp, T. L. M. (2019). Haggling Highlanders: Marketplaces, Middlemen and Moral Economy in the Papua New Guinean Betel Nut Trade. *Oceania, 89*(2), pp. 182–204. doi.org/10.1002/ocea.5221

Skrzypek, E. (2020). *Revealing the Invisible Mine: Social Complexities of an Undeveloped Mining Project, Vol. 8.* Berghahn Books. doi.org/10.2307/j.ctv287sjfm

Smith, G. (2013a). Nupela Masta? Local and Expatriate Labour in a Chinese-Run Nickel Mine in Papua New Guinea. *Asian Studies Review, 37*(2), pp. 178–95. doi.org/10.1080/10357823.2013.768598

Smith, G. (2013b). Beijing's orphans? New Chinese investors in Papua New Guinea. *Pacific Affairs, 86*(2), pp. 327–49. doi.org/10.5509/2013862327

Smith, G., & Dinnen. S. (2015). And then there were three: a new Chinese miner in Papua New Guinea. *Australian National University Department of Pacific Affairs In-Brief 2015/48.* Australian National University.

Thompson, E. P. (1971). The moral economy of the English crowd in the eighteenth century. *Past and Present, 50*(1), pp. 76–136. doi.org/10.1093/past/50.1.76

Triandis, H., & Vassilou, V. (1972). A comparative analysis of subjective culture. In H. C. Triandis (Ed.), *The analysis of subjective culture* (pp. 299–335). Wiley.

Velupillai, V. (2015). *Pidgins, Creoles and Mixed Languages: An Introduction* (Vol. 48). John Benjamins Publishing Company.

Wu, D. (1982). *The Chinese in Papua New Guinea: 1880–1980.* The Chinese University Press.

Zimmer-Tamakoshi, L. (1997). When land has a price: ancestral gerrymandering and the resolution of land conflicts at Kurumbukare. *Anthropological Forum, vii*(4), pp. 649–66. doi.org/10.1080/00664677.1997.9967478

Zimmer-Tamakoshi, L. (2001). Development and Ancestral Gerrymandering: Schneider in Papua New Guinea. In R. Feinberg & M. Ottenheimer (Eds.), *The Cultural Analysis of Kinship: The Legacy of David M. Schneider* (pp. 187–203). University of Illinois Press.

8

Trade, mines and language: The Chinese in Papua New Guinea

Alexandra Y. Aikhenvald

Section 1: The many faces of a colonial alien: The Papua New Guinea context

The island of New Guinea is the locus of extreme linguistic and cultural diversity: about a thousand languages spoken there belong to at least sixty families, in addition to quite a few isolates (linguistic 'orphans' with no known relatives). The advent of the European coloniser has added an extra dimension to this diversity. The emergence and spread of Tok Pisin— a national language and a lingua franca of Papua New Guinea (PNG), based on English—has affected the linguistic ecosystem of the country. What about the Chinese, a major group of expatriates?

The growth of Chinese immigration to PNG over the past few decades and the rapid establishment of Chinese-run enterprises are likely precursors to the emergence of special registers and new ways of speaking—a further splash of colour in the patchwork quilt of the diverse linguistic ecosystem in PNG. Two contributions to this volume, by I-Chang Kuo and by Shaun Gessler, focus on newly arising means of communication between Chinese and Papua New Guineans in the Basamuk nickel refinery in Madang Province.

When groups of people speaking different languages interact in a work or trade environment, new codes and ways of talking come about. A brief background on a few recurrent options—pidgins, creoles and foreigner talk—is in Section 2. We then offer a glimpse into Chinese-based pidgins across the Pacific and the Far East of Eurasia in Section 3. The following section addresses the 'old' and the 'new' Chinese in PNG. The Basamuk 'workplace pidgin' (addressed in Kuo's chapter) is the topic of Section 5. In Section 6, we turn to the features of the language of the Marmar market around Basamuk (the topic of Gessler's chapter). The last section contains a summary.

Section 2: Pidgins, creoles and foreigner talk: A backdrop

Throughout the process of European colonisation, people from different language groups were forced to work together as slaves or indentured workers. They would communicate with each other and with their masters using a simplified language, for limited purposes—simple commands, questions and statements. Such makeshift means of communication is known as *pidgin language* (ultimately from English *business*). A pidgin will be used in limited circumstances, most frequently for trade, and will never develop first-language learners. It will not be native to anyone (more on the development of pidgins and their linguistic features is in Parkvall & Bakker, 2013a; Winford, 2003, pp. 268–303; Mesthrie, 2008; Smith, 2002; Markussen-Daval & Bakker, 2017; and a summary in Aikhenvald, 2014, pp. 306–8; Parkvall & Bakker, 2013b contains a comprehensive bibliography on the subject).

Numerous pidgins—also referred to as trade jargons—sprang up spontaneously in various parts of the world, following the need for simple, yet efficient, communication. As Stefánsson (1909, p. 217) put it in his discussion of an Eskimo-English trade jargon of Herschel Island in Alaska,

> wherever white men have remained for a year or more in definite contact with the Eskimo people there has sprung up a more or less complete system of jargon talk mutually serviceable to both parties … At the root of many nouns … lies an English word, but it is usually so metamorphised as to be well-nigh unrecognizable.

The 'jargon talk' in question was short-lived. None of the Eskimo-based pidgins (recorded from the seventeenth century until the twentieth century) have survived (van der Voort, 2013; Bakker & Grant, 1996).

A few indigenous pidgins developed outside the European colonial rule, following the need to communicate within the context of trade. These include Pidgin Swahili in Africa and Chinook Jargon in the Pacific Northwest of North America. Trade pidgins used between speakers of neighbouring unrelated languages in New Guinea include Yimas-Arafundi Pidgin (Foley, 2013), Arafundi-Enga Pidgin (Williams, 1995), Pidgin Iatmul in the Middle Sepik region of New Guinea (Foley, 1986) and the putative Kwoma-Manambu Pidgin (Bowden, 1997; Aikhenvald, 2008). These pidgins stand apart from European trade jargons in that they developed between traditional trade partners rather than in the situations of new contacts (Parkvall & Bakker, 2013a, 2013b). The impending spread of Tok Pisin, the ubiquitous lingua franca of the country, as well as English, have taken their toll; the New Guinea pidgins went into decline, and are now only remembered by a few old people.

Once speakers of a pidgin start marrying each other, a pidgin may become the main language spoken by the next generation of children (while their indigenous languages start to wither). It then expands into a fully-fledged language that would be used for all purposes—telling stories, gossiping and talking about all sorts of topics. The pidgin grows into a creole, a language that can fulfil all the functions needed. Much of the vocabulary of European-based creoles comes from a European language (their 'lexifiers'). They will also bear the mark of those indigenous languages that must have been there in the minds of the earlier speakers of its predecessor, a pidgin. Tok Pisin is an example of a creole with English lexifier. It is believed to have emerged over a hundred years ago, on the plantations of Samoa and other areas of Melanesia, including New Britain. Its vocabulary is mostly English, with a few words from German (who controlled large areas of the New Guinea island until World War I) and Austronesian languages spoken in its birthplace.[1]

---

1   More on the evolution of Tok Pisin is in Smith (2002), Winford (2003, pp. 289–97), and Smith and Siegel (2013). An alternative hypothesis regarding the origins of Tok Pisin in Queensland is in Baker (2001). Informal reference to Tok Pisin as 'Pidgin' obscures the status of the language as a fully-fledged creole, the first language, and a mark of identity, for many. The same applies to the Solomon Islands Pijin, also a creole. Another creole language, Unserdeutsch (literally, 'our German'), or Rabaul Creole German (the only attested creole with a German lexifier), evolved in New Britain under a different set of circumstances. Unserdeutsch was developed by children from varied linguistic backgrounds in a boarding school environment as an in-group language. Following the decolonisation of Papua New Guinea, most members of the Unserdeutsch community migrated to various locations to Australia, and the language is severely endangered. A comprehensive analysis of the history and the properties in Unserdeutsch is in Maitz and Volker (2017) and Maitz (2016).

Tok Pisin is estimated to have over a hundred thousand first-language speakers, plus several million who speak it as a second language. Notably, it is the main language for workers at the Basamuk nickel refinery (Kuo, this volume) and for the women at Marmar market (Gessler, this volume)—the focus of Sections 5–6 in this chapter.

Communication between those who speak different languages may take other forms. In Ferguson's (1996, p. 177) words,

> many, perhaps all, speech communities have registers of a special kind for use with people who are regarded for one reason or another as unable to readily understand the normal speech of the community (e.g. babies, foreigners, deaf people). These forms of speech are generally felt by their users to be simplified versions of the language, hence easier to understand, and they are often regarded as imitation of the way the person addressed uses the language himself.

A register of simplified speech that 'seems quite widespread and may even be universal is "foreigner talk" which is used by speakers of a language to outsiders who are felt to have very limited command of the language or no knowledge of it at all' (see Ferguson, 1996, 1981; Fedorova, 2015). Several varieties of 'foreigner talk' are in use by native speakers who communicate with immigrant workers in European countries, and in the context of teaching, occasional encounters and tourism (see Fedorova, 2015 and references there).

The mining industry offers a fertile ground for developing new means of multi-ethnic communication. The multi-ethnic composition of the workforce and specific working conditions are conducive to creating special registers and mixed dialects, often akin to 'foreigner talk' (see an overview in Cornips & Muysken, 2019; Knotter, 2015). Different mining settings produce different results. A special mining register, known as *Cité Duits,* was developed as an in-group coalminers' language in the town of Eisden in Belgium (Pecht, 2019). *Cité Duits* combines features of Southern Dutch, German and the Maaslands dialect of Flemish spoken in the area, in addition to traits not found in any of these varieties. The new varieties may serve as in-group identity marks, setting the speakers apart from the mainstream. *Cité Duits* is now moribund, due to the decline of the coalmine, not unlike special mining varieties of Dutch in the south-eastern province of Limburg in the Netherlands, of Swahili in the Katanga Region in the southeast of the Democratic Republic of Congo (DRC) and a mixed language based on

Quechua, Aymara and Spanish in the mines of Potosí in Bolivia (Muysken, 2019). This contrasts with Fanakalo Pidgin, which developed into a creole after being chosen as the main language of the mines (Mesthrie, 2019).

Section 3: Chinese pidgins and trade languages

The spread of the Chinese diaspora, and the increase in trade and workplace relationships between the Chinese and the local populations, have created propitious conditions for the development of a wide variety of new languages and registers.

The best-known Chinese-based trade language is the China Coast Pidgin, or Chinese Pidgin English, sometimes referred to as 'the mother of all pidgins' (Ansaldo, Matthews & Smith, 2012; Matthews & Li, 2013; Mühlhäusler et al., 1996; Li, 2016, on trade pidgins in China). The language was first attested in the early-to-mid eighteenth century. The pidgin evolved as the China trade was developing, 'with British, other European and later American Ships visiting Macau, Whampoa (now Huangpu) and Canton (now Guangzhou)' (Matthews & Li, 2013, p. 206). The pidgin was 'used primarily between European traders and Chinese merchants in the limited settings in which such trade was permitted', including the treaty ports, which ceased to operate in 1949. Its main substrate language was Cantonese, with a few lexical items from Hindi, Scandinavian languages and Portuguese. World War II and the closure of the treaty ports following the Chinese Civil War:

> saw the end of the linguistic ecology which had supported Chinese Pidgin English. In Hong Kong, Chinese Pidgin English continued to be used between Europeans and Chinese servants throughout the 1960s ... but was in effect extinct by the 1990s. (Matthews & Li, 2013, p. 207)

Chinese-Russian Pidgin is another well-documented instance of a simplified language variety spontaneously evolved for the purposes of trade. The pidgin—referred to as *lomanɔj jazyk* ('broken language') or *lomanɔj russkij* ('broken Russian') and known as Kyahta language—

> was spoken between the last decades of the eighteenth and the middle of the twentieth centuries in the vast territories along the Russian-Chinese border in southern Siberia and the Russian Far East,

northern China in the city of Harbin, and along the Chinese Far
East Railway built by Russia in Manchuria in 1903. (Perekhvalskaya,
2013, p. 69)

With the development of trade throughout the nineteenth century, the
pidgin spread along the whole extent of the Russian-Chinese border,
and was in use by various local indigenous groups, besides Chinese
traders and Russian colonial settlers (Shapiro, 2010, p. 9). Inter-ethnic
communication on the Russian-Chinese border was 'abruptly interrupted
in the 1930s: the border between China and the USSR was closed, many
Chinese were deported from the border regions, and any such trade contacts
as had previously existed became impossible' (Fedorova, 2018, p. 84). This
led to the demise of the pidgin—now extinct (with just a few representatives
of Siberian minorities in the region remembering a little of it).

Chinese-Russian Pidgin was used exclusively for the purposes of trade
between various groups and the collection of fur taxes in the region. As there
was 'no mass resettling of people of different nations who would have to use
pidgin as the unique means of communication', this pidgin never acquired
first-language learners and thus never grew into a Creole—in contrast to
Tok Pisin in PNG or the many Creoles in the Caribbean (Perekhvalskaya,
2013, p. 69).

Numerous other Chinese-based pidgins have been attested across the world.
In the nineteenth century, a series of pidgins emerged in the Philippines
because of trade contacts between Spanish, local languages and Chinese
dialects spoken by traders and settlers (known as Bamboo-Spanish) (Penny,
2002, pp. 29–30). The status of a Chinese-Spanish pidgin reported to have
been spoken in Manila in the early eighteenth century remains a matter
of some controversy, centred around whether it did exist as an established
or 'stabilised' means of communication, or was a mere 'unstable jargon'
(Fernández, 2018). A pidgin Hawaiian developed because of early contact
between Hawaiians and outsiders in the 1790s, based on the Hawaiian
language. By the 1880s, it became the primary means of communication
with, and for, Chinese, Portuguese and Japanese labourers employed in
the sugar industry. The language is currently extinct; its last speaker passed
away in the 1980s (Roberts, 2013; see also Mühlhäusler et al., 1996, on
Parau Tihito, a Chinese-Tahitian pidgin, also on the verge of extinction; and
Mühlhäusler, 1983, on the Pidgin German developed in the former German
protectorate of Kiatschou (Jiaozhou) in central eastern China between 1898

and the Japanese occupation of the area in 1914). None of these pidgins evolved into a Creole, in contrast to Tok Pisin in PNG, Solomon Islands Pijin and Bislama in Vanuatu.

The development of pidgins is a common but hardly universal consequence of trade relationships. One prerequisite for a development of a pidgin is verbal communication. No pidgins developed in the situations of 'silent markets' where the exchange of products was done without verbal interaction (described for the Sawos and the Chambri peoples in the Middle Sepik: see Gewertz, 1983; Schindlbeck, 1980 and M. Schindlbeck, personal communication, 20 July 2016; Bowden, 1984). Nowadays, communication in the market-place is conducted in Tok Pisin, the language known to all parties (see Aikhenvald, 2018).

Another prerequisite for the development of pidgins by diverse groups of people speaking different languages is the existence of established relationships between them over several years—be it in the context of trade, joint work on plantations, mines or other environments. Occasional trade-based communication may not lead to the development of a pidgin. In the situation of newly emergent contexts of trade and joint employment we may be faced with instances of people spontaneously adapting their language to a foreign partner, creating foreigner talk. This communicative strategy may develop into a stabilised pidgin in the long run.

An instructive example comes from the Russian-Chinese border area in the Zabaikalskii territory of Russia and especially the Chinese border town Manzhouli. The Chinese foreign workers have limited, if any, command of Russian but pick up some words and expressions necessary for day-to-day communication. The emergent 'Chinese-Russian' variety is perceived by Russian native speakers as a 'broken language' and is the object of derision and mockery (Fedorova, 2015, pp. 144–6; Fedorova, 2011a, 2011b; Yang, 2007; Shapiro, 2010, pp. 11–2). In their interactions with Russians, Chinese speakers are looked down upon and 'are treated as non-equals to their Russian speaking interlocutors both linguistically and socially: one cannot expect full understanding from them, but, at the same time, they are not "important" enough for the Russian speakers to make serious efforts to be understood' (Fedorova, 2015, p. 144). This is iconically reflected in the way Russians address the Chinese. The polite form *Vy*, 'plural second person pronoun', is a norm in addressing an adult stranger. The Russians of the region consistently talk to Chinese immigrant workers using the familiar second singular form *ty*—a mark of lack of respect and a 'linguistic way of domineering' (Fedorova, 2015, p. 146).

Russians involved in ongoing business or personal relations with the Chinese modify their language by simplifying it and speaking ungrammatically, as if to 'imitate' their Chinese partners' imperfect speech. A first-person singular form may be used in a question to a second person . Second person singular imperative forms are preferred in declarative clauses; for example, *ne rabotaj* (negation work.second.person.imperative)—'it does not work'. In the normative Russian this can only be understood as a command: 'you (familiar) don't work!' Second person singular imperatives—which consist of the bare root and replace every verb form—are considered the 'proper way' to speak to the Chinese. These same forms were typical of the Chinese-Russian Pidgin of the olden days (Fedorova, 2012), and other Russian-based pidgins, including *govorka* (developed in long-term trade communication between Russians and the local Samoyedic-speaking populations on the Taymyr peninsula: Stern, 2005). The current Chinese-Russian emergent pidgin is in flux—its characteristics 'will be clearer when (and if)' it 'stabilises' (Shapiro, 2010, p. 13).

We now turn to the Chinese diaspora in PNG, and their communicative practices.

Section 4: In with the new: The Chinese in Papua New Guinea

The presence of the Chinese in PNG has a long history, starting from 1888 when the German New Guinea Company imported hundreds of Chinese indentured workers (most of them men) from Xiamen (formerly Amoy), Singapore, Hong Kong and Sumatra to work on sugar and coconut plantations. The Chinese population kept expanding, with different dynamics in the territory of New Guinea (formerly a German colony) and in Papua (a possession of Australia since 1906: see Wood & Backhaus, this volume, on the ways in which the Chinese were treated by the Australian Government throughout the history of the colonial occupation).

There is one major division among the Chinese in PNG. The PNG-born Chinese who were in PNG at the time of Independence and who had lived in PNG for several generations are known as 'old' Chinese' (Chin 2008 and this volume; Cahill, 2012). As Chin (this volume) puts it, 'their spiritual "home" was Rabaul, East New Britain'—where the settlers formed a community-based organisation in the early twentieth century (see Inglis, 1972, on the Chinese in PNG before Independence).

In the words of Wood and Backhaus (this volume), ever since the establishment of the Chinese in the region, 'Chinese life in New Guinea was defined primarily as within an urban enclave linked to systematic exclusions from an economy and social order largely defined by white plantations and a governing bureaucracy'. Almost all the 'old' Chinese are Christians, and they use English, even among themselves. They tend to send their children to Australia to study. Many took out Australian citizenship after Independence (Chin, 2008, this volume; see Wood & Backhaus, this volume, on the colonial character of the policies relative to extending Australian citizenship to the New Guinea Chinese).

The 'old' Chinese used to be hard-working and industrious. They ran trade-posts and shops, frequented by indigenous people. They have played a substantial role in the economy of the country, but appear to have kept themselves to themselves and presumably used English and Tok Pisin in interacting with their indigenous and expatriate clientele. The trade and employment relationships between the 'old' Chinese and the rest of the population did not appear to have resulted in the creation of a pidgin, or of any other specific communicative code.

Why so? We can suggest two possible reasons. If communication between the Chinese and the other groups was only sporadic, no specific register may have arisen, become stabilised or developed into a pidgin.

Alternatively, patterns and forms of communication between the Chinese and other groups in the early colonial periods may have 'fallen between the cracks'. In other words, nothing is known about them because no one bothered to look or document them. This resonates with the point made by Henry, Vávrová and Bragge (this volume): the 'old' Chinese 'have been largely rendered invisible in colonial and post-colonial histories of PNG'. In Laurie Bragge's words, during his time as a patrol officer just before Independence, 'the Chinese were a fact of life but were ignored basically'. The 'old' Chinese were disregarded and rendered invisible in archives, historical accounts and traditional lore. This is in stark contrast to the representation of white people across Papua New Guinean traditions. The 'meaning of a white man' (along the lines of Bashkow, 2006) is part of traditional lore and representation of histories for many indigenous societies.

A 'white man'—a European coloniser—can be viewed as an ancestral spirit (as is the case among the Ku Waru: Rumsey, 1999, similar to large portions of Australia: Dixon, 2019, pp. 156–7) or even as a cannibal or a dangerous ghost. So, the early Europeans were referred to by the Kamula of Western Province as 'aiyaluma men'—a term that means 'prohibited', 'taboo' and can be used to refer to the evil spirit that inhabits a witch's heart (Wood, 1995, p. 29; see Rumsey, 1999, on 'white man' as a cannibal).

The Kwoma of the Middle Sepik use the term *gaba* 'ghost, soul of a person who died', as an alternative to *waitman* 'European, white man or woman'. As Bowden (1997, p. 42) explains, during the early years of European contact the Kwoma thought white people were ghosts and referred to them as such. They occasionally still refer to Europeans as ghosts, though not normally in their presence. A young child, seeing a European approach, might call to its mother: *'Awi, gaba yato!'*, 'Mother, a ghost is coming!' The Yalaku, a Ndu-speaking group in contact with the Kwoma, employ the term *kaba* 'ghost' (a borrowing from Kwoma) to refer to white people and objects associated with them; for example, *kaba takwa* (ghost woman), 'a white woman', *kaba yuwa* (ghost brideprice), 'money', *kaba nagu* (ghost sago), 'bread, biscuit', *kaba mi* (ghost tree/slit.drum), 'phone, guitar' (see also Aikhenvald, 2018). The term *kaba* has derogatory overtones: the late Anna Mongowur (my classificatory mother in the Yalaku community and the oldest woman in the village) insisted on referring to me as *wama-sefi* (white-skin) rather than as *kaba takwa* (ghost woman), saying that I was too nice to be called *kaba*.

White people were integrated into the cosmology of some groups. The Manambu refer to white people and objects associated with them as *wali* 'coming from east'; for example, *wali-du* (east-man), 'white man' and *wali-kudi* (east-language), 'white people's language (English or Tok Pisin)'. White people are typically adopted into the Wulwi-Ñawi clan group (whose totems include the eastward wind and direction, and everything bright and of white colour: see Harrison, 1990; Aikhenvald, 2008). This echoes Leavitt (2000, p. 306) on 'Europeans as relatives' incorporated into the kinship and exchange system.

In contrast, the Chinese—and Asians in general—are consistently left out. They do not appear to be given any special name, other than descriptive terms; for example, Manambu *Saina-ke-de du* (China-belonging-masculine. singular man) or Yalaku *Saina* 'Chinaman, Asian'. Neither do they appear to be integrated into mythologies or totemic systems.

This is, again, in contrast to Europeans. Wood (1995, p. 23) argues that, through their narratives and attitudes, the indigenous Kamula, the 'real people', 'are capable of transforming the otherness of Europeans into something more like themselves'. The Chinese remain 'a non-transformable other'—'the outsiders are not homogenous or interchangeable because "white skins", most other humans and quasi humans are potentially transformable liminal entities, but the Chinese are not' (Wood, 1995, p. 41). Do these trends reflect a relatively shallow time–depth of interactions between the Chinese and the indigenous peoples (compared with the time–depth and the intensity of the European contact)? This question remains open.

The Chinese presence across PNG has dramatically increased since the early 2000s, with an influx of many mainland Chinese, especially the Chinese state-owned enterprises, and Chinese traders who 'started to flood the market with cheap Chinese products' (Chin, this volume; Connolly, 2020). These 'new' Chinese 'have now cemented their position as the most influential group among the Chinese community in PNG—both in politics and the economy' (Chin, this volume). A general perception nowadays is that the PNG economy is likely to eventually be overtaken by the mainland Chinese (resonating with the policies of the mainland Chinese government: see Chin, this volume). As employers and as traders, the 'new' Chinese are here to stay, and to expand.

The mainland Chinese have gradually become a dominant economic and political force in PNG. Many Chinese-owned enterprises are now major employers for the indigenous people, especially so in and around mining. The Ramu Nickel mine in Madang Province, the largest single outbound direct investment project by a Chinese company in the Pacific with its many locations (Smith, 2013, p. 180), is a case in point.

Section 5: A language in the making: Basamuk Pidgin

New workplace environments provide new requirements for communication. Within the Chinese-run Ramu Nickel mine, different worksites tend to have 'a distinctive work culture, and a distinctive set of local identities, based on shared work histories, shared cultural preferences, and often a shared local dialect' (Gessler, this volume). A source of tension in the context of the

Basamuk nickel refinery is a communication barrier between the locals and the 'new' Chinese workers and managers, who either do not know enough English or Tok Pisin to communicate, or they pretend they do not (Smith, 2013, p. 185). Papua New Guineans employed at the refinery are aware of the necessity to adapt to the new requirements by learning how Chinese expatriates work and what their work ethics is. The linguistic outcome of this is a new 'workplace pidgin' (Kuo, this volume).

This 'workplace pidgin' is described as a mixture of Tok Pisin, Chinese and English, with a strong gestural component. Learning takes place on the job. The new employees stay together and try and guess what their Chinese supervisor is saying, in addition to taking advice from other PNG staff. This learning method is described in Tok Pisin—a common language for all PNG employees within the refinery—as *wokim aksen* (make action) and *bihainim aksen* (follow action). When speaking to the Chinese staff, PNG workers state that they speak in simple sentences, and use only very specific nouns and verbs, often repeated.

A short text provided to Kuo by Nathan, a PNG employee, includes adjectives *broken* and *no good* (it is not clear from Kuo's discussion whether we are dealing with an English *no good* or Tok Pisin *nogut*, as Nathan is competent in both). Adjectives and verbs are repeated, to convey intensive meaning as in *talk talk*, 'have a discussion', and joint action as in *wok wok*, 'work together'. There are no markers of tense or aspect; the English and Tok Pisin verbs are used in their root form. An example is *we talk talk and maintenance, ah, come, ah, fix* meaning 'Let us have a discussion and inform the maintenance team to come and fix (the valve)'. Locals appear to frequently use the Mandarin Chinese *la* 'OK' at the end of a sentence. Other frequently used Mandarin words are *yǒu*, 'have', *méi yǒu*, 'not have', *hǎo,* 'good' and *huài le*, 'broken'.

A close set of frequently used Chinese words include a demonstrative *nà gè*, 'that one' (pronounced without tones, as [na ge]). In Mandarin Chinese, this form is composed of *nà*, 'that (distal demonstrative)' and *gè*, 'generic classifier'. In Mandarin, the distal demonstrative *nà* can be considered functionally unmarked, especially in combination with the generic form *gè*, in that most of its uses 'pertain to the more semantically neutral' domain. This form is used if the distance or proximity of the object is irrelevant or unknown, and as a hesitation mark (Saillard, 2014; Tseng, 2017; see Dixon, 2010, pp. 223–57 on functional markedness in demonstrative systems).

Across the world, pidgin and creole languages tend not to have classifiers or grammatical gender (see Aikhenvald, 2016, p. 71, 75; Baker, 2001; Parkvall, 2017, and references there).[2]

The Chinese 'workplace pidgin' preserves just one Mandarin classifier form—the most neutral and the most frequent one, *gé*, which is extended to all the referents. This is reminiscent of the Ethiopian-Chinese Pidgin (Driessen, 2020, p. 7) where the verb forms of Amharic origin occur in the formally and functionally less marked masculine singular form. Alternatively, the exclusive use of masculine singular forms in Ethiopian Pidgin may be the artefact of an all-male environment in which the pidgin is currently used. Synchronically, the form *ge* in the Chinese 'workplace pidgin' of Basamuk cannot be considered a classifier, since this form occurs with any referent independently of its properties.

Specialised terms—different for different departments of the refinery— come from Chinese. Examples include *chái yóu*, 'diesel fuel', in the limestone mill, or *pí dài*, 'conveyor belt', *bāng pǔ*, 'pump' and *qiú mó jī*, 'ball mill' in the limestone processing plant (Kuo, personal communication, December 1, 2020). To remember the Chinese terms, Nathan writes them down as he hears them (without paying attention to tones, e.g., /pidai/ for *pí dài*, 'conveyor belt'). Lack of tones is a typical feature of all pidgins including the Chinese-based pidgins (Perekhvalskaya, 2013; Driessen, 2020, p. 12). So is the absence of various morphological markers.

The resulting blend of English, Tok Pisin and toneless Mandarin Chinese forms in the workplace pidgin of Basamuk is different from each of the component languages. As Kuo puts it, 'It is hard to say whether an employee speaks English or Mandarin Chinese when using this workplace pidgin'. This resonates with Stefánsson's (1909) observation (Section 2), that English words within the Eskimo jargon are 'usually so metamorphised as to be well-nigh unrecognizable'. The new code with its limited vocabulary and grammar is taking on a life of its own. The workplace pidgin at Basamuk differs from codes of communication described for the languages of the mines: users of the Basamuk Pidgin do not involve actual miners and underground communication (where gestures are of limited use: Cornips & Muysken, 2019).

---

2   I am grateful to Chris Holz for bringing this to my attention and sharing the references with me.

The pidgin of Basamuk is referred to as a 'workplace language'. Attitudes to it are somewhat ambiguous. Some locals see it as a part of a pathway to get a chance to learn technical skills that would allow them to get better jobs, and to obtain a promotion within the Ramu mining network. Others—especially those with a more advanced level of education—voice a negative attitude to it: they feel as if they were 'talking down' to the interlocutors, as they must speak slowly and simplify their language.

It is instructive to compare the pidgin of Basamuk with another workplace pidgin used on Chinese-run construction sites in Ethiopia (Driessen, 2020). A Chinese-Ethiopian pidgin has gradually evolved in a variety of Chinese-run building sites in Ethiopia (including Addis Ababa, Raya, the Lower Omo River, Afar and Amhara) since the mid-2000s. The pidgin is based on three languages—Amharic, Chinese and English (with some influence from Oromo and Tigrinya: Driessen, 2020). Similar to Basamuk Pidgin, names for construction machinery come from Chinese. The terms for construction material and building tools are Amharic, and denominations of professionals are of English origin. The Chinese-Ethiopian pidgin has time words, from Amharic, and number words from English, in addition to Mandarin sentence particles such as *ma* for questions and *a* as a discourse marker and attention getter (see Li, 2006, pp. 28, 37, 50–7 on their functions in Chinese). Similar to Basamuk Pidgin, gestures are central to supplementing communication (Driessen, 2020, p. 9). Both pidgins share a few grammatical features, typical of pidgins in general—including reduplication and lack of person marking on verbs.

A common Mandarin Chinese term shared by both pidgins is 'stealing, thief'. Driessen (2020, p. 14) indicates a similarity between this word and the Amharic *léba*, 'thief'. According to her results, 'Most Ethiopians insisted the term comes from Chinese, whereas most Chinese asserted that it must be an Amharic word', with only two people pointing out its Arabic origin. In all likelihood, the term *alibaba* made its way to Basamuk though the intermediary of the Chinese.[3]

---

3   It remains unclear how this usage could be related to the name of the woodcutter, *Ali Baba,* in the folktale *Ali Baba and the Forty Thieves,* part of *One Thousand and One Nights.* In all likelihood, the use of *alibaba* in a derogatory way meaning 'thief' is associated with a mock-'Uyghur' comic and somewhat crooked character, Uncle Alibaba, a lamb kebab peddler (Chen, 2020, pp. 8–9). The name *Alibaba* must have come to be associated with Uyghurs and cultural misappropriation of their practices by the Han Chinese (see also Section 6, on 'Mock-Uyghur'). An association between *Ali Baba* and stealth may have been influenced by the title of the folk tale itself where the name Ali Baba appears in the context of 'thieves' (Peter Bakker, personal communication, December 3, 2021). Along similar lines, Driessen (2020, p. 14) reports that 'the Han Chinese used the concept of *alibaba* to address Uyghurs in western China' in Xinjiang in the early 2000s.

In contrast to Basamuk Pidgin, whose use is limited to the Ramu Nickel mining area,[4] Chinese-Ethiopian Pidgin is used across various locations in the country. When construction work finishes in one place, the workers—both the Chinese and the locals—move to another one, taking the pidgin with them. Consequently, the Ethiopian pidgin is richer in its lexical stock and ways of saying things than Basamuk Pidgin, a language in the initial stages of its making.

Basamuk Pidgin and Chinese-Ethiopian Pidgin are unlike most pidgin languages. Both are based on three lexifier languages, rather than just two as is typical (see Daval-Markussen & Bakker, 2017, on the linguistic composition of pidgins and creoles).[5] Words and grammatical forms from Mandarin, Amharic and English form Chinese-Ethiopian Pidgin. Basamuk Pidgin combines Mandarin, English and Tok Pisin as its lexifiers. This is a rare pidgin, which includes a creole language (Tok Pisin) as one of its lexifiers (the other known example is the Ndyuka-Trio Pidgin in Surinam).

Both Chinese-Ethiopian Pidgin and Basamuk Pidgin are used in a predominantly male environment—a feature shared with the emerging Chinese-Russian Pidgin. In contrast to Chinese-Ethiopian Pidgin and Basamuk Pidgin, Chinese-Russian Pidgin is predominantly used in the context of trade. The longevity of each of the pidgins is contingent on the external conditions—the activities of the Chinese construction companies in Ethiopia, the continuity of Chinese-Russian trade in the border regions, and Chinese expansion in the PNG mining industry. As mainland Chinese investment in PNG economy shows no sign of abating (Chin, this volume, and Hayes, this volume), a Chinese-based workplace pidgin may be here to stay. Its durability is enhanced by the development of positive attitudes to the Chinese as employers and as work colleagues, and the necessity to acquire it to further one's career in the mining industry is felt and voiced by local employees (as pointed out by Kuo, this volume).

A rather different communicative code is being developed outside the refinery—the Marmar market run by women sellers.

---

4   This pidgin appears to be in use at the Kurumbukari mining site, also within the Ramu Nickel mine (Kuo, personal communication, December 1, 2020).
5   A new incipient pidgin is in the process of developing in Guangzhou, as a consequence of recent interactions between African traders and the local Chinese (Liu, 2013). The pidgin appears to be based upon a number of varieties of African English and West African Pidgin English, alongside French, Mandarin and Cantonese. If this pidgin stabilises, its comparison with Basamuk Pidgin will be instructive.

Section 6: The language of Marmar market: A gendered foreigner talk

Trade relations and markets are fertile ground for developing a common way of speaking. We can recall that many pidgins, including the Chinese-Russian varieties, have evolved in the context of trade. A further aspect of communication around the Chinese-run Ramu Nickel Cobalt refinery in Basamuk involves trade between Chinese workers and local women—fish and vegetable sellers. In contrast to Basamuk Pidgin and Chinese-Russian Pidgin—both used in an all-male environment—trade between Chinese and locals in the *Marmar* market around Basamuk involves local women interacting with Chinese men.

As Gessler (this volume) points out, markets are 'critical to the livelihoods of rural Papua New Guineans', especially women. Women are excluded from employment in what Gessler refers to as 'the highly masculinised refinery workforce'. They rely on the success of their market produce to cover their expenses, especially school fees for children. The interaction between Chinese male buyers and local female sellers takes place within a limited time-frame, each day, during the refinery's shift rotation time between 6 a.m. and 8 a.m. After that, Chinese workers go back to the refinery, and Marmar continues as a typical PNG market selling betelnut to Papua New Guinean nationals.

The way in which women sellers talk to their Chinese customers contains several features of 'foreigner talk' (in the sense of Ferguson, 1996; Fedorova, 2015; see Section 2). Typical features of 'foreigner talk' across the world include simplified grammatical forms, loud speech and overuse of gestures. In their interactions with the Chinese buyers, women—all with native proficiency in Tok Pisin—use short sentences, accompanied by gestures, with a prevalence of short verbless commands that are supposed to be understood contextually.[6] An example is *faiv kina moa*, '(Add) five kina more!'—a command hard to understand outside the context in which it was used. Some further sentences quoted by Gessler are short and ungrammatical in Tok Pisin; for example, *no wasi wasi, nogat*, 'no soap, no!' Women employ a substantial amount of repetition, ostensibly to make themselves understood. Many use the term *okela*, imitating the way in which the Chinese use this word, their adaptation of Tok Pisin *olgeta*,

---

6   As reflected in the transcripts of marketplace interactions, in Gessler (this volume).

'all, every'. *Okela*—which is neither Tok Pisin nor Mandarin—is a salient feature of the Marmar foreigner talk. Some of the women employ terms for Chinese currency adapted to Tok Pisin phonology, to negotiate prices more efficiently and thus empower themselves against aggressive bargaining; for example, Mandarin *yī máo,* pronounced by the local women as [ee-mo] 'ten cents', Mandarin *liǎng máo,* pronounced by the local women as [lay-mo] 'twenty cents'. Whether or not the women-only foreigner talk will ever develop into a more conventionalised, pidgin-like variety is contingent on the stability of trade relations with the Chinese in the Marmar context. So far, Marmar foreigner talk appears to be the only instance of such a register based on a creole language (Tok Pisin).

The female-only foreigner talk by local women reflects a strong cultural friction and gendered tension between the sellers and the buyers. Following their own cultural practices, the expatriate Chinese men try and engage in haggling and bartering (see Orr, 2007)—a practice considered inacceptable and offensive by women sellers. As Gessler puts it, 'developing social relations and mutual obligations is central to the Melanesian marketplace'. In contrast, Chinese expatriate workers aim to seek the best price for a commodity they are after, not to build social relationships. In Tok Pisin, this attitude and emphasis on gain by the Chinese is referred to, rather derogatorily, as *mani pes* (money face). Some women are quite direct in audibly scolding the Chinese as being *bargain lain* (haggler) and even *idiot* (all produced in the presence of Gessler, an Australian researcher). The gendered attitude towards the Chinese at the Marmar market is strikingly different from the Russians' attitude to the Chinese they are in contact with, in the context of the newly emerging Chinese-Russian Pidgin: Russian women, especially middle-aged ones, appear to be more patronising and forgiving of the Chinese than Russian men, who are overly negative (Fedorova, 2013).

The clash of values at the Marmar market highlights a further aspect of language use. Women sellers imitate—and mock—the Chinese and their ways of speaking. The Chinese rendering of Tok Pisin *no gut*, 'no good, bad', as *nogudi* or *no guda* is parodied by a seller (Transcripts 1 and 3, Gessler, this volume). A Chinese buyer was explicitly addressed as '*No cheapey-cheapey!*', as a mock imitation of how a Chinese person would pronounce the English word *cheap*. In another instance, a woman seller addressed a buyer as *Yu cheapa-cheapa man kam yu noken toktok!,* meaning either 'You cheap cheap man come, you cannot speak', or 'You cheap cheap man come, don't you speak!', to the delight of other women sellers. This sentence is ambiguous: it can be understood either as a criticism of the Chinese man for his lack of proficiency in Tok Pisin, or as a command not to talk; that is, not to haggle. Another seller openly mocked Chinese pronunciation of a PNG brand of soap 'Was Was' (lit. washing) offered in exchange for her goods, as 'no wasi wasi, nogat!'. The way Chinese-like pronunciation of the Tok Pisin or English words is parodied by the woman, and the repetition of the form okela overused by the Chinese, are reminiscent of the phenomenon known as a 'mock language'.

'Mock languages' involve 'linguistic appropriation' of somewhat skewed forms in the other's language forms, to further emphasise the abyss between the superior 'us' and the inferior 'them' (cf. Hill, 2008, pp. 158–9; Rosa & Flores, 2017). 'Mock language' consists of purposeful mispronunciation of the 'other' language forms, to create a comic effect or, less overtly, as a means of perpetuating negative linguistic and racial attitudes. For instance, mock Spanish is a comic device that involves deliberate linguistic modification aimed at transmitting a negative ethnic stereotype, relegating Spanish speakers 'to a zone of foreignness and disorder' (Hill, 2008, pp. 128–9, 133, 146–7). Numerous Chinese TV shows imitate and mock the imperfect ways the Uyghur speak Mandarin, with a Uyghur accent. Deliberate mispronunciation and outré quasi-Uyghur features reinforce ethnic stereotyping of a hapless minority as incapable and inferior to the mainstream population (Chen, 2020, pp. 8–11).

'Mock Asian' (including 'Ching-Chong English', discussed by Chun 2004, 2009, 2016)—used in comedies and in day-to-day racist discourse—has several specific features, including neutralisation of the phonemic distinction between /r/ and /l/ and the insertion of an epenthetic vowel at the end of a word ending in a consonant. This has been documented for the female foreigner talk in Marmar: guda, nogudi, wasi wasi and cheapey and cheapa.

The growing presence of the Chinese in the DRC has seen the development of mock Chinese in Lingala, the main language of the capital Kinshasa (Nassenstein, 2020, pp. 197–203). Parodies of the Chinese ways of speaking Lingala (often exaggerated) appear to be a direct reflection of a generally hostile attitude towards the Chinese and their presence within the context of the region.

'Mock Chinese' is reflected in several Russian set expressions that parody foreigners (Shapiro, 2012, pp. 17–8; many of those appear in the literature 'quoting' Chinese-Russian pidgin forms or representing Chinese speech). Among Russian speakers on the China–Russia border, jocular imitations of the Chinese-Russian pidgin are a popular form of 'language play', used when talking about contacts with Chinese while shopping at Chinese markets or about border crossing practices (Fedorova, 2015, pp. 144–5; see also examples in Fedorova, 2018). 'Mock Chinese'—or mock Chinese-Russian Pidgin—is essentially a racist device aimed at demeaning the Chinese, who are considered inferior by the domineering Russians (see Fedorova 2011a, 2011b, 2015, and Section 3).

Joking behaviour and derision on Chinese-run construction sites across Ethiopia (referred to as 'pidgin play' by Driessen, 2020) point in a similar direction. The pidgin term *alibaba*, 'thief'—extended to refer to any morally suspicious person—is applied to the Chinese by Ethiopian workers (even within their hearing). Chinese words in the pidgin itself acquire derogatory and offensive meanings. The habits of the Chinese are parodied by using intonational or pitch contours: for instance, a worker said to his Chinese foreman, with his voice rising in pitch, so as 'to jest with the supposedly formal and respectful form of address', 'Mrrr Li, no lunch go?!'. This is a way of 'ridiculing Chinese punctuality when it came to lunch time' (Driessen, 2020, p. 16). Mocking the Chinese employers and foremen in the Ethiopian context can be seen as a means of subverting power relations in the workplace. This is comparable to the functions of 'mock Portuguese' forms inserted into the discourse of the Tariana of northwest Amazonia in a derisory fashion. Such insertions function as a semiotic index employed to reproduce 'a negative stereotype of a white person and of an Indian who wants to be like a hated white person and shows off his or her superiority' by overusing the white man's language, Portuguese, and thus tacitly subverting the dominance of the colonial invader (Aikhenvald, 2003, p. 16).

'Foreigner talk' and 'mock language' have different functions. Foreigner talk can be considered a specific form of convergent accommodation between two parties: a native speaker will adjust their speech in ways that make it more easily understood by a non-native interlocutor: the use of foreigner talk generally 'conveys a native speaker's willingness to engage in a successful communication' (Chun, 2009, p. 20). In the context of a market, this successful communication is a prerequisite to a successful business transaction. Mocking the interlocutor and the use of 'mock language' in the sense of Hill (2008) produces the opposite effect. It attributes negative value to a mocked target, often through outré mimicry of what is perceived as typical features of the way the interlocutor speaks.

In Marmar we find both. On the one hand, women are trying to learn the terms for Chinese currency to facilitate business transactions. On the other hand, there is overt mockery of Chinese ways of pronouncing Tok Pisin and English words, in rendering *gut* as *gudi*, *nogut* as *nogud*, or *was was* as *wasi wasi*. We hypothesise that the prevalence of the mock Chinese in Marmar is a direct consequence of a cultural clash between different market-place behaviours and expectations of the sellers and the buyers. So far, no such conflict has been described for the male-only environment at the Basamuk nickel refinery, and no mock Chinese has been documented.

The degree of awareness of the importance of Basamuk Pidgin (referred to as a 'workplace language'), as reflected in self-reports by its speakers to Kuo, appears to be higher than that of the Marmar foreigner talk, for which no term exists. The materials available so far are useful but far from comprehensive. More studies are needed on further features of and aspects of use for Basamuk Pidgin and Marmar foreigner talk (including the role of expatriate researchers) and their place within the context of linguistic ideologies—'an essential aspect of how people recognise their own "identity" revealed through language' (Silverstein, 1999, p. 101)—before we get a complete picture.

Section 7: Conclusion

The spread of the Chinese diaspora and Chinese workers across the world has resulted in the emergence of numerous pidgins—simplified communication codes used in trade and workplace environments. The Chinese presence in PNG goes back to the late nineteenth century, yet no Chinese-based pidgins have been documented. This is what makes Kuo's account of a male-only workplace pidgin based on Mandarin Chinese, Tok Pisin and English so significant. Basamuk Pidgin is unique in that one of its lexifiers is a creole language. The expansion of Chinese-run enterprises may well see the emergence of similar workplace pidgins. Consistent interaction in workplaces and growing trade have provided a ready setting for a new means of communication—Basamuk Pidgin.

An unusual gender-based register, a foreigner talk, is in use in the Marmar market outside the refinery. Used by women sellers to communicate with their Chinese customers (employees of the refinery), this register combines elements of simplified Tok Pisin, English and Mandarin. Cultural tensions and differences in market practices between the Chinese and the Melanesian women introduce another dimension to this foreigner talk. It has features of a 'mock language', whose function is to ridicule and belittle the aggressive and haggling business partners by mimicking their language practices.

The exact role and distribution of newly emergent Chinese-based pidgin(s) and foreigner talk registers—and their stability—within the linguistic ecology of multi-lingual and multi-cultural PNG are a matter for further studies. The investigations by Kuo and Gessler are part of discovering and disclosing the 'meaning of Chinese' in PNG, along the lines of Bashkow (2006). With its linguistic diversity in terms of genetic groupings and areal clusters of varied extent and antiquity, the island of New Guinea remains the most challenging testing ground. The newly documented varieties—each unique in their own way—add a further linguistic dimension to the 'land of the unexpected'. Gessler's and Kuo's materials open possibilities for the emergence of a new wave of studies on Chinese linguistic communication in PNG within the context of increasing global interest in new forms of Chinese-based pidgins and other codes across the world. We are off to a good start.

Acknowledgements

I am grateful to Rosita Henry, Michael Wood and Anna Hayes for involving me in the workshop on which the volume and the paper are based, and for their insightful comments. Special thanks go to R. M. W. Dixon, for comments and encouragement, to my Manambu and Yalaku families for sharing their remarkable languages and insights with me, and to Peter Bakker, Kapitolina Fedorova, I-Chang Kuo, John H. McWhorter, Shaun Gessler, Chris Holz, Craig Volker and Jingting Ye for comments and help with references and sources.

References

Aikhenvald, A. Y. (2003). Multilingualism and ethnic stereotypes: the Tariana of northwest Amazonia. *Language in Society, 32*, pp. 1–21. doi.org/10.1017/s0047404503321013

Aikhenvald, A. Y. (2008). Language contact along the Sepik River. *Anthropological Linguistics, 50*, pp. 1–66.

Aikhenvald, A. Y. (2014). Language contact. In C. Genetti (Ed.). *How languages work* (pp. 295–317). Cambridge University Press.

Aikhenvald, A. Y. (2016). *How gender shapes the world.* Oxford University Press.

Aikhenvald, A. Y. (2018). Worlds apart: language survival and language use in two Middle Sepik communities. *Journal de la Société des Océanistes, 146*, pp. 203–12. doi.org/10.4000/jso.8148

Ansaldo, U., Matthews, S., & Smith, G. (2012). China Coast Pidgin. Texts and contexts. In U. Ansaldo (Ed.). *Pidgins and Creoles in Asia* (pp. 59–90). John Benjamins. doi.org/10.1075/bct.38.03ans

Baker, P. (2001). No creolisation without prior pidginisation. *Te Reo, 44*, pp. 31–50.

Bakker, P., & Grant, A. P. (1996). Interethnic communication in Canada, Alaska and adjacent areas. In S. A. Wurm, P. Mühlhäusler, & D. T. Tryon (Eds.). *Atlas of languages of intercultural communication in the Pacific, Asia, and the Americas* (pp. 1107–69). Mouton de Gruyter. doi.org/10.1515/9783110819724.3.1107

Bashkow, I. (2006). *The meaning of Whiteman: race and modernity in the Orokaiva cultural world.* The University of Chicago Press. doi.org/10.7208/chicago/9780226530062.001.0001

Bowden, R. (1997). *A Dictionary of Kwoma, a Papuan Language of North-east New Guinea.* Pacific Linguistics.

Bowden, R. (1984). Art and gender ideology in the Sepik. *Man, New Series, 19*, pp. 445–58. doi.org/10.2307/2802182

Cahill, Peter. (2012). *The Chinese in Rabaul 1914–1960: Needed but not wanted.* CopyRight Publishing.

Chen, Y. (2020). From 'Lamb Kebabs' to 'Shared Joy': Cultural appropriation, ignorance, and the constrained connectivity within the 'One Belt, One Road' initiative. *Journal of Contemporary China, 29*(121), pp. 1–16. doi.org/10.1080/10670564.2019.1621526

Chin, J. (2008). Contemporary Chinese Community in Papua–New Guinea: Old Money versus New Migrants. *Chinese Southern Diaspora Studies, 2*, pp. 117–26.

Chun, E. W. (2004). Ideologies of legitimate mockery: Margaret Cho's revoicings of Mock Asian'. *Pragmatics, 14*, pp. 263–89. doi.org/10.1075/prag.14.2-3.10chu

Chun, E. W. (2009). Speaking like Asia immigrants: intersections of accommodation and mocking at a U.S. high school. *Pragmatics, 19*, pp. 17–38. doi.org/10.1075/prag.19.1.02chu

Chun, E. W. (2016). The meaning of Ching-Chong. Language, racism, and response in new media. In H. Samy Alim, J. R. Rickford, & A. F. Ball (Eds.), *Raciolinguistics* (pp. 81–96). Oxford University Press. doi.org/10.1093/acprof:oso/9780190625696.003.0005

Connolly, P. (2020). The Belt and Road comes to Papua New Guinea. *Security Challenges, Geo-Economies in the Indo-Pacific, 16*(4), pp. 41–64.

Cornips, L., & Muysken, P. (2019). Introduction: Language in the mines. *International Journal of the Sociology of Language, 258*, pp. 1–11. doi.org/10.1515/ijsl-2019-2026

Dixon, R. M. W. (2010). *Basic linguistic theory* (Vol. 2, Grammatical topics). Oxford University Press.

Dixon, R. M. W. (2019). *Australia's original languages.* Allen and Unwin.

Driessen, M. (2020). Pidgin play: linguistic subversion on Chinese-run construction sites in Ethiopia. *African Affairs, 119*(476), pp. 432–51. doi.org/10.1093/afraf/adaa016

Fedorova, K. (2011a). Language contacts on the Russian-Chinese border: the 'second birth' of Russian-Chinese Trade Pidgin. In T. Bhambry, C. Griffin, T. Hjelm, and O. Voronina (Eds.), *Perpetual motion? Transformation and transition in Central, Eastern Europe and Russia* (pp. 72–84). School of Slavonic and East European Studies, University College London.

Fedorova, K. (2011b). Transborder trade on the Russian-Chinese border: Problems of interethnic communication. In B. Bruns & J. P. Miggelbrink (Eds.), *Subverting borders. Doing research on smuggling and small-scale trade* (pp. 107–28). Springer. doi.org/10.1007/978-3-531-93273-6_6

Fedorova, K. (2012). Interethnic communication and cultural memory in the Russian-Chinese border area. In C. Hogan, N. Rentel, & S. Schwerter (Eds.), *Bridging cultures: intercultural mediation in literature, linguistics, and the arts* (pp. 197–214). Ibidem Verlag.

Fedorova, K. (2013). Speaking with and about Chinese. Language attitudes, ethnic stereotypes and discourse strategies in interethnic communication on the Russian-Chinese border. *Civilisations, 62*, pp. 71–89. doi.org/10.4000/civilisations.3334

Fedorova, K. (2015). Foreigner talk: a register or registers?. In A. A. Frog (Ed.), *Registers of Communication* (Vol. 18, pp. 138–49). Finnish Literature Society. doi.org/10.2307/j.ctvggx2qk.11

Fedorova, K. (2018). Interethnic communication on the Russian-Chinese border: its past and present. *REGION: Regional Studies of Russia, Eastern Europe, and Central Asia, 7*, pp. 83–103. doi.org/10.1353/reg.2018.0005

Ferguson, C. A. (1981). 'Foreigner talk' as the name of a simplified register. *International Journal of the Sociology of Language, 28*, pp. 9–18. doi.org/10.1515/ijsl.1981.28.9

Ferguson, C. A. (1996). *Sociolinguistic perspectives: Papers on language in society, 1959–1994.* Oxford University Press.

Fernández, M. (2018). El pidgin chino-español de Manila a principios del siglo XVIII. *Zeitschrift für romanische Philologie, 134*, pp. 137–70. doi.org/10.1515/zrp-2018-0006

Foley, W. A. (1986). *The Papuan languages of New Guinea.* Cambridge University Press.

Foley, W. A. (2013). Yimas-Arafundi pidgin. In S. M. Michaelis, P. Maurer, M. Haspelmath, & M. Huber (Eds.), *The survey of pidgin and creole languages* (Vol. 3, Contact Languages Based on Languages from Africa, Asia, Australia, and the Americas, pp. 105–13). Oxford University Press.

Gewertz D. B. (1983). *Sepik River societies. A historical ethnography of the Chambri and their neighbors.* Yale University Press.

Harrison, S. (1990). *Stealing people's names. History and politics in a Sepik River cosmology.* Cambridge University Press. doi.org/10.1017/cbo9780511521096.012

Hill, J. H. (2008). *The everyday language of White racism.* Wiley-Blackwell.

Inglis, C. (1972). Chinese. In P. Ryan (Ed.), *Encyclopaedia of Papua and New Guinea* (pp. 170–74). Melbourne University Press.

Knotter, A. (2015). Migration and ethnicity in coalfield history: Global perspectives. *International Review of Social History, 60*, pp. 13–39. doi.org/10.1017/s0020859015000413

Leavitt, S. (2000). The Apotheosis of white Men: A Re-examination of Beliefs about Europeans as Ancestral Spirits. *Oceania, 70*(4), pp. 304–16. doi.org/10.1002/j.1834-4461.2000.tb03069.x

Li, B. (2006). *Chinese Final Particles and the Syntax of the Periphery* [Doctoral thesis, University of Leiden]. www.lotpublications.nl/Documents/133_fulltext.pdf

Li, M. (2016). Trade pidgins in China: Historical and grammatical relationships. *Transactions of the Philological Society, 114*(3), pp. 298–314. doi.org/10.1111/1467-968x.12066

Liu, Y. (2013). Marketplace communication between Africans and Chinese in Guangzhou: An emerging pidgin? [Unpublished Master of Philosophy thesis]. The University of Hong Kong.

Maitz, P. (2016). Unserdeutsch. Eine vergessene koloniale Varietät des Deutschen im melanesischen Pazifik. In A. N. Lenz, (Hrsg.): *German Abroad—Perspektiven der Variationslinguistik, Sprachkontakt- und Mehrsprachigkeitsforschung* (pp. 211–40). Vienna University Press. doi.org/10.14220/9783737005975.211

Maitz, P., & Volker, C. A. (2017). Documenting Unserdeutsch: Reversing colonial amnesia. *Journal of Pidgin and Creole Languages, 32*(2), pp. 365–97. doi.org/10.1075/jpcl.32.2.06mai

Markussen-Daval, A., & Bakker, P. (2017). Typology of Creole languages. In A. Y. Aikhenvald, & R. M. W. Dixon (Eds.), *The Cambridge Handbook of Linguistic Typology* (pp. 254–86). Cambridge University Press. doi.org/10.1017/97813 16135716.009

Matthews, S., & Li, M. (2013). Chinese Pidgin English. In S. M. Michaelis, P. Maurer, M. Haspelmath, & M. Huber (Eds.), *The survey of pidgin and creole languages* (Vol. 1, English-based and Dutch-based languages, pp. 206–13). Oxford University Press.

Mesthrie, R. (2008). Pidgins/Creoles and contact languages: an overview. In S. Kouwenberg, & J. V. Singler (Eds.), *The Handbook of Pidgin and Creole Studies* (pp. 263–86). Wiley-Blackwell. doi.org/10.1002/9781444305982.ch11

Mesthrie, R. (2019). Fanakalo as a mining language in South Africa: A new overview. *International Journal of the Sociology of Language, 258*, pp. 13–33. doi.org/10.1515/ijsl-2019-2027

Mühlhäusler, P. (1983). Notes on the Pidgin German of Kiautschou. *Papers in pidgin and creole linguistics, Series A, Number 65*(3), pp. 139–42.

Mühlhäusler, P., Dutton, T. E., Tryon, D. T., & Wurm, S. A. (1996). Post-contact pidgins, creoles, and lingue franche, based on non-European and indigenous languages. In S. A. Wurm, P. Mühlhäusler, & D. T. Tryon (Eds.), *Atlas of languages of intercultural communication in the Pacific, Asia and the Americas* (pp. 439–70). Mouton de Gruyter. doi.org/10.1515/9783110819724.2.439

Muysken, P. (2019). Multilingualism and mixed language in the mines of Potosí (Bolivia). *International Journal of the Sociology of Language, 258*, pp. 121–42. doi.org/10.1515/ijsl-2019-2031

Nassenstein, N. (2020). Mock Chinese in Kinshasa: On Lingala speakers' offensive language use and verbal hostility. In N. Nassenstein & A. Storch (Ed.), *Swearing and Cursing—Contexts and Practices in a Critical Linguistic Perspective* (pp. 185–208). De Gruyter Mouton. doi.org/10.1515/9781501511202-009

Orr, W. W. F. (2007). The bargaining genre: a study of retail encounters in Traditional Chinese Local markers. *Language in Society, 36*, pp. 73–103. doi.org/10.1017/s0047404507070042

Parkvall, M. (2017). Pidgin Languages. In M. Aronoff (Ed.), *Oxford Research Encyclopedia of Linguistics*. Oxford University Press. doi.org/10.1093/acrefore/ 9780199384655.013.58

Parkvall, M., & Bakker, P. (2013a). Pidgins. In Y. Matras & P. Bakker (Ed.), *Contact languages* (pp. 15–64). Mouton de Gruyter. doi.org/10.1515/9781614513711.15

Parkvall, M., & Bakker, P. (2013b). Pidgins. In M. Aronoff (Ed.), *Oxford bibliographies online—Linguistics*. Oxford University Press. doi.org/10.1093/obo/978019977 2810-0034

Pecht, N. (2019). Grammatical features of a moribund coalminers' language in a Belgian *cité*. *International Journal of the Sociology of Language, 258*, pp. 71–98. doi.org/10.1515/ijsl-2019-2029

Penny, R. J. (2002). *A history of the Spanish language*. Cambridge University Press.

Perekhvalskaya, E. (2013). Chinese Pidgin Russian. In S. M. Michaelis, P. Maurer, M. Haspelmath, & M. Huber (Eds.), *The survey of pidgin and creole languages* (Vol. 3, Contact Languages Based on Languages from Africa, Asia, Australia, and the Americas, pp. 69–76). Oxford University Press.

Roberts, S. J. (2013). Pidgin Hawaiian. In S. M. Michaelis, P. Maurer, M. Haspelmath, & M. Huber (Eds.), *The survey of pidgin and creole languages* (Vol. 3, Contact Languages Based on Languages from Africa, Asia, Australia, and the Americas, pp. 119–27). Oxford University Press.

Rosa, J., & Flores, N. (2017). Unsettling race and language: Toward a raciolinguistic perspective. *Language in Society, 46*, pp. 621–47. doi.org/10.1017/s00474045 17000562

Rumsey, A. (1999). The White Man as Cannibal in the New Guinea Highlands. In L. Goldman (Ed.), *The anthropology of Cannibalism* (pp. 108–21). Bergin and Garvey.

Saillard, C. (2014). From demonstrative to definite and beyond: the case of *nage* 那個 in spoken Taiwan Mandarin. *Faits de Langues, 43*(1), pp. 41–59. doi.org/ 10.1163/19589514-043-01-900000004

Schindlbeck, M. (1980). Sago bei den Sawos (Mittelsepik, Papua New Guinea). *Ethnologisches Seminar der Universität und Museum für Völkerkunde, Basel, 19*, pp. 562–6.

Shapiro, R. (2010). Chinese Pidgin Russian. *Journal of Pidgin and Creole Studies, 25*, pp. 5–62. doi.org/10.1075/jpcl.25.1.02sha

Shapiro, R. (2012). Chinese-Pidgin Russian. In U. Ansaldo (Ed.), *Pidgins and Creoles in Asia* (pp. 1–58). John Benjamins. doi.org/10.1075/bct.38.02sha

Silverstein, M. (1999). NIMBY goes linguistic: conflicted 'voicings' from the culture of local language communities. In S. J. Billings, J. P. Boyle, & A. M. Griffin (Eds.), *CLS 35. The Panels. Language, identity and the other* (pp. 101–23). Chicago Linguistic Society.

Smith, G. (2013). Nupela Masta? Local and Expatriate Labour in a Chinese-Run Nickel Mine in Papua New Guinea. *Asian Studies Review, 37*(2), pp. 178–95. doi.org/10.1080/10357823.2013.768598

Smith, G. P. (2002). *Growing up with Tok Pisin. Contact, creolization, and change in Papua New Guinea's national language.* Battlebridge Publications.

Smith, G. P., & Siegel, J. (2013). Tok Pisin. In S. M. Michaelis, P. Maurer, M. Haspelmath, & M. Huber (Eds.), *The survey of pidgin and creole languages* (Vol. 1, English-based and Dutch-based Languages, pp. 214–22). Oxford University Press.

Stefánsson, V. (1909). The Eskimo trade jargon of Herschel Island. *American Anthropologist, New Series, 11*, pp. 217–32. doi.org/10.1525/aa.1909.11.2.02a 00050

Stern, D. (2005). Taimyr Pidgin Russian (Govorka). *Russian Linguistics, 29*, pp. 289–318. doi.org/10.1007/s11185-005-8376-3

Tseng, S. C. (2017). Chinese Demonstratives and Their Spoken Forms in a Conversational Corpus. *Journal of the Phonetic Society of Japan, 21*(3), pp. 41–52.

van der Voort, H. (2013). Eskimo Pidgin. In S. M. Michaelis, P. Maurer, M. Haspelmath, & M. Huber (Eds.), *The survey of pidgin and creole languages* (Vol. 3, Contact Languages Based on Languages from Africa, Asia, Australia, and the Americas, pp. 166–73). Oxford University Press.

Williams, J. P. (1995). A note on the pronominal system of Arafundi-Enga Pidgin. *Journal of Pidgin and Creole Languages, 10*, pp. 171–5. doi.org/10.1075/jpcl. 10.1.09jef

Winford, D. (2003). *An introduction to contact linguistics.* Blackwell.

Wood, M. (1995). 'White skins', 'real people' and 'Chinese' in some spatial transformations of the Western Province, PNG. *Oceania, 66*(1), pp. 23–50. doi.org/10.1002/j.1834-4461.1995.tb02529.x

Yang, J. (2007). Transbaikalian Manchu Pre-Pidgin. Towards a sociolinguistic study (Zabajkaljsko-manchzhurskij pre-pidgin. Opyt sociolingvisticheskoyo issledovanija). *Voprosy jazykoznania, 2*, pp. 67–74.

9

The New Cold War, great power rivalry and Papua New Guinea

Anna Hayes

Xi Jinping's China Dream constitutes a grand strategy by Beijing to displace the liberal world order and to disrupt the balance of power globally. Xi's signature policy, the Belt and Road Initiative (BRI) is the blueprint for achieving Xi's China Dream. When 'Xi Jinping Thought on Socialism with Chinese Characteristics for a New Era' was introduced into the Chinese constitution in 2018, it cemented pursuit of the BRI into China's foreign policy and investment goals for both state-owned enterprises and individual entrepreneurs. While Beijing promotes the BRI as a cooperative development project, BRI-branded development projects attract significant scrutiny because they often involve high-modernist development approaches centred upon expensive large-scale infrastructure, industrialisation, natural resource extraction and in some instances, military agreements (Chellaney, 2017; He, 2019; Hillman, 2020; McCahill, 2017; Rudd, 2022; Thornton & Thornton, 2018).[1] Given Beijing seeks to extend its military reach into

---

1   Scott (2020, p. 4) defined development undergirded by high-modernist ideology as 'best conceived as a strong, one might even say muscle-bound, version of the self-confidence about scientific and technical progress, the expansion of production, the growing satisfaction of human needs, the mastery of nature (including human nature), and, above all, the rational design of social order commensurate with the scientific understanding of natural laws'. Moreover, Scott (2020, p. 89) argued that 'many of the great state-sponsored calamities of the twentieth century have been the work of rulers with grandiose and utopian plans for their society', also noting its links to authoritarian states and the influence of Soviet high modernism. The Chinese Dream, which is undergirded by the BRI and its high-modernist development, is both grandiose and utopian.

the Pacific, it appears the southern extension of Beijing's 21st Century Maritime Silk Road is attempting to extend China's Island Chain Strategy beyond the South China Sea, unlocking all of the Pacific and challenging United States (US) predominance within the Pacific. Due to its strategic geographic location, and its status as a BRI partner state, Papua New Guinea (PNG) is attracting more interest within examinations of the BRI, and it is increasingly finding itself in the middle of the rapidly unfolding great power rivalry of the New Cold War or Cold War II.

This chapter is divided into two sections. The first section identifies the stated objectives of both the China Dream and the BRI, identifying how they fit within China's grand strategy, and outlines some of the concerns and debates within contemporary international relations pertaining to the BRI. It identifies that a New Cold War is unfolding and how this may impact BRI partner states. In section two, the chapter shifts its focus to PNG. This section examines important dynamics on how the BRI has been rolled out in PNG and some of the concerns raised about the BRI. This chapter argues that the US–China strategic competition, and the resultant New Cold War, is drawing other states into the unfolding great power tensions. In this New Cold War, non-alignment may not be as achievable compared to the previous Cold War due to the tech and cyber domains, as well as conditions contained within BRI agreements. For the Pacific region, and PNG in particular, geography is another critical dynamic drawing it into the conflict, despite Prime Minister Marape wanting PNG to remain neutral (Lyons, 2022). Therefore, understanding this rapidly evolving geostrategic competition is imperative for BRI partner states, like PNG, who must now consider how their foreign relations may be impacted by the New Cold War and the great power rivalry between China and the US, and their associated allies and partners.

The return of great power rivalry

The China Dream and the Belt and Road Initiative

China's leader, Xi Jinping, has repeatedly defined the China Dream as the 'great rejuvenation of the Chinese nation', with hopes that China would become prosperous and powerful again (Xi, 2014, 2017a, 2019). However, it is increasingly understood that this great rejuvenation involves a grand strategy for displacement of the US as the world's leading power and a restructuring of global norms, rules and order (Connolly, 2020; deLisle & Goldstein, 2021; Doshi, 2021; Hayes, 2020; Schuman, 2020).[2] Rush Doshi argues that Beijing seeks to eventually 'project leadership over global governance and international institutions, split Western alliances, and advance autocratic norms at the expense of liberal ones' (2021, pp. 4–5). These shifts from China have seen US–China relations move from engagement to post-engagement.[3]

Xi's signature strategy, the BRI, is integral to achieving the China Dream. Officially described in 2013 as a revitalisation of the land and sea-based Old World trading networks into a twenty-first century Silk Road, the BRI contains the hallmarks of an imperial endeavour (Hillman, 2020). Michael Schuman assesses the BRI as being a deliberate recreation of:

> the China-centric trade links of the overland Silk Road and the old maritime routes once sailed by the mariner Zheng He by building ports, roads and other infrastructure across the Eurasian landmass and beyond. And much like Zheng He's treasure fleets, Belt and Road is meant to be a grand pronouncement of the revival of Chinese power in the world and to entice foreigners to come running to Beijing to pay their respects to the new son of Heaven. (2020, p. 314)

Through the BRI, Xi has walked away from Deng Xiaoping's cautionary approach of 'Hide your strength; bide your time; never take the lead' and in 2021 he told provincial and party leaders that 'time and momentum are on our side' to challenge the US and the liberal world order (Cited in Rudd, 2022, p. 9). He has also linked the China Dream to military modernisation. China's defence forces have received significant spending boosts, increasing Chinese capacity in nuclear, space, cyber and electronic warfare domains as well as considerably expanding its blue water navy (Garamone, 2022; Grady, 2023). Xi reported to the 2017 National Congress that China was 'building a powerful military with Chinese characteristics' and that 'a strong military in the new era' means 'world-class forces that obey the Party's

---

2   For an overview of these changes, see deLisle & Goldstein (2021).

3   The engagement strategy began during the Nixon presidency, undergirded by hopes that economic integration of China into the global economy would encourage Beijing to liberalise politically. The goals of this strategy have not materialised, and this realisation has been especially pronounced under the increasingly authoritarian presidency of Xi Jinping. The shift to a post-engagement strategy of strategic competition between the US and China began in the final years of the Obama presidency, escalated during the Trump presidency, and have continued under the Biden presidency. Post-COVID, the US has also looked towards de-risking the relationship, meaning more diversified supply chains, greater resistance to economic coercion from China, and prioritising US national interests when dealing with China on sensitive matters.

command, can fight and win, and maintain excellent conduct' combined with 'military-civilian integration' and a stronger role of the Party in the military (Xi, 2017b, pp. 5–48). While Chinese leaders since the Qing Dynasty have desired a rejuvenation of China, restoring Chinese greatness, Xi's BRI is the most comprehensive blueprint on how to achieve this goal.

The China Dream also seeks to significantly alter existing international institutions. The BRI has deliberately side-stepped established lending norms and institutions, lacks transparency and accountability, and encourages corruption (Rajah, Dayant & Pryke, 2019; Hillman, 2020). In 2016, Su Ge identified it was China's time to build a 'new type of global governance system', explaining that the BRI was the mechanism for this displacement (2016, pp. 9–10). Wang Fan argued 'China should deeply participate in global governance and actively guide the reform of the international order', concluding that China's rise is 'bound to impact the existing international power and interest structures and *brings a tremendous shock to the international system*' (2018, pp. 38–41, emphasis added by Hayes). The BRI, combined with the increasingly assertive and aggressive rhetoric and actions from Beijing, has intensified US–China competition. This competition includes an ongoing trade war between the two powers and warnings the world has already descended into a New Cold War (deLisle & Goldstein, 2021, p. 13).[4] Hence, early assessments that argued the BRI sought to reshape globalisation into Sino-globalisation under a Sino-led international order, making China the global hegemon, are ringing true (Wang, 2016; McCahill, 2017; Thornton & Thornton, 2018; He, 2019).

The New Cold War

The New Cold War divisions are increasingly between the world's democracies including, for example, the US, United Kingdom (UK), France, Germany, Japan, South Korea, Taiwan and Australia (all of whom support existing international institutions and the liberal world order), as well as those that oppose both democracy and the liberal world order (such as China, Russia, Saudi Arabia, Egypt, North Korea and Pakistan). For decades, China has forged the like-minded group (LMG)—an informal and loosely aligned group of states also seeking to avoid external criticism of their human rights

---

4   Not all scholars are convinced a New Cold War has emerged, or if it does, that bipolarity will result. See: Zhao, S. S. (2021). The US–China Rivalry in the Emerging Bipolar World: Hostility, Alignment, and Power Balance. *Journal of Contemporary China, 31*(134), pp. 169–85. doi.org/10.1080/10670564. 2021.1945733

violations and poor governance practices domestically—who work together as a voting bloc to defend member-states from external criticism and censure (Chen, 2021; Economy, 2018). Like China, these states prioritise high-modernist development, non-interference in their 'domestic affairs', and they have shared identities as mostly authoritarian and hybrid regimes. Via the BRI and the Asian Infrastructure Investment Bank, this cooperation is also transactional, with states supporting Beijing on international forums to ensure continued loans from Beijing (ibid.). However, this transactional relationship with China via the BRI and the LMG also means these states are increasingly being drawn to the Chinese side of the New Cold War.

Already, Chinese academics like Wang Fan have considered the possibility of conflict in the New Cold War. Acknowledging that the possibility of great power war has been reduced due to mutually assured destruction (and China's second-strike nuclear capabilities), he identified that, like the previous Cold War, '"proxy wars" involving smaller nations' are the likely theatres for great power conflict in the New Cold War (Wang, 2018, p. 33).[5] However, he also added that 'non-traditional kinds of "war" in trade, cyberspace and financial area will become the main forms of great power competition, and the damage caused therefrom may be higher than traditional wars' (Wang, 2018, p. 33). Already, these non-traditional kinds of war are playing out in real time. For example, the 'Network Wars' between Chinese and Western tech companies are part of the New Cold War and countries that accepted or repelled Huawei and ZTE may be impacted by, or become beneficiaries of, such decisions in years to come (Economy, 2018; Hillman, 2021; Rudd, 2022).[6] Moreover, China has also already used economic sanctions and trade wars against states that have displeased them, including Norway, Japan, South Korea, the Philippines, Mongolia, Taiwan, Australia and Lithuania, demonstrating the aforementioned non-traditional kinds of war are already being deployed by Beijing against other states (Miller, 2022). With specific reference to the focus of this chapter, Wang identified that for China to maximise 'the present period of strategic opportunity', its strategic choices mean that 'the Asia-Pacific region will remain its geopolitical priority' (2018, p. 40). Therefore, it is imperative

---

5   Ukraine appears to be the first proxy war of the New Cold War.
6   In fact, the division of the world began to be drawn in the early 2000s when China, aided by Western tech companies, sought to establish a separate version of the internet via censorship controls and internet surveillance systems and has since exported such technologies to other authoritarian states wanting to control their own domestic internet access (Economy, 2018; Hillman, 2021).

that China's grand strategy via the China Dream and the BRI receives more attention in regional considerations and there needs to be a growing awareness that we have already entered a New Cold War.

Other challenges and considerations

The BRI has also triggered concern over debt-trap diplomacy.[7] Brahma Chellaney, the progenitor of that term, warned that China has engaged in deliberate debt-trap strategies with BRI partner states that could result in them surrendering territory or other assets to China in the future due to their inability to service their debts.[8] Although Hillman has argued that those who agree with the debt trap theory 'give China too much credit' (2020, p. 12), Holslag (2017) disagrees, arguing the BRI includes offensive mercantilism with debt trap just one of its features. Nonetheless, the debt trap question remains a key focal point because many BRI partner states are considered by the Organisation for Economic Co-operation and Development to be countries with increased risk of being overwhelmed by large external debts, preferring instead to adopt a sustainable debt approach with such countries. Many are also serious human rights abusers with poor governance records, opening up Beijing to accusations of assisting those states to defy existing international rules, norms and institutions (Zhao, 2010). Since COVID-19, concerns over the debt trap have increased with numerous BRI partner states and projects experiencing vulnerability to debt and currency crisis (Buckley, 2020). However, as the lead creditor country, COVID-19 has also exposed China financially and there are concerns its economy could become increasingly unstable (Reilley, 2021; Buckley, 2020; Crawford & Gordon, 2020).

---

7   At its core, debt-trap diplomacy refers to poor lending conditions between a creditor country and a debtor country, with the creditor country providing excessive credit to the debtor country. The excessive nature of the loans, combined with the credit insecurity or unreliability of the debtor country, is not of a serious concern to the creditor country as the investment loans contain conditions that allow for the extraction of economic or political concessions from the debtor country should it be unable to keep up repayments on the loans. Another condition of debt-trap diplomacy agreements include that debtor countries are required to use and pay contractors from the creditor country, over their own workers, thereby increasing the win for the creditor country and decreasing the win for the debtor country.

8   Not all share Chellaney's assessment, however, with some scholars arguing: the evidence to conclusively prove the debt trap remains elusive; that the debt trap 'myth' has been debunked (which seems a little premature given the BRI has only been in play for a decade); or that it is the partner states, not China, that are responsible for their debt traps because they signed up to heavy loans they are unable to manage. See: Jones, L. & Hameiri, S. (2020, August). Debunking the myth of China's 'debt-trap diplomacy'. *Chatham House.* www.chathamhouse.org/2020/08/debunking-myth-debt-trap-diplomacy; Rajah, Dayant, & Pryke (2019, October 21), and Sims, K. (2020, October 31). Laos set its own debt trap. *East Asia Forum.* www.eastasiaforum.org/2020/10/31/laos-set-its-own-debt-trap/

Prior to COVID-19, there were already concerns inside China over the BRI's reckless spending to fiscally vulnerable states and how it might cripple the Chinese economy. These concerns resulted in tighter lending conditions for BRI agreements to be included in China's fourteenth Five-Year Plan (2021–2025).[9] Given the high risk of past BRI lending, combined with the substantial drop in China's foreign reserves in 2015, even prior to COVID-19, Beijing was pulling back on some BRI projects (CEIC, 2023; Hillman, 2020; Tao, 2021).[10] These changes signalled that even Beijing had realised the BRI could be a potential 'lending trap' for Beijing (Reilley, 2021, p. 347). In response to such concerns, the Taihe Institute inside China identified several Pacific Island countries (PICs), including PNG, as being 'bad or risky investments for Belt and Road projects' (Finin, 2021, p. 179). Hence, future funding may be more conservative, centred on the provision of 'basic needs' over major funding projects (ibid.). Moreover, Chinese spending in the Pacific peaked in 2018, falling 15 per cent in 2019 (Pryke & Dayant, 2021). This decline was partly due to a drop-off in lending because the costly, large-scale infrastructural projects identified above had already received their funding in the preceding years, with no new major multilateral projects being announced and funded in 2019 (ibid.). However, it has also resulted due to belt-tightening from Beijing, driven by increased concerns stemming from Beijing's risky lending and China's own domestic debt crisis. Chinese lending to the Pacific is now lower than in 2012 (Dayant, Keen & Rajah, 2023; Deng, 2022).

---

9   See: Proposal XI:40 in Central Committee of the Communist Party of China. (2020, November 3). Proposals of the Central Committee of the Communist Party of China on Formulating the Fourteenth Five-Year Plan for National Economic and Social Development and Long-Term Goals for 2035. *Xinhua*. web.archive.org/web/20201104114039/http://www.xinhuanet.com/politics/zywj/2020-11/03/c_1126693293.htm

10   Loan default has already occurred in Sri Lanka, which resulted in a debt-equity swap where a port and surrounding land was leased to China for 99 years as part repayment of the defaulted loan (Amit, 2019). Countries such as Tonga have been granted loan repayment extensions, while others such as Malaysia have renegotiated loan terms and conditions that are more favourable to them ("Tonga gets five years' grace on Chinese loan as Pacific nation joins Belt and Road initiative", 2018; Parameswaran, 2019). In early 2021, debt-ridden Pakistan sought concessional rates from China on existing loans, a request that at the time of writing, had stalled BRI frameworks between the two states (Aamir, 2021). In December 2021, fears over Uganda's Entebbe Airport have also sharpened focus on the BRI, low-income countries and their ability to repay excessive loans to China. See: Ojambo, F. (2021, December 3). Uganda Can Meet China Loan Terms, Keep Airport, Legal Head Says. *Bloomberg*. www.bloomberg.com/news/articles/2021-12-02/uganda-can-meet-china-loan-terms-keep-airport-legal-head-say

By removing term limits for President and Vice President from the Chinese constitution, Xi has cemented his power as President for life, evidencing China's new hard authoritarianism (deLisle & Goldstein, 2021).[11] In his assessment of these changes, Richard McGregor (2019, pp. 11–12) identified China as being 'a geopolitical challenge to the West'. Hence, concerns have been growing over the nature and intentions of Xi Jinping's China and his BRI. However, the onset of the global pandemic hit the pause button for some states and much has happened in the meantime. How they engage with the post-COVID BRI against the backdrop of a rapid escalation of great power rivalry and a New Cold War will be of great importance. This chapter now moves to section two, where it will focus on Chinese engagement with PNG.

The Chinese in Papua New Guinea

PNG signed a BRI agreement in 2018 during Peter O'Neill's term as Prime Minister (Connolly, 2020). Like all BRI agreements, considered to be state secrets by Beijing, exact details of what it contained are not publicly available.[12] Beijing's lending to PICs has increased because Oceania is both a source of natural resources for China and it provides new markets for domestic over-consumption (Wesley-Smith, 2013; Hillman, 2020).[13] Between 2011 and 2018, more than US$6 billion was pledged in loans to PICs, roughly 21 per cent of the regional GDP (Rajah, Dayant & Pryke, 2019). Of that total, US$4.46 billion was pledged to PNG to cover three main projects. They include the PNG-China Integrated Agriculture Industrial Park, the Goroka Town Water Supply Upgrade Project and the High Priority Economic Roads Project (Kenneth, 2017; O'Dowd, 2021, p. 400). There remains a lack of transparency on actual figures of indebtedness, which is further complicated by the grouping of China and

---

11   The author argues that examinations of the BRI prior to the constitutional changes announced by Xi Jinping in 2018 have underestimated the political climate of Beijing and Xi's political aspirations both within and outside of China.

12   The secrecy of such agreements extends to countries such as Australia. In 2019, the Australian state of Victoria signed a BRI MOU with Beijing without consulting the Federal Government or relevant government departments. Canberra was displeased with the Victorian agreement, which the Prime Minister stated was 'inconsistent with the Australian government's policy' and 'Australia's national interest' (Scott Morrison cited in Varano, 2021). After the passage of the Foreign Relations Bill through Australian parliament, the Federal government cancelled the Victorian BRI MOU with Beijing.

13   PICs with BRI agreements include Cook Islands, Fiji, Kiribati, Federated State of Micronesia, New Zealand, Niue, PNG, Solomon Islands, Samoa, Tonga and Vanuatu (International Institute of Green Finance, 2021).

Taiwanese debts under one figure in the 2020 PNG National Budget, but Beijing's spending in PNG is concentrated in 'resource-intensive, extractive and polluting industries', thereby replicating its domestic development model (O'Dowd, 2021, p. 399).

Australia–China competition and 'information deficits'

In 2019, Wang Shiming identified that Australia and PNG have 'close ties' and that via the BRI, PNG offered avenues for third-party cooperation between China and Australia. He also identified the significance of the Pacific region in 'Australia's foreign aid strategy' and that '[a]s one of the southern routes of the 21st Century Maritime Silk Road, the Pacific island [*sic*] counties have *unique location advantages* and convenience to connect with the initiative' (Wang, 2019, p. 96, emphasis added by Hayes). After making a case for why Australia has misjudged Chinese motives in the region and thus far missed out on the BRI opportunity, Wang accused Australia of having a 'rigid biased approach and Cold War mentality' towards China, which he concluded would negatively affect China–Australia cooperation in PNG (2019, p. 99). Tellingly, he also discussed how 'Oceania is regarded as a space where great powers insert their geostrategic, geopolitical, and geo-economic influence', and acknowledged there is a 'mutual trust deficit' between Australia and China in the present era. Despite these concerns, Wang expressed his hope that Australia would cooperate with China inside of PNG so China could learn from Australia how to operate more effectively there.

Wang's framing of Australia as having a 'Cold War mentality' is hypocritical given his published article came at a time when Beijing was entreating Australia to 'choose a side' in the US–China competition—that is, China's side. In 2019, Beijing sent a delegation of Chinese academics to Australia on a speaking tour. The academics deployed wedge politics while in Australia, warning it would be a 'frontier region' should war break out between China and the US (ie. a territory for 'proxy war'), that Australia was 'naïve' to trust its alliance with the US and it would be 'the first sacrifice for this war' (Wang Yiwei, cited in Greenbank, 2019). In April 2020, China launched a trade war against Australia, following Canberra's calls for an independent investigation into the origins of COVID-19. In November 2020, Beijing issued a list of '14 grievances' to Canberra, demanding they had to be resolved before normal relations between the two states could be restored.

All of the alleged grievances interfered with Australian domestic security and the free flow of Australian democracy, hence they all constituted Chinese interference in the domestic affairs of the Australian state. At the 2021 G7 summit in Rome, Australia highlighted Beijing's interference and coercion by distributing the list of '14 grievances' to those in attendance (Wilson, 2021). Therefore, Beijing's punitive measures against Australia reflect a change in China's approach to Australia. Beijing has adopted a more assertive and aggressive foreign policy towards Australia, and its actions also reflect a hierarchical positioning of Australia as being a 'little brother' to China in need of corrective reprimand and punishment.

According to O'Dowd (2021, p. 401, emphasis added by Hayes), although Australia 'is the main financial backer in the South Pacific, China is the Pacific's and PNG's largest bilateral creditor'. Following on, she posits that the competition between Australia and China may enable PNG to 'attain more preferable lending arrangements' by going between Australia and China seeing which state will offer more to PNG (ibid., p. 416). This kind of strategy works up to a point. However, because the current US–China great power competition is intensifying, decisions made now could determine where states are positioned in the New Cold War because non-alignment could be quite different to the previous Cold War, if even possible at all, due to state reliance on digital communications technologies and artificial intelligence—which already constitute a new '"arms race" between Washington and Beijing' (Kania & Segel, 2021, p. 301; Thomas-Noone, 2021; Zhao, 2019; Mascitelli & Chung, 2019, Wesley-Smith, 2021). Indeed, debt-trap diplomacy could extend beyond Chellaney's current definition to include strategic dimensions that draw BRI partner states into conflict via the BRI's port-based infrastructure projects, which frequently reflect Beijing's 'first civilian, later military' approach (Kuhara, 2022). With specific reference to the 'win-win' rhetoric espoused by Beijing in reference to BRI projects, Kohji Kuhara (2022, p. 12) warned that 'Despite this innocuous framing, China gradually may expand the civil facilities that it builds overseas for use by its military, relying on the host state's growing economic dependence on China to ensure continued access'. States in this position may quickly find themselves being a 'smaller nation' on which great power 'proxy war' is waged due to dual use ports and infrastructure that have both commercial and military capacities (Wang, 2018).

In her analysis, O'Dowd also identified the Pacific as being of 'somewhat peripheral importance to Beijing' (2021, p. 407). This may have been the case decades earlier, but it has not been the case for at least the past decade. Due to the escalating great power competition, the Pacific has become of vital strategic importance as Beijing seeks to extend its power and control across multiple island chains in both the Pacific and Indian oceans, breaking free from the first island chain (Espena & Bomping, 2020; VornDick, 2018; Zhang, 2020). The Island Chain Strategy emerged in US foreign policy circles in 1951. It proposed that the US establish multiple bases across the West Pacific to contain Soviet and Chinese ambitions in the Pacific Ocean region. Despite the dissolution of the Soviet Union, it has remained a focal point within American and Chinese geo-political strategies.[14] Dominant presence within the island chains determines which power has control over the Pacific Ocean and its important sea lines of communication. The PICs play a critical role in unlocking the region and this is why they are fast becoming a site of great power competition. In his research, Zhang Denghua noted that multiple Chinese academics have identified the need for China to break through the first and second island chains—thereby unlocking the Pacific—with some scholars suggesting that Beijing should establish 'strategic pivot ports'—commercial ports that can double as military ports— across the region. Moreover, Zhao Minghao (2019, p. 389) identified that 'the Western Pacific and Indo-Pacific will be the focal points of US–China strategic competition in the decades to come', hence the building of artificial islands in the South China Sea should be recognised as integral elements within China's existing Island Chain Strategy deployment (Andrew Erikson, cited in Cavas, 2016). Consequently, the PICs are of critical strategic importance as, after Taiwan, their territories further unlock the Pacific, allowing China to have strategic presence across the region.[15]

---

14 Although not an official policy of China, Island Chain Strategy influences how Beijing views its geostrategic constraints and influences their outlook. Between 2015 and 2019, the author participated in multiple Track 1.5 events in Beijing. Chinese presenters at those events frequently raised the Island Chain Strategy in their discussions, signalling that Beijing is well aware of the Island Chain Strategy and how it either locks or unlocks the Pacific Ocean. It has long featured in PLA Navy discussions. See: Huang, A. (1994). The Chinese Navy's Active Offshore Defence Strategy: Conceptualization and Implications. *Naval War College Review, 47*(3), pp. 1–26. digital-commons.usnwc.edu/nwc-review/vol47/iss3/2/.

15 Taiwan is outside of the scope of this chapter. However, should China take possession of Taiwan it then breaks free from the first island chain.

Investment opportunities: 'everything depends on favours'

Beijing's 2017 Ministry of Commerce report on PNG (hereafter referred to as the 'Guide') is a publication produced annually to provide companies and investors with information on PNG. The Guide (Ministry of Commerce, 2017) noted the strategic importance of PNG as the 'junction of Asia and the Pacific', identifying it as being central to the 'southern extension of the "21st Century Maritime Silk Road"'. It also noted PNG 'has close military cooperation with Australia', receives significant military assistance and training from Australia, and that it has defence relationships with the UK and US (Ministry of Commerce, 2017). Given the 'many suitors' seeking 'bilateral engagements' with PICs, including Australia, New Zealand, the US, Indonesia, South Korea, Taiwan, the UK *and* China, the New Cold War environment increases the stakes of such engagements, particularly those that involve military and policing elements (Szadziewski, 2021, p. 307). As a result, the US and Australia have increased high-level diplomatic engagement within the region as they attempt to deter China from increasing its military footprint in the Pacific. This is a point the chapter will return to shortly.

Recognising the complexity of PNG's population and operational environment, the Guide encouraged Chinese companies to adopt a 'three-skinned team' approach in their operations, meaning recruitment of Papua New Guineans, Chinese and 'white' workers—a category that includes white Papua New Guineans and expatriate workers from mostly Australia, New Zealand and the UK (Ministry of Commerce, 2017). The 'three-skinned team' approach replaces earlier desires to exclude Australian workers and likely stems, in part, from Beijing's realisation that some PNG nationals are white. Graeme Smith provides an account from a white PNG national working at Chinese-owned Ramu Nickel who reported the Chinese managers 'nearly fell off their chairs' when he entered the room due to his appearance (Smith, 2013, p. 340, also see Kuo, this volume). The same worker also identified Ramu Nickel's early approach was to exclude Australian workers. The later acceptance of some Australian workers demonstrates Beijing recognised Australian workers and other white workers were needed to help them overcome their information deficits in PNG, especially those related to mining industry regulations and safety standards in PNG, which are modelled on Australian and New Zealand safety standards and are stringently applied (see Kuo this volume).

The Guide also identified that investment opportunities in PNG are possible, but difficult, and they are 'guided by the construction of the "Belt and Road"' with direct reference to the aforementioned report to the Nineteenth National Congress by Xi Jinping (Ministry of Commerce, 2017, p. ii). Key problems facing investors identified in the Guide included violence, social unrest and instability, the under-development ('backwardness') of the region, poor road and infrastructural facilities, PNG's legal system, work visa requirements and the rights of the landowners. Identified investment opportunities included forestry, fisheries, petroleum, minerals and agriculture (ibid., pp. 14–5). It also noted that PNG has access to approximately 20 per cent of the world's total tuna reserves and is rich with prawns and lobsters (ibid., pp. 3, 14–5). Other noted export goods included gold, silver, copper, liquified natural gas, crude oil, cocoa, palm oil, coffee, timber and diamonds (ibid., p. 13). The report identified PNG's 'specialty is low barriers to entry', but noted 'a firm foothold is difficult', and that 'everything depends on favours' (ibid., p. v). Hence, while PNG is ruled by law, approval processes based on 'favours' are conducive to existing Chinese business practices such as *guanxi*, corruption and crony capitalism.[16] Therefore, it could be argued that 'the extensive corruption in PNG bureaucracy' identified by Chin (2008, and this volume), provides a familiar operating environment for mainland Chinese investors (Pei, 2016).

Given corruption is a 'feature' of the BRI, and it has been found to 'linger after project implementation has ended', the lack of transparency and accountability of BRI projects is cause for concern (Hillman, 2020, p. 9; Varrall, 2021, p. 114). O'Dowd (2021, p. 415) argued that BRI investments 'may exacerbate PNG's challenges with corruption, public sector management and poor governance by offering less regulated funding opportunities for projects of dubious development value'. Whether the PNG government and regulatory bodies are up to the task is a critical question. It appears Papua New Guineans have already expressed concern over their government's handling of BRI agreements, reflected in the downfall of O'Neill in 2019. Peter Connolly (2020, pp. 53–8) argued that inside PNG, O'Neill was 'perceived to have been unduly influenced by the

---

16 *Guanxi* translates as 'connections' or 'networks' and is an important feature within Chinese society. It ranges from simple introductions and network connections through to rampant corruption and crony capitalism in its most virulent application. However, it is important to recognise that *guanxi* is integral to an individual's personal social networks and is intricately linked to power and hierarchy within Chinese culture and how individuals can elevate their standing within that system.

Chinese', with his successor Prime Minister James Marape pledging to 'Take back PNG' upon assuming office, part of which has involved a focus on official corruption (Kama, 2019). While perceived Chinese influence was not the only factor in O'Neill's downfall, it was *a* factor, reflecting that in PNG, government interactions with Beijing and the BRI can have political ramifications for PNG's ministers and government officials.[17]

Despite his pledge to PNG, upon becoming Prime Minister, Marape initially looked to China for an $11.8 billion loan so he could refinance PNG's national debt (Grigg, 2019). Walking away from that idea, he later switched to Australia, seeking $1.5 billion in loans from Canberra (ibid.). In response to these events, PNG's Commerce Minister Wera Mori stated that it was his personal view that PNG had 'too much [financial] exposure to China' and it was instead looking to its 'friend' Australia (cited in Grigg, 2019). In August 2020, Australian Prime Minister Scott Morrison and Prime Minister Marape agreed to a new Comprehensive Strategic and Economic Partnership between Australia and PNG focused on security, trade and investment considerations (Economist Intelligence Unit, 2020). In June 2021, Marape expressed his continued commitment to the PNG–China bilateral relationship, stating he wanted 'to place on the record the excellent relations that PNG continues to enjoy with the People's Republic of China' and that PNG does not 'perceive China as a security threat, but rather as an important development, investment and trade partner with shared values conducted under mutual friendship and understanding' (Department of Prime Minister and National Executive Council, 2021). These comments followed the publication of alleged statements made by PNG Defence Force Commander Major General Gilbert Toropo that the growing Chinese presence was 'a challenge' for PNG, and that he welcomed the joint Australian–PNG upgrade of Lombrum Naval Base, which would increase PNG's naval capabilities (Faa, 2021).

---

17 Angola may hold some lessons for both PNG and Beijing. President José Eduardo Dos Santos negotiated many of Angola's loans with Beijing (like O'Neill's alleged 'closed door' discussions with Xi at APEC 2018—see discussion later in this chapter under sub-heading: 'Trickle-down economics, 'sub-optimal' aid and taking stock of the BRI in PNG'). However, after standing down in 2017, Angola's new President, João Lourenço, sought market diversification to provide a lifeline to Angola's poorly performing economy, to tackle widespread corruption, and to respond to 'the problem of unbalanced relations with China' (like Marape's 'Take back PNG' approach) (de Carvalho, Kopinski & Taylor, 2021, p. 2). This has resulted in Beijing finding 'itself over-exposed in Angola, leading to an intention to reduce its engagement' (ibid., p. 17). A similar pattern appears to be taking place in PNG following O'Neill's downfall and Marape's diversified market approach.

Toropo's comments were preceded by the announcement of a signed Memorandum of Understanding (MOU) between China's Fujian Zhonghong Fishery Company, the Governor of Western Province and PNG's Fisheries Minister. The MOU proposed a $30 billion port city development on Daru Island, including a $200 million fisheries port (Strangio, 2021). The proposal was downplayed by Morrison as 'speculation' and unsurprising, while Marape stated it was still in its 'concept stage' and had not yet been 'considered by the national government' (Strangio, 2021; Whiting, 2021). Nonetheless, Daru landowners were concerned that they had not been consulted about the proposal, also fearing that if implemented, the proposal 'could "destroy" fishing stocks and the environment', a fear also shared by Australia's Department of Foreign Affairs and Trade with regards to possible impacts on the Torres Strait region (Whiting, 2021). While the outcome of the MOU remains unresolved, Marape's post-election rhetoric has been very much focused on positioning PNG as 'a friend to all, enemy to none' and he too has courted both China and Australia, following in the footsteps of his predecessor (ibid.).

The 'landowner problem'

The Guide repeatedly singles out PNG's landowners as a problem to Chinese investors and highlights the landowner issue as reflecting a crucial difference between China and PNG when it comes to land use and development. Since the 1990s, land seizures and underpaying the value of the land have been common features of domestic Chinese development (Pei, 2016, pp. 58–9). Therefore, land issues in China are politicised and frequently corrupt, and there is little or no consideration of existing land users in these types of development projects. In its discussion of landowners in PNG, the Guide highlighted stark contrasts between the land system in China compared to PNG. In China, the government holds the power, whereas the Guide stated that in PNG 'landowners have absolute rights to their own land. The government does not have enough right to speak' (Ministry of Commerce, 2017, p. 48). It also detailed the legal parameters of the Land Law 1996, noting that the PNG 'government can expropriate private land, but it must be based on public and other legitimate purposes, and appropriate compensation should be given to private landowners' (ibid., p. 37). The Guide identified PNG's landowner system as 'not conducive to foreign investment', highlighting that '97 [per cent] of PNG's land is occupied by various tribes' under customary land rights with the government owning only three per cent, urging readers to 'pay attention to land disputes' (ibid., p. 48, v).[18] In this volume, Chin identifies similar comments having been made about the 'landowner problem' by Chinese officials and non-officials conducting business in PNG.

In his opening remarks to the Guide, Liu Linlin, the Economic Counselor at the Embassy of the PRC in PNG, identified the landowners as 'a major problem that *plagues* foreign investors' and that 'landowner *interference*' can cause problems for investors (Liu Linlin, cited in Ministry of Commerce, 2017, p. v, emphasis added by Hayes). The Guide also stressed the importance of proper handling of the relationship with landowners to avoid the kinds of problems that had occurred in the past. Prior to the BRI, in 2004, there was a serious breach when China's Metallurgical Construction Company (MCC) made an agreement with the government over the Ramu Nickel mine, but not the landowners, hence the project was stalled. This case was the proof for Beijing that, unlike in China, in PNG the landowners truly do hold the power. MCC's oversight resulted in serious local tensions, as well as a lengthy and costly court battle (Kemish, 2020). The Guide also identified that only 'PNG citizens can own land and foreigners cannot obtain PNG land ownership' (Ministry of Commerce, 2017, p. 37). Hence, PNG's land laws were a critical focal point within the Guide, but they may also protect Papua New Guineans against the excesses of the BRI experienced in other states, such as Djibouti, Sri Lanka and Tajikistan, all of which have already lost some territory to China due to debt-for-land swaps when they have been unable to make loan repayments.[19]

---

18 PNG's customary land ownership and its possible role in constraining development is also contested within academia. In 2004, such a debate played out in the *Pacific Economic Bulletin*. It appears both sides of the debate reached a similar conclusion: PNG would need to transition to a system that includes more individual land titles, but this process would need time and adequate protections, and the process should not be rushed. See: original article, Gosarevski, S., Hughes, H., & Windybank, S. (2004). Is Papua New Guinea viable?. *Pacific Economic Bulletin, 19*(1), pp. 134–48; response to original article, Fingleton, J. (2004). Is Papua New Guinea viable *without* customary groups?. *Pacific Economic Bulletin, 19*(2), pp. 96–103; and authors' response to Fingleton, Gosarevski, S., Hughes, H., & Windybank, S. (2004). Is Papua New Guinea viable *with* customary land ownership?. *Pacific Economic Bulletin, 19*(3), pp. 133–6.

19 The Edevu Hydropower Project may signal how the 'landowner problem' will be handled by China into the future. In this case, the Chinese investor worked with the Koiari landowners to develop the project, a move that has been praised by Marape as 'a wonderful example to other landowners right across our country' and that 'land sitting idle is of no use to us' (cited in *PNG Business News*, 2023). He also called on other investors to follow this model. If this continues to happen, the potential shield provided by landowner rights to prevent debt-for-land swaps will be eroded.

Defence relations and the further deployment of Island Chain Strategy

In an article published in *China Military Science,* China's most prestigious military journal, Xu Qi (2004, pp. 13–4, emphasis added by Hayes), a Senior Captain in the People's Liberation Army (PLA) Navy, stated:

> For the past few years, China has provided aid to the South Pacific region and also strengthened economic and trade ties … These [achievements have] all contributed to the development of China's maritime geostrategic relationships … the Chinese nation's existence, development and *great resurgence* [national rejuvenation] [all] increasingly rely on the sea.

He identified that China's maritime geostrategic development was spurred on by the 'collapse of the Soviet Union' and '9/11' and that China's 'passage in and out of the [open] ocean is obstructed by two island chains' (ibid., p. 9). His article demonstrates the geostrategic importance of the Pacific region to China's maritime geostrategic goals. However, to facilitate such goals, China requires military presence within the region, and the PLA has been working to establish such links. It already has established defence links with the PNG Defence Force (PNGDF). Currently, these links include an annual meeting and equipment procurements for PNG within a defined Chinese budget, reciprocal defence attachés, military aid, and deepening military and police bonds between China and PNG (Connolly, 2020, p. 60; Dziedzic, 2022a, 2022b; Luo, 2018; Zhang, 2020). These links also include training PNG military officers in Chinese military colleges where they study China's 'Party-Army model' and civil–military corporatism, enabling Beijing to forge relations with PNG's military elites (in addition to political elites) (Doran, 2018; Li, 2019; Tylecote & Rossano, 2021). PNG police officers are also being trained in China (Dziedzic, 2022a; Luo, 2018). According to Connolly, these kinds of arrangements could exacerbate Australian–Chinese tensions over PNG because:

> [s]uch representation will enable persistent Chinese influence via security cooperation with military and police forces of the Pacific Island Countries … It will therefore enable China to have a more comprehensive approach to the execution of its grand strategy in the Pacific, which will intensify competition between China and PNG's traditional partners. (2020, p. 60)

Moreover, increased PNGDF–PLA military ties could result in a securitisation of BRI projects inside of PNG, similar to what occurred in Pakistan. This likelihood increases should Papua New Guineans damage or destroy BRI projects, which a senior government official foreshadowed is possible: 'Don't worry about the Chinese investments in PNG: if they do anything wrong, the landowners will deal with them—they will burn everything down' (cited in Connolly, 2020, p. 59). The problem with this scenario is that, like in Pakistan, attacks against BRI projects are not something Beijing is prepared to weather. To protect BRI projects in Pakistan, an army division numbering 15,000 troops was formed by the Pakistani government at Beijing's insistence. Alongside these troops, China has also engaged private security contractors to secure Chinese interests and investments inside of Pakistan (Hillman, 2020, p. 145). This could be replicated in PNG, particularly the use of private security contractors.[20]

The growing defence links between China and PNG are also problematic within the New Cold War environment and they demonstrate that Beijing's plan for the 'southern extension' of the 21st Century Maritime Silk Road contains both economic and military goals. I argue that those military goals constitute the start of a further deployment of Island Chain Strategy as Beijing tries to increase its defence footprint beyond the South China Sea and the first island chain, thereby attempting to unlock Oceania.[21] In his analysis of this region, and the rising great power tensions, Kevin Rudd (2022) argued that alongside agricultural lands, natural resources and fisheries, Beijing's engagement with PICs has also been centred upon intelligence, security and communications interests. He stated:

> Chinese military academics have also argued the advantages of developing military bases among the island states, particularly in Papua New Guinea, Fiji, and Vanuatu, among other locations. This would allow China to secure strategic proximity to the Bismark Sea and the Vitiaz Strait, through which three of Australia's five

---

20   The use of private security contractors could result in a Sandline Affair-like event re-occurring in PNG. For an overview of the conflict in Bougainville and the Sandline Affair see: Adamo, A. (2018). A Cursed and Fragmented Island: History and Conflict Analysis in Bougainville, Papua New Guinea. *Small Wars and Insurgencies, 29*(1), pp. 164–86. doi.org/10.1080/09592318.2018.1404765

21   The Solomon Islands is outside of the scope of this paper. However, it is also central to this discussion, particularly the Solomons–China 2022 security pact. For a detailed discussion of the Solomon Islands and China, see: Fraenkel, J. & Smith, G. (2022). The Solomons-China 2022 security deal: extraterritoriality and the perils of militarisation in the Pacific Islands. *Australian Journal of International Affairs, 76*(5), pp. 473–85. doi.org/10.1080/10357718.2022.2085243

major sea trade routes pass, including those supporting the supply
of 60-70 percent of Japan's total imported coal and iron ore needs.
(ibid., p. 215)

Hence, this is a region that is already of critical geostrategic importance
to Australia, Japan and the US. Recent developments, like the progress
on the Australia–PNG Bilateral Security Treaty, are significant and these
kinds of arrangements need to extend to other suitable Pacific states. The
draft principles of the treaty highlight important areas of cooperation that
will benefit both PNG and Australia in areas of both traditional and non-
traditional security realms. This includes more meaningful partnerships
within the region, enhanced multilateralism and a deeper understanding
of the opportunities and challenges of the region.[22] For PICs, dominant
security challenges are human security concerns such as climate change,
economic insecurity, and law and order issues (Albiston, 2023). Hence,
these kinds of agreements must contain an over-arching security framework
that encompasses elements of both state and human security.

Trickle-down economics, 'sub-optimal aid' and taking stock of the BRI in PNG

The Guide acknowledges that China is new to the region and has much
to learn about entering PNG. China's information deficits have already
caused some problems on the ground and, according to Zhang, China
has found it difficult to gain a 'social license' within the region, due to
pervasive negative views over its motivations and modus operandi (2022,
p. 590). Zhang interviewed a Papua New Guinean scholar who claimed:
'China wants Pacific countries to sign on to the BRI as a condition to get
aid', indicating there may be some coercion by Beijing and that China's
so-called 'no strings attached' aid does indeed have some strings attached
(2022, p. 579). Already, some Papua New Guineans believe Chinese
spending in PNG is 'sub-optimal', with some BRI projects simply 'vanity
projects' (B4 cited in Pan et al., 2019, p. 394). According to Pan Chengxin
et al. (2019, p. 394), some Papua New Guineans believe that because such
projects use 'Chinese labor and materials' the perceived benefit to local
populations is minimised. One of their interviewees concluded 'Sometimes
you wonder if you're looking at aid-funded projects, or just pure commercial

---

22   See: Prime Minister of Australia. (2023, January 12). Joint Statement Prime Minister of Papua New
Guinea. www.pm.gov.au/media/papua-new-guinea-australia-bilateral-security-agreement.

activities' (L11 cited in Pan et al., 2019, p. 395). Unsurprisingly, some Papua New Guineans are also identifying the problems of unfulfilled promises of trickle-down economic benefits: 'China may spend a lot, but it has not trickled down' (C3 cited in Pan et al., 2019, p. 394). Others are concerned PNG is being drawn into a 'debt trap' with Beijing via the BRI (Zhang, 2022). Hence, rather than pursing projects for 'political symbolism', Beijing needs to rethink its approach and be more responsive to the needs of local communities if it wants the social license to operate within PNG (Pan et al., 2019, p. 397).

Transparency is also critical in bilateral agreements and for gaining a social license among the people. However, PNG's full promises to Beijing remain opaque because O'Neill deliberately sidelined other politicians in his negotiations with China. According to a senior government official in PNG, O'Neill and Xi had 'fleshed out' the details of their bilateral partnership at APEC 2018 without input from other ministers (cited in Connolly, 2020, p. 59). Moreover, he stated: 'The political courtship [over two years leading up to APEC] was disturbing because we abandoned our traditional friends. They said this was because Chinese aid was cheaper to get. If you're looking for cheaper aid, you're looking for things for yourself as well'. Without a public release of the details of the PNG–BRI agreement it is very difficult to determine the nature of such projects, their benefits to PNG or their challenges. If Beijing truly wanted to promote openness, transparency and accountability within its BRI agreements, it would remove the condition that such agreements be kept secret (Buckley, 2020, p. 312).[23] Without such openness, questions of corruption and debt trap will continue to plague Beijing and social license from the people will remain elusive.

Finally, BRI agreements must be open and transparent because of the geostrategic nature of the BRI. Signing on to the BRI is drawing states into the unfolding New Cold War between China, the US and other great powers. This is already causing some Papua New Guineans to weigh up the costs and benefits of the BRI. According to one PNG official, 'PNG is at a cross-roads', and has undergone significant change since APEC, adopting a fresh approach to BRI projects, and that PNG:

---

23   BRI agreements are so secretive that when Pakistan applied to the IMF for a loan, even the IMF was unable to access all the China-Pakistan Economic Corridor agreements (Buckley, 2020).

now needs to develop a "filtering mechanism" that allows them to conduct a "stock take" of the good and the bad, and *what PNG may have missed, in order to preserve their national interest in the relationship with China.* (cited in Connolly, 2020, p. 60, emphasis added by Hayes)

Such a stocktake also requires thinking about the increased authoritarian power of Xi Jinping and exactly what 'national rejuvenation' entails. Via the BRI, China is far more than an alternative source for development lending. Through its southern extension of the Maritime Silk Road, it is drawing states into its attempts to displace the US, the liberal world order, and to greatly disrupt the balance of the Pacific, including important sea lines of communication. Due to PNG's geographic location, where it is the linchpin between the second and third island chains, it will increasingly be drawn into this great power rivalry as Beijing tries to secure a dominant strategic presence in the region. The increased high-level diplomatic engagement it has received over 2022 and into 2023 provides further evidence of the geostrategic importance of the region. PNG is now in negotiations for bilateral security treaties with both the US and Australia (Albiston, 2023; Dziedzic, 2022b; Whiting, 2023). In September 2022, the Biden administration hosted a delegation of leaders from PICs to Washington in the first US–Pacific Summit (Lyons, 2022). This built on the US's 2019 partnership with PNG under the Global Fragility Act, whereby the US implemented a ten-year strategy for addressing the drivers of instability inside PNG, alongside Haiti, Libya, Mozambique and Coastal West Africa (Collins, 2022). Biden was scheduled to make an historically significant visit to PNG in May 2023, in between the G7 meeting in Hiroshima and a Quad meeting in Sydney (Dziedzic, 2023). However, his visit was cancelled due to US domestic affairs and US Secretary of State, Anthony Blinken, attended in his place. During Blinken's visit, a defence and maritime surveillance agreement between the US and PNG was signed. Blinken's visit coincided with a planned visit by India's Prime Minister Narendra Modi, who was meeting with several leaders from PICs in PNG (Needham, 2023). This engagement was further bolstered when President Biden hosted Pacific leaders for the second US-Pacific Summit in Washington in September 2023.

Conclusion

Prior to O'Neill's downfall and the onset of COVID-19, the 2010s saw Chinese investment in PNG grow considerably. Beijing saw PNG as integral to achieving its BRI goals in the South Pacific. PNG looked to China as an additional source for development loans. However, because the strategic and military dimensions of the BRI are now becoming more apparent, and there is growing recognition that Xi's China Dream seeks to displace the US as the global leader, overturning the liberal world order and significantly altering or dismantling international institutions, states must recognise the BRI as a deeply complex initiative that goes well beyond trade and development. With the rapidly unfolding New Cold War in play, BRI partner states must prioritise 'their continuation as a state' as the principal interest underpinning their negotiations with other states, taking what is of benefit to them and their national interests while at the same time avoiding excessive loans that could threaten their sovereignty in future years (Ping, 2019, p. 212).

By virtue of its geographic location, PNG is of critical strategic importance to both sides in the New Cold War. While it may want to remain neutral or non-aligned, given the shape and form of the New Cold War is different to the previous Cold War, it is still uncertain how non-alignment could work or if it is possible. New domains of warfare also mean states are incredibly vulnerable within this changing strategic landscape. Beijing's 'southern extension' of its 21st Century Maritime Silk Road has pulled this region into that conflict and the unfolding great power competition. China's desires for greater defence and policing presence within the region, as well as commercial ports that can become military ports, show that it seeks to extend its Island Chain Strategy deployment beyond the South China Sea to include the Pacific, thereby unlocking the region. Therefore, understanding this rapidly evolving geostrategic competition is imperative for BRI partner states, like PNG, who must now consider how their foreign relations may be impacted by the New Cold War.

Acknowledgements

The author is a Senior Fellow at the East Asia Security Centre and wishes to acknowledge the Centre's role in enabling the insights contained within this chapter. The author also thanks Professor Rosita Henry, Associate Professor

Jonathan Ping, Dr. Michael Wood and two anonymous reviewers for their helpful comments on the chapter. The author thanks Professor Alexandra Aikhenvald and Professor Robert Dixon for their invitation to present a paper in the Language and Culture Research Group, which generated deeper thinking by the author around the significance of *tianxia* in understandings of both the BRI and the China Dream. Finally, the author would like to thank Professor Rosita Henry, Dr. Michael Wood and Dr. Vincent Backhaus for their invitation to participate in the 'Re-visualising the Past & Imagining the Future of Race, Governance and Development in Papua New Guinea' workshop, which extended the author's thinking to include PNG's position within the BRI.

References

Albiston, L. (2023, January 9). Australia's close bonds with Papua New Guinea can help build a stronger nation. *The Strategist*. www.aspistrategist.org.au/australias-close-bonds-with-papua-new-guinea-can-help-build-a-stronger-nation/

Aamir, A. (2021, January 19). China and Pakistan fall out over Belt and Road Frameworks. *Nikkei Asia*. asia.nikkei.com/Spotlight/Belt-and-Road/China-and-Pakistan-fall-out-over-Belt-and-Road-frameworks

Amit, R. (2019). China's Infrastructure Projects in South Asia under BRI: An Appraisal. *Contemporary Chinese Political Economy and Strategic Relations*, 5(3), pp. 1079–110.

Buckley, P. (2020). China's Belt and Road Initiative and the COVID-19 crisis. *Journal of International Business Policy*, 3, pp. 311–14. doi.org/10.1057/s42214-020-00063-9

Cavas, C. (2016, February 1). Powers Jockey for Pacific Island Chain Influence. *Defence News*. www.defensenews.com/global/asia-pacific/2016/02/01/powers-jockey-for-pacific-island-chain-influence/

CEIC (Census and Economic Information Centre). 2023. China Foreign Exchange Reserves from January 1989 to February 2023. www.ceicdata.com/en/indicator/china/foreign-exchange-reserves

Chellaney, B. (2017, January 23). China's debt-trap diplomacy. *Project Syndicate*. www.project-syndicate.org/commentary/china-one-belt-one-road-loans-debt-by-brahma-chellaney-2017-01?barrier=accesspaylog

Chen, Y. J. (2021). "Authoritarian International Law" in Action? Tribal Politics in the Human Rights Council'. *Vanderbilt Journal of Transnational Law, 54*(5), pp. 1203–55.

Chin, J. (2008). Contemporary Chinese Community in Papua-New Guinea: Old Money versus New Migrants. *Chinese Southern Diaspora Studies, 2*, pp. 117–26.

Collins, J. (2022, October 11). The Global Fragility Act in PNG: can the US succeed?. *The Interpreter.* www.lowyinstitute.org/the-interpreter/global-fragility-act-png-can-us-succeed

Connolly, P. (2020). The Belt and Road comes to Papua New Guinea. *Security Challenges, 16*(4), pp. 41–64.

Crawford, N., & Gordon, D. (2020, April 10). China Confronts Major Risk of Debt Crisis on the Belt and Road due to Pandemic. *The Diplomat.* thediplomat.com/2020/04/china-confronts-major-risk-of-debt-crisis-on-the-belt-and-road-due-to-pandemic/

Dayant, A., Keen, M., & Rajah, R. (2023, January 25). Chinese aid to the Pacific: decreasing, but not disappearing. *The Interpreter.* www.lowyinstitute.org/the-interpreter/chinese-aid-pacific-decreasing-not-disappearing

de Carvalho, P., Kopinski, D., & Taylor, I. (2021). A Marriage of Convenience on the Rocks? Revisiting the Sino-Angolan Relationship. *Africa Spectrum*, pp. 1–25. doi.org/10.1177/00020397211042384

deLisle, J., & Goldstein, A. (2021). Rivalry and Security in a New Era for US-China Relations. In J. deLisle & A. Goldstein (Eds.), *After Engagement: Dilemmas in US-China Security Relations* (pp. 1–49). Brookings Institution Press.

Deng, J. (2022, November 9). An explanation for the decline of China's aid to the Pacific. *The Interpreter.* www.lowyinstitute.org/the-interpreter/explanation-decline-china-s-aid-pacific

Department of Prime Minister and National Executive Council. (2021, June 16). 'Prime Minister Marape dispels perception of China as a Security Threat to PNG'. Media Statements. web.archive.org/web/20210812114047/www.pmnec.gov.pg/index.php/secretariats/pm-media-statements/319-prime-minister-marape-dispels-perception-of-china-as-a-security-threat-to-png

Doshi, R. (2021). *The Long Game: China's Grand Strategy to Displace American Order.* Oxford University Press.

Doran, S. (2018, July 26). China and Africa: the Zimbabwe file. *The Strategist.* www.aspistrategist.org.au/china-and-africa-the-zimbabwe-file/

Dziedzic, S. (2022a, October 13). Australia, PNG inch closer to inking security treaty as defence minister tours the Pacific island nation. *ABC News*. www.abc.net.au/news/2022-10-13/richard-marles-defence-security-deal-papua-new-guinea/101531650

Dziedzic, S. (2022b, November 23). China hosts meeting with senior police officers and diplomats from six Pacific nations. *ABC News*. www.abc.net.au/news/2022-11-23/china-hosts-meeting-with-pacific-police-officers-and-diplomats/101686126

Dziedzic, S. (2023, February 14). Pacific Island leaders announce US President Joe Biden will visit the region. *ABC News*. www.abc.net.au/news/2023-02-14/joe-biden-pacific-islands-visit-pif-summit-micronesia/101974228

Economist Intelligence Unit. (2020, August 6). PNG and Australia sign economic partnership. Country report.

Economy, E. (2018). *The Third Revolution: Xi Jinping and the New Chinese State*. Oxford University Press.

Espena, J., & Bomping, C. (2020, August 13). The Taiwan Frontier and the Chinese Dominance for the Second Island Chain. Australian Institute of International Affairs. www.internationalaffairs.org.au/australianoutlook/taiwan-frontier-chinese-dominance-for-second-island-chain/

Faa, M. (2021, June 15). Australian Defence Force to fund $175 million major upgrade for Papua New Guinea's naval base on Manus Island. *ABC News*. www.abc.net.au/news/2021-06-15/major-naval-base-on-png-manus-island-lombrum-adf/100216040

Finin, G. (2021). Associations Freely Chosen: New Geopolitics in the North Pacific. In G. Smith, & T. Wesley-Smith (Eds.), *The China Alternative: Changing regional order in the Pacific Islands* (167-96). ANU Press. doi.org/10.2307/j.ctv1h45mkn.9

Garamone, J. (2022, November 29). China Military Power Report Examines Changes in Beijing's Strategy. *Department of Defence News*. www.defense.gov/News/News-Stories/Article/Article/3230682/china-military-power-report-examines-changes-in-beijings-strategy/

Grady, J. (2023, January 16). China Undergoing "Build-Up in Every Warfare Area," Says ONI Commander'. *US Naval Institute News*. news.usni.org/2023/01/16/china-undergoing-build-up-in-every-warfare-area-says-oni-commander

Greenbank, A. (2019, September 25). China-based academic says Australia is naive to rely on US, after Morrison's comments on trade. *ABC News*. www.abc.net.au/news/2019-09-25/china-academic-responds-to-scott-morrison-trade-comments/11546900

Grigg, A. (2019, August 20). PNG seeks $1.5 billion in loans from Australia, dropping China debt plan. *The Australian Financial Review.*

Hayes, A. (2020). Interwoven 'Destinies': The Significance of Xinjiang to the China Dream, the Belt and Road Initiative, and the Xi Jinping Legacy. *Journal of Contemporary China, 29*(121), pp. 31–45. doi.org/10.1080/10670564.2019.1621528

He, B. (2019). The Domestic Politics of the Belt and Road Initiative and its Implications. *Journal of Contemporary China, 28*(116), pp. 180–95. doi.org/10.1080/10670564.2018.1511391

Hillman, J. (2020). *The Emperor's New Road: China and the Project of the Century.* Yale University Press.

Hillman, J. (2021). *The Digital Silk Road: China's Quest to Wire the World and Win the Future.* Profile Books.

Holslag, J. (2017). How China's New Silk Road Threatens European Trade. *The International Spectator, 52*(1), pp. 46–60. doi.org/10.1080/03932729.2017.1261517

International Institute of Green Finance. (2021). Countries of the Belt and Road Initiative (BRI). Green Belt and Road Initiative Centre, Central University of Finance and Economics, Beijing. doi.org/10.1007/978-981-16-3188-7

Kama, B. (2019, August 8). 'Take Back PNG': Prime Minister Marape and his audacious vision for PNG. *Devpolicy Blog.* devpolicy.org/take-back-png-prime-minister-marape-and-his-audacious-vision-for-png-20190808/

Kania, E., & Segel, A. (2021). Globalized Innovation and Great Power Competition: The US-China Tech Clash. In J. deLisle & A. Goldstein (Eds.), *After Engagement: Dilemmas in US-China Security Relations* (pp. 298–329). Brookings Institution Press.

Kemish, I. (2020, July 3). China's push into PNG has been surprisingly slow and ineffective. Why has Beijing found the going so tough?. *The Conversation.* theconversation.com/chinas-push-into-png-has-been-surprisingly-slow-and-ineffective-why-has-beijing-found-the-going-so-tough-140073

Kenneth, G. (2017, November 17). Multi-billion Kina Deal Signed to Strengthen PNG and China Relations. *Post Courier.* postcourier.com.pg/multi-billion-kina-deal-signed-strengthen-png-china-relations/

Kuhara, Kohji. (2022). Countering China's "Trident" Strategy—Frustrating China's Aims in the East and South China Seas and the Indian Ocean. *Naval War College Review, 75*(2), pp. 1–24. digital-commons.usnwc.edu/nwc-review/vol75/iss2/4/

Li, J. (2019, March 4). First Chinese trained military doctor commissioned to Papua New Guinea Defense Force. *China Military.* eng.chinamil.com.cn/CHINA_209163/TopStories_209189/9440292.html

Luo, P. (2018, May 9). Papua New Guinea dignitaries security training course held in Sichuan Police Academy. *China News.* www.chinanews.com.cn/gn/2018/05-09/8509786.shtml

Lyons, K. (2022, December 6). Papua New Guinea can't afford Australia and US standoff with China, James Marape warns. *The Guardian.* www.theguardian.com/world/2022/dec/05/papua-new-guinea-cant-afford-australia-and-us-standoff-with-china-james-marape-warns

Mascitelli, B., & Chung, M. (2019). Hue and cry over Huawei: Cold war tensions, security threats or anti-competitive behaviour? *Research in Globalization, 1,* pp. 1–6. doi.org/10.1016/j.resglo.2019.100002

McCahill, W. (2017, October 24). China's 'New Era' and 'Xi Jinping Thought'. *The National Bureau of Asian Research.* www.nbr.org/publication/chinas-new-era-and-xi-jinping-thought/

McGregor, R. (2019). *Xi Jinping: The Backlash.* Penguin.

Miller, C. (2022). Explaining China's strategy of implicit economic coercion. Best left unsaid?. *Australian Journal of International Affairs, 76*(5), pp. 507–21. doi.org/10.1142/9789813146310_0021

Ministry of Commerce, 2017, 对外投资合作国别（地区）指南: 巴布亚新儿内亚, *(Guide to Foreign Investment Cooperation Countries (Regions): Papua New Guinea).* The Economic and Commercial Counsellor's Office of the Chinese Embassy in Papua New Guinea, Institute of International Trade and Economic Cooperation, Ministry of Commerce Department of Foreign Investment and Economic Cooperation, Ministry of Commerce, Beijing.

Needham, K. (2023, April 27). Biden to make historic visit to Papua New Guinea next month - PNG officials. *Reuters.* www.reuters.com/world/biden-visit-papua-new-guinea-next-month-png-official-2023-04-27/

O'Dowd, S. (2021). Bridging the Belt and Road Initiative in Papua New Guinea. In G. Smith & T. Wesley Smith (Eds.), *Changing Regional Order in the Pacific Islands* (pp. 397–425). ANU Press. doi.org/10.22459/ca.2021.13

Pan, C. X., Clarke, M., & Loy-Wilson, S. (2019). Local agency and complex power shifts in the era of Belt and Road: Perceptions of Chinese aid in the South Pacific. *Journal of Contemporary China, 28*(117), pp. 385–99. doi.org/10.1080/10670564.2018.1542220

Parameswaran, P. (2019, April 23). Malaysia's Evolving Approach to China's Belt and Road Initiative. *The Diplomat.* thediplomat.com/2019/04/malaysias-evolving-approach-to-chinas-belt-and-road-initiative/

Pei, M. X. (2016). *China's Crony Capitalism: The Dynamics of Regime Decay.* Harvard University Press. doi.org/10.4159/9780674974340

Ping, J. H. (2019). Middle power hybridisation and China. In T. S. de Swielande, D. Vandamme, D. Walton, & T. Wilkins (Eds.), *Rethinking Middle Powers in the Asian Century: New Theories, New Cases* (pp. 210–23). Routledge. doi.org/10.4324/9780429463846

PNG Business News. (2023, April 24). PM Marape thanks Koiari landowners and investor for K770 million hydropower project. www.pngbusinessnews.com/articles/2023/4/pm-marape-thanks-koiari-landowners-and-investor-for-k770-million-hydropower-project

Pryke, J., & Dayant, A. (2021, September 30). China's declining Pacific aid presence. *The Interpreter.* www.lowyinstitute.org/the-interpreter/china-s-declining-pacific-aid-presence

Rajah, R., Dayant, A., & Pryke, J. (2019, October 21). Ocean of Debt? Belt and Road and Debt Diplomacy in the Pacific. *Lowy Institute Analyses.* www.lowyinstitute.org/publications/ocean-debt-belt-and-road-and-debt-diplomacy-pacific#_edn1

Reilley, J. (2021). China's Belt and Road Initiative. In J. deLisle, & A. Goldstein (Eds.), *After Engagement: Dilemmas in US-China Security Relations* (pp. 330–60). Brookings Institution Press.

Rudd. K. (2022). *The Avoidable War: The Dangers of a Catastrophic Conflict between the US and Xi Jinping's China.* Hachette.

Schuman, M. (2020). *Superpower Interrupted: The Chinese History of the World.* Public Affairs.

Scott, J. C. (2020). *Seeing Like a State: How Certain Schemes to Improve the Human Condition Have Failed.* Yale University Press. doi.org/10.12987/9780300252989

Strangio, S. (2021, February 9). Why China's 'Island city' in Papua New Guinea is a Mirage. *The Diplomat.*

Szadziewski, H. (2021). A Search for Coherence: The Belt and Road Initiative in the Pacific Islands. In G. Smith, & T. Wesley-Smith (Eds.), *The China Alternative: Changing regional order in the Pacific Islands* (pp. 283–317). ANU Press. doi.org/10.22459/ca.2021.09

Smith, G. (2013). Beijing's Orphans? New Chinese Investors in Papua New Guinea. *Pacific Affairs, 86*(2), pp. 327–49. doi.org/10.5509/2013862327

Su, G. (2016). The Belt and Road Initiative in Global Perspectives. *China International Studies, 57*, pp. 5–27.

Tao, Y. F. (2021). The Political Economy of Xi Jinping's Political Rollback. *Issues and Studies: A Social Science Quarterly on China, Taiwan, and East Asian Affairs, 57*(2), pp. 1–20. doi.org/10.1142/s1013251121500077

Thomas-Noone, B. (2021, January 12). What the Cold War can teach Washington about Chinese tech tensions. Tech Stream, Brookings Institution. www.brookings.edu/techstream/what-the-cold-war-can-teach-washington-about-chinese-tech-tensions/

Thornton, W., & Thornton, S. (2018). Sino-globalisation: The China Model after Dengism. *China Reports, 54*(2), pp. 213–30. doi.org/10.1177/0009445518761087

Tonga gets five years' grace on Chinese loan as Pacific nation joins Belt and Road initiative. (2018, November 18). ABC News. www.abc.net.au/news/2018-11-19/china-defers-tongas-loan-payments-as-nation-signs-up-to-bri/10509140

Tylecote, R., & Rossano, H. (2021, November). China's military education and Commonwealth countries. *Civitas: Institute for the Study of Civil Society.* www.civitas.org.uk/publications/discussion-paper-chinas-military-education-and-commonwealth-countries/

Varano, J. (2021, May 6). Tearing Up the Belt and Road Initiative: Australia's Rejection of China's New Silk Road in Victoria. *Australian Outlook.* www.internationalaffairs.org.au/australianoutlook/tearing-up-the-belt-and-road-initiative-australias-rejection-of-chinas-new-silk-road-in-victoria/

Varrall, M. (2021). Australia's Response to China in the Pacific: From Alert to Alarmed. In G. Smith, & T. Wesley-Smith (Eds.), *The China Alternative: Changing regional order in the Pacific Islands* (pp. 107–41). ANU Press. doi.org/10.22459/ca.2021.03

VornDick, W. (2018, October 22). China's reach has grown; so should the island chains. *Asia Maritime Transparency Initiative.* Centre for Strategic and International Studies. amti.csis.org/chinas-reach-grown-island-chains/

Wang, F. (2018). Recognizing and Maintaining the Period of Strategic Opportunity for Development. *China International Studies, 73*, pp. 26–41.

Wang, S.M. (2019). Open Regionalism and China-Australia Cooperation in the South Pacific Islands Region. *China International Studies, 75*, pp. 84–108.

Wang, Y. W. (2016). *The Belt and Road Initiative: What will China offer the world in its rise.* New World Press.

Wesley-Smith, T. (2013). China's rise in Oceania: Issues and perspectives. *Pacific Affairs, 86*(2), pp. 351–72. doi.org/10.5509/2013862351

Wesley-Smith, T. (2021). A New Cold War? Implications for the Pacific Islands. In G. Smith, & T. Wesley-Smith (Eds.), *The China Alternative: Changing regional order in the Pacific Islands* (pp. 71–105). ANU Press. doi.org/10.22459/ca.2021.02

Whiting, N. (2021, February 10). Locals in Papua New Guinea speak out as China's proposed industrial fishing park sets off alarm bells in Canberra. *ABC News.* www.abc.net.au/news/2021-02-10/png-daru-fishing-park-china-australia-tensions-james-marape/13136188

Whiting, N. (2023, January 20). PNG prepares to sign Defence Cooperation Agreement with US as it finalises security treaty with Australia. *ABC News.* www.abc.net.au/news/2023-01-20/png-prepares-to-sign-a-defence-cooperation-agreement-with-us/101871422

Wilson, J. (2021, November 9). Australia Shows the World What Decoupling From China Looks Like. *Foreign Policy.* foreignpolicy.com/2021/11/09/australia-china-decoupling-trade-sanctions-coronavirus-geopolitics/

Xi, J. P. (2014). *The Chinese Dream of the Great Rejuvenation of the Chinese Nation* (compiled by the Party Literature Research Office of the Central Committee of the Communist Party of China). Foreign Languages Press.

Xi, J. P. (2017a). *The Governance of China, Volume II.* Foreign Languages Press.

Xi, J.P. (2017b, October 18). Secure a Decisive Victory in Building a Moderately Prosperous Society in All Respects and Strive for the Great Success of Socialism with Chinese Characteristics for a New Era. *19th National Congress of the Communist Party of China.* www.xinhuanet.com/english/download/Xi_Jinping%27s_report_at_19th_CPC_National_Congress.pdf

Xi, J. P. (2019). *The Belt and Road Initiative.* Foreign Languages Press.

Xu, Qi 2004, Maritime Geostrategy and the Development of the Chinese Navy in the Early Twenty-first Century (Andrew S. Erickson & Lyle J. Goldstein, Trans.). *Naval War College Review, 59*(4), pp. 1–22. digital-commons.usnwc.edu/nwc-review/vol59/iss4/5/

Zhang, D. H. (2020). China's Military Engagement with Pacific Island Countries. *In Brief.* Department of Pacific Affairs. No. 22. dpa.bellschool.anu.edu.au/sites/default/files/publications/attachments/2020-08/dpa_in_brief_202022_zhang_0.pdf

Zhang, D. H. (2022). China's influence and local perceptions: the case of Pacific island countries. *Australian Journal of International Affairs, 76*(5), pp. 575–95. doi.org/10.1080/10357718.2022.2112145

Zhao, M. H. (2019). Is a New Cold War Inevitable? Chinese Perspectives on US–China Strategic Competition. *The Chinese Journal of International Politics, 12*(3), pp. 371–94. doi.org/10.1093/cjip/poz010

Zhao, S. S. (2010). The China Model: can it replace the Western model of modernization?. *Journal of Contemporary China, 19*(65), pp. 419–36. doi.org/10.1080/10670561003666061

10

Conclusion: Imagining a Chinese future in PNG

Michael Wood, Anna Hayes
and Rosita Henry

Our initial intentions for this collection were ambitious. We thought of chapters that would contribute to making the Chinese more central to the history of PNG, and that would enable reflection on what this history might mean for a Chinese future in PNG. The chapter by Hayes effectively concludes our collection because she poses epochal questions about this future amid the backdrop of intensifying geo-political competition within the region and an unfolding New Cold War. Interest in this subject matter has also intensified since our initial workshop in 2020.

In combination, the chapters in this volume reveal that the Chinese in PNG have never been a homogenous assemblage, but are a succession of distinct groups with different origins, languages, aspirations and political histories. By emphasising the internal diversity of the Chinese who have resided in PNG, we seek to provide impetus for further systematic exploration of this topic.

We have highlighted the diversity of the Chinese inter-cultural interactions in workplaces, markets, economic and political spheres, and in other contexts and across different time periods in PNG. In their chapters, the authors view the topic through different disciplinary lenses, but in combination the volume provides a valuable multidisciplinary perspective on the Chinese past, present and future in PNG. Some contributors emphasised the multilingual practices of the Chinese in PNG. Others emphasised how the Chinese experience in PNG was a multi-state phenomenon and highlighted the importance of the circulation of the Chinese between different nation-states as much their circulation within PNG. Such diasporic histories point to different forms of citizenship and claims to sovereignty that external states have at various times claimed over the Chinese in PNG.

While both Hayes and Chin suggest that the Chinese state is a significant and increasingly dominant actor in PNG politics, it is never an autonomous solitary actor, but is modulated by various entanglements with the other states, international norms and actors that in various ways co-occupy with China the field that constitutes the state and sovereignty of PNG. In other chapters, the Chinese state appears as significantly absent. This suggests that the Chinese state in PNG is perhaps a bit like the PNG state—in some contexts it is present and growing in influence, but in other contexts it is an absent presence (Bainton & Skrzypek, 2021) and in yet other contexts it may be a weakening presence. Clearly, accounts of China's increasing dominance in PNG need to be supplemented by detailed descriptions of the interactions of Chinese state agents in different contexts within PNG. Such research might reveal that both the PNG and the Chinese nation-states are not as much discrete manifestations of national power as composite and dynamic entanglements of competing powers, structures of sovereignty and channels of interaction.

Our collective aim was to present Chinese-centric narratives that could displace dualistic accounts of PNG history centred on PNG and European interactions and social categories of difference. Such stories, we suggest, enable some forms of PNG politics and sociality to be conceptualised as a three-body problem (Liu, 2016), rather than just repeat dualisms concerning black and white bodies. At the same time, we are aware that others have already attempted something similar even if they deployed different approaches to the material and analysis (Bashkow, 2006; Smith, 2013; Wolfers, 1975; Wood, 1995). However, the Chinese and the Papua New Guineans are often placed jointly in a colonial waiting room of history where both come too late to an already partially developed European modernity (Fanon, 1967, p. 92; Chakrabarty, 2008).

In this volume, we have not presumed to define something like a distinct Chinese temporality or historicity (Ballard, 2014). Nor have we attempted in our selection of stories to head towards a unified pre-determined conclusion. The idea of increasing Chinese influence, power and control in PNG is variously assumed, qualified and rejected by different contributors. Chinese domination in PNG's future is treated in some chapters as conditional or even indefinite, as not an inevitable but a contingent product of future political debate and conflict. On pragmatic political grounds of opening a future for PNG, it is perhaps important to disrupt the pessimistic idea that PNG is running towards an inevitable future even if that future turns out to have contingently emerged. It is not inevitable that PNG will be dominated or threatened by China or by an Australian–US alliance.

This ambivalence about the future of PNG also motivates us now, in the current political context defined by various understandings of Chinese expansionism, to present the narratives as both extensions of existing accounts of the Chinese in PNG and as openings to developing new narratives and chronologies of the Chinese experience of living in PNG. This will involve actively facilitating further Chinese accounts of these experiences. It should also involve creating and narrating other pasts and futures for the Chinese in PNG to those outlined here. We hope that others, with different interests, positions and qualifications to us, will continue to demonstrate the multiplicity and creativity of Chinese engagements in PNG's past, present and future.

References

Bainton, N., & Skrzypek, E. (Eds). (2021). *The Absent Presence of the State in Large-Scale Resource Extraction Projects*. ANU Press. doi.org/10.2307/j.ctv1zcm2sp

Ballard, C. (2014). Oceanic Historicities. *The Contemporary Pacific, 26*(1), 96–124. doi.org/10.1353/cp.2014.0009

Bashkow, I. (2006). *The Meaning of the Whiteman: Race and Modernity in the Orokaiva Cultural World*. University of Chicago Press. doi.org/10.7208/chicago/9780226530062.001.0001

Charkrabarty, D. (2008). *Provincialising Europe: Postcolonial Thought and Historical Difference*. (New Edition). Princeton University Press.

Fanon, F. (1967). *Black Skin White Masks*. Pluto Press.

Liu, C. (2016). *The Three-Body Problem*. Tor Books.

Smith, G. (2013). Beijing's Orphans? New Chinese Investors in Papua New Guinea. *Pacific Affairs, 86*(2), 327–49. doi.org/10.5509/2013862327

Wolfers, E. P. (1975). *Race Relations and Colonial Rule in Papua New Guinea*. Australia and New Zealand Book Company.

Wood, M. (1995). 'White Skins', 'Real People' and 'Chinese' in some Spatial Transformations of the Western Province, PNG. *Oceania, 66*(1), 23–50. doi.org/10.1002/j.1834-4461.1995.tb02529.x

www.ingramcontent.com/pod-product-compliance
Lightning Source LLC
Chambersburg PA
CBHW051959270326
41929CB00015B/2714